Readings in Caribbean History and Economics
An Introduction to the Region

CARIBBEAN STUDIES

A series of books edited by Roberta Marx Delson, *Associate Director, Latin American Institute, Rutgers University, New Jersey* and Arnaud F. Marks, *Director of Caribbean Studies, Royal Institute of Linguistics and Anthropology, Leiden, Netherlands.*

International Standard Serial Number (ISSN): 0275-5793

VOLUME 1

READINGS IN CARIBBEAN HISTORY AND ECONOMICS
Edited by Roberta Marx Delson

Additional volumes in preparation

This book is part of a series. The publisher will accept continuation orders which may be cancelled at any time and which provide for automatic billing and shipping of each title in the series upon publication. Please write for details.

Readings in Caribbean History and Economics
An Introduction to the Region

ROBERTA MARX DELSON
Rutgers University

GORDON AND BREACH SCIENCE PUBLISHERS
New York   London   Paris

Copyright © 1981 by Gordon and Breach, Science Publishers, Inc.

Gordon and Breach, Science Publishers, Inc.
One Park Avenue
New York, NY10016

Gordon and Breach Science Publishers Ltd.
42 William IV Street
London, WC2N 4DE

Gordon & Breach
7-9 Rue du Emile Dubois
F-75014 Paris

Library of Congress Cataloging in Publication Data
Main entry under title:

Readings in Caribbean history and economics.

    (Caribbean studies, ISSN 0275-5793; v.1)
    Bibliography: p. 329
    Includes index.
    1. Caribbean area — History — Addresses, essays, lectures.
    2. Caribbean area — Economic conditions — Addresses —
essays, lectures. I. Delson, Roberta Marx. II. Series:
Caribbean studies; v. 1.
F2156.R4   972.9'05   81-6302
ISBN 0-677-05280-4   AACR2

Library of Congress catalog card number 81-6302 ISBN 0 677 05280 4.
ISSN 0275-5793. All rights reserved. No part of this book may be
reproduced or utilized in any form or by any means, electronic or
mechanical, including photocopying, recording, or by any information
storage or retrieval system, without permission in writing from the
publishers. Printed in the U.S.A.

In Memory of My Father

Now the island rose in a blaze of morning, riding at ease through treacherous currents of wind and water. Hurricanes had often disfigured its face. Floods . . . would carry huge proportions of soil into the sea. But it would grow again, as though its hopes were never wholly out of favour. Its history had been a swindle of treaties and concessions. Its sovereignty was no more than an exchange of ownership. There had been no end to the long and bitter humiliations of foreign rule. The battles for ascendency were too numerous to be remembered. But its habits of submission had suffered a terrible blow. The meek flame started at San Souci had spread beyond . . . wildest expectations. Now this name San Cristobal had become a warning everywhere . . .

George Lamming
Water With Berries

Contents

vii

Introduction

Caribbean Studies is a series of monographs devoted to an examination of the Caribbean in pan-regional focus. The purpose of the series is to provide a forum in which the major themes and trends affecting the entire region will be explored in depth. Thus, while the island-specific approach is not eschewed, the aim is to develop perspectives on problem-solving in the area as an entirety, both on the local level and in the international context. Hence the emphasis is on the qualitative and quantitative interpretation of the economic and political culture in which the modern Caribbean operates. Historical, demographical and sociological issues, when relevant to the central focus of the series, will also be examined.

The series is designed as a vehicle for academic scholars publishing in the region, as well as Caribbeanists internationally. Simultaneously, it is anticipated that the monographs will function as a reference data source for libraries, foundations and government agencies with an interest in the Caribbean either exclusively or peripherally.

It is the coeditors' hope that the series will not only launch comprehensive Caribbean studies internationally, but that it will similarly stimulate innovative research and the development of methodology suitable to comparative perspectives. Only when the Caribbean is evaluated in its broadest panorama can the true global importance of the region be appreciated.

Manuscripts may be sent to either of the two coeditors (who will be assisted by an advisory board to be selected from internationally recognized scholars). Their addresses are as follows:

Prof. Roberta Marx Delson   Prof. Arnaud F. Marks
Associate Director   Director of Caribbean Studies
Latin American Institute   Royal Institute of Linguistics
Rutgers University   and Anthropology
180 College Avenue   Postbus 9507
New Brunswick,   2300 RA Leiden,
    NJ 08903 USA   NETHERLANDS

Preface

In a commencement address presented at the University of
Guyana, the distinguished statesman, William G. Demas,
cautioned that the "New Caribbean Man" was obliged to
develop a sensitivity to his own history.[1] Emphasizing the
necessity of searching for self-identity and drawing strength
from the discoveries thus revealed, Demas made the point
that

> to be acquainted with our history and to know that we have survived
> the moral and psychological travail of slavery and indentureship, Crown
> Colony Government, and cultural deprivation and have retained our
> vitality, our élan and our creativity . . . ought to give us a tremendous
> amount of self-confidence. We ought to feel elated rather than depressed
> by knowing that we have the greatest gift a group of human beings can
> have — moral and psychological resilience.

Although Demas' remarks were addressed to an English-
speaking Caribbean audience, his counsel is clearly relevant
for the non-Anglophone units of the West Indies as well.
The weaving of historical analogies through political jargon
and ideological treatises has become a commonplace phenomenon within the region, with local leaders as diverse in their
views as Fidel Castro of Cuba and Joaquín Balaguer of the
Dominican Republic frequently calling upon the historical
past to inspire (and often legitimize) their current actions.
That history has emerged as the handmaiden of politics is no
coincidence: the twin themes of slavery and extractive
plantation monoculture invite easy comparison and analogy
with modern day variants of socio-economic organization.
Too often, however, the attempt to invoke the horrors and
injustices of the past to underscore the inequities and depen-
dencies of today obscures the true matrix in which events and

people have been juxtaposed. Speculations based on mythical interpretations of the past have found their way into the dialogues of even the most informed individuals, and it is a mere truism to state that, in general, the more geographically removed the audience is from the Caribbean itself, and the more closely it is affected by frequently non-sympathetic metropolitan historiography, the more prominent the myths and delusions become.

This collection of readings is intended primarily for such an overseas audience and especially for students of Caribbean background (whether themselves emigrants or the descendants of the on-going Caribbean diaspora) who are now living in metropolitan centers of Canada, the United Kingdom and the United States. Naturally, there is no attempt to exclude students without previous Antillean experience and conversely, students within the Caribbean will hopefully discover much that is unknown to them about their territorial neighbors. It would be pure folly to suggest that a single, introductory anthology could correct all false interpretations and misconceptions about the Caribbean past; years of study have not prevented some scholars from obscuring issues and accepting 'conventional wisdom' as *prima facie* evidence. Nevertheless, the value of compiling such a collection of interpretive essays lies in guiding the new student into an understanding of the basic themes and issues of the Caribbean past and initiating the process by which 'island insularity' (both in the region and abroad) may eventually be eliminated.

A readings format allows an editor considerable leeway in the selection and arrangement of data. As with a more restricted historical monograph, however, the articles that appear in this collection, as well as the themes which are emphasized reflect my personal choice and consequently my own bias. In this instance, I have been most concerned with presenting the region as a comprehensive entity and have thus chosen to play down the particularistic histories of individual political subdivisions. Accordingly, although I have tried to incorporate into the chronological framework of this volume as many of the germane categories and issues as space permitted, there will undoubtedly be many missing names, as well as events. Similarly, I have attempted to be catholic in my coverage of the various ethnic components that comprise the Caribbean totality, but I have also purposefully chosen material that relates to specific themes and topics of broad comparative significance. Thus, many excellent works have been rejected because they were either too island-specific, or at least not directly applicable to the broader themes under discussion. The articles themselves represent the recent and wide range of talent of scholars from the Caribbean as well as foreign researchers. It is imperative that students not only gain insight into the patterns of the historical past, but also that they be aware of the way modern Caribbeanists analyse the region's background and shape future interpretations.

The decision to treat the Caribbean as a regional unit deserves some explanation and, perhaps, some justification. Any researcher in the area would be hard pressed to accept the notion of the Caribbean and the circum-Caribbean region as a monolith; the range of ethnic, political and economic differences is too great to allow for conceptual fusion without clear intent. Indeed, the noted Dominican historian, Frank Moya Pons, has recently suggested that the idea of a Caribbean whole may exist only in the minds of three groups: 'sales managers of the great local and multi-national corporations, Washington policy makers [and] local and foreign intellectuals and scholars, who, for analytical purposes, strive to give a conceptual coherence to a region'.[2]

While this collection clearly falls into this last category, and notwithstanding the apparently growing consensus among academics that the pan-Caribbean approach is productive,[3] few scholars have actually developed textual material that fits into this range. There are only a handful of contemporary surveys that treat the area as a whole.[4] One of the most successful in these, Franklin Knight's *The Caribbean: The Genesis of a Fragmented Nationalism* suggests in contrast to Moya Pons that the

sum of common experience and understanding of the Caribbean outweighs the territorial and insular differences and peculiarities. To speak therefore of Haitian, Jamaican, Cuban or Caribbean characteristics should not be to speak of them as mutually exclusive; the first are merely variations or components of the last.[5]

On a purely academic level, then, the comprehensive
Caribbean approach represents an attempt to bring heuristic
coherency (in this case via thematic organization) to a
plethora of nations, ethnic identities and ideologies. The
conscientious instructor in Caribbean history must aim for a
geographical definition which includes the neighboring territories (the Guiana Highlands and the Venezuelan coast) as
well as the Antilles themselves. Obviously, one can make
sense out of this enormously expansive region only if
common historical denominators are established. Such
categories, which automatically invite comparative perspective, may include institutions, labor patterns, political structures and race relations, among others.

The only inherent difficulty in opting for this approach is
the understandable tendency for the institution of slavery to
overshadow other underlying commonalities. While much
recent scholarship has focused on local variations of this
broadly experienced institution,[6] the similarities of shared
characteristics of slavery as practiced in the West Indies have
long been singled out under the labels of 'slave culture',
'sugar culture' or 'plantation culture'.[7] Thus, scholars have
acknowledged for some time the socio-economic traits
commonly associated with slavery including the oppression
of African slaves relocated on plantations, the development of a highly stratified and caste-conforming society
and the concomitant official disinterest in land and society
not directly involved in monocultural enterprise. These
variables, of course, are not strictly the possession of
the Caribbean past; such characteristics link the southern
portions of the United States as well as Brazil and other
nations of Latin America intrinsically to the slave experience.

But, to focus exclusively on slavery, while fascinating and
academically valid in itself, is potentially dangerous for the
new student since it automatically suggests too broad an
historical and geographical spectrum for evaluation. The
other alternative, examining the differences among slave
systems, is counterproductive for an introductory text, since
it would lead the uninitiated student away from a general
understanding of the region as a whole.

Fortunately for analytical purposes, the threads of shared

Caribbean history do not begin or end with slavery itself; closer scrutiny of the Antillean past reveals that the modern political units of the West Indies have jointly experienced the annihilation of the Amerindian populations, an external dependence on the economy of the metropolitan country, a growth of the peasant sector in the nineteenth century, an intellectualization of 'creole culture' in the present century, accompanied by the growth of nationalism and the radicalization of the 'have-nots' in recent years and the phenomenon of out-migration of the economically depressed (both intra-regional and overseas). Similarly, even a cursory attempt at periodization suggests that Caribbean territorial units have followed one another (albeit at different rates and times) through the stages of what may be termed Spanish sub-culture, the Enlightenment, European free-trade liberalism, United States 'Manifest Destiny' and so on.

If there is one underlying *leitmotif* to the entire panorama of Caribbean history, it is the observation that economic patterns forged in the early years of colonization have wielded unparalleled influence in shaping the societies of today. The organization of labor and production for the benefit of particular segments of society to the exclusion of others is a pervasive theme in the region, whether one is considering the familiar sugar, tobacco or cotton monopolies of the past or the operation of extractive industries (including tourism) in the present. Thus, this volume is intentionally designed to allow the student to associate economic with historical phenomena by focusing on the economic dimensions of specific time periods.

Many of the issues dealt with in this reader will not be directly pertinent to a discussion of economic organization or growth. Yet in an area as historically rich as the Caribbean, economic, political and social phenomena are rarely mutually exclusive. The problems faced by an indentured East Indian sugar worker in nineteenth-century Trinidad, for example, were labor specific but also of sociological significance, as the system of indentureship was established to replace an emancipated slave-labor force. There is a similarly cohesive relationship between economic organization and political ideology seen in the role exerted by labor unions in

the English-speaking Caribbean and Puerto Rico in fostering
nationalistic goals.

Let me underscore one point. While the well known fusion
of land and labor into monocultural export-production
units is all-pervasive, to single out specific bedevilments with
a view to exposing companies or nationalities is not the role
of an introductory text. This collection is therefore not
arranged to either support or discredit structuralist, deter-
minist, dependency or neo-Marxist paradigms of historical
economic development. Rather, I think it imperative to allow
the new student in the area to sort out the patterns comparatively and then to draw his own conclusions (no matter how
self-evident) about the dynamics of economic growth. If
one model must be singled out for the selection of material
contained in this reader, then the notion of 'political economy' is most appropriate since its major concern is the
historical matrix. This approach, recently defined:

. . . concerns itself with the social relations between individuals, em-
ploys real historical causes, and its causal variables are not abstractions
such as the interest rate, the supply of money, and the level of prices,
but rather human agents . . . political economy is a critical science in
the sense that it views the capitalist mode of production (including
private property, wage labor, profits and so on) as a historical phenomenon.[8]

The articles selected for this reader clearly echo this line
of thought. They have been chosen for the student with a
non-technical background, but are nonetheless sophisticated
and sufficiently informative to acquaint the reader in a
systematic fashion with the major economic patterns visible
in the Caribbean over the past five centuries. My aims have
been to draw attention to the manner in which labor has
been organized, to consider the sectors of the economy
which attract and provide investment, to evaluate the continuing battle to reconcile industrial growth in areas possessed
of historically large and vital peasant populations, and to
introduce other related topics.

The broad chronological divisions and themes utilized in
this reader, whether specifically concerned with historical
phenomena, economic organization or the interface between

the two, are designed to bring the student from a study of the past into contemplation of the present and future, and from the Caribbean to the overseas context. It is my personal conviction that the 'New Caribbean Man', if he is ever to emerge, will be forged from the input of the experience of the diaspora as well as the influence of the region itself. The shared experiences of the diaspora can serve as a guard against the latent parochialism that isolates Caribbean groups from each other, and the recognition of common historical bonds can do much to cement regional integration.

To borrow a metaphor from evolution, I suggest that students just entering into the polemical and controversial maze which constitutes Caribbean historiography, should be trained as 'lumpers' rather than 'splitters' of the Caribbean past. While the pan-regional outlook is certainly not an end in itself, it is imperative that the student first determine the strong 'family' ties that override, and are of greater initial conceptual importance (particularly to an overseas audience) than, local 'speciation'; the student must instinctively seek to understand what Cuba, Haiti, Surinam and Barbados, for example, have experienced in common, as well as what makes each unique.

A word about the arrangement of articles is in order. Where a topic is of a magnitude sufficiently broad to warrant separate coverage, I have devoted an entire section to a specific theme, for example, the Spanish world of the sixteenth century and the section entitled Slave Emancipation and Changing Economic Patterns of the British West Indies: The Emergence of the Peasantry. The remaining sections, however, explore critical themes and concepts in a pan-regional perspective. A few of the selections are excerpts from travel accounts, personal letters, speeches, etc. of historical significance. Although much of the material is recent, some of the selections are well-known classics of the area. The balance is supplemented by the use of non-traditional historical materials, including poetry and literary analysis. Such 'data' can have a profound bearing on the understanding of the past and may enable the student to grasp the subject in a non-chronological context.

Each section begins with an editorial introduction, at the

end of which is a brief selection of suggested further readings. While the choice of published materials is indeed vast, I have indicated material that would be easily understood by the new student and is available outside the Caribbean region. This is by no means a comprehensive bibliography, but merely an attempt to whet the student's appetite to future explorations of the historical literature. Each article is preceded by a brief editorial note highlighting the significance of its contents.

I am indebted to the numerous scholars who graciously gave consent to have excerpts of their work reproduced in this collection. Similarly, I gratefully acknowledge the co-operation of the permissions and rights departments of the publishers of the original material. The staff at Gordon and Breach must be singled out for continual support and en-couragement in the face of seemingly endless paperwork. Of the scholars not directly involved by way of article selection there are many who have been particularly help-ful Dr Barry Higman, of the University of the West Indies, Jamaica, has lent historical acumen and bibliographic know-ledge in abundance, and Drs Vera Rubin and Lambros Comitas, both of the Research Institute for the Study of Man, New York, gave enthusiastic responses to early outlines of the project. Dr Jay Mandle, of Temple University, kindly read and commented upon my section and article introduc-tions. Technical assistance in proof-reading, reproduction of materials and preparation of the index was provided by Lisa Belkin, Ted Povinelli, Elizabeth Strasser and Dr Eric Delson. To all these individuals, and to my ever-patient family, I offer my heartfelt thanks; the responsibility for data selection and the editorial interpretations are entirely my own.

ENDNOTES

1. W.G. Demas (1971), 'The New Caribbean Man', *Caribbean Quar-terly*, 7, Nos. 3 and 4 (September–December), pp. 7–14. See Section 10.1.
2. F. Moya Pons (1979), 'Is there a Caribbean consciousness?', *The Americas*, 3, No. 8, August, pp. 33–36.
3. In the Spring of 1977, I conducted a survey on the teaching of Caribbean history in universities of the United States. Out of a sample of fifty-four courses with Caribbean content, twenty-six

(or about half) were devoted to presenting the region as an entirety, while the remaining courses of the sample were either island-specific or included Mexico and Central America in their coverage. See R.M. Delson (1978), 'Teaching Comprehensive Caribbean history in the North American context', in N. Niles and T. Gardner (eds.), *Perspectives in West Indian Education*, Michigan State University Press, East Lansing, Michigan, pp. 187-94.

4. For example, E. Williams (1970), *From Colombus to Castro: The History of the Caribbean, 1492-1969*, Harper and Row, New York; J.H. Parry and P. Sherlock (1971), *Short History of the West Indies* (St. Martins, New York); F.W. Knight (1978), *The Caribbean: The Genesis of a Fragmented Nationalism*, Oxford Unversity Press, New York; D.A.G. Waddell (1967), *The West Indies and the Guinas*, Prentice-Hall, Englewood Cliffs, New Jersey. In 1974, L. Comitas and D. Lowenthal edited a four volume anthology entitled *West Indian Perspectives*, Anchor Doubleday, Garden City, which, as Gordon Lewis has pointed out, contains some excellent material but is largely concerned with the English-speaking units of the Caribbean: see G.K. Lewis (1974), 'On the dangers of composing a West Indian anthology', *Caribbean Studies*, 14, No. 1 (April). The same comment may be made for the recent collection *Africa and the Caribbean* (Johns Hopkins Press, Baltimore, 1979) edited by F.W. Knight and M. Crahan, which (its name notwithstanding), focuses on the Anglophone Caribbean.

5. F.W. Knight (1978), *op cit.*, p. x.

6. For example, G. Midlo Hall (1972), *Social Control in Slave Plantation Societies: A Comparison of St. Domingue and Cuba*, Johns Hopkins Press, Baltimore (see section 3.7). E.V. Goveia (1970), *The West Indian Slave Laws of the Eighteenth Century*, Caribbean Universities Press, Barbados, presents comparative perspectives within the context of the English colonial domain.

7. Much of the credit for the popularization of this latter term may be attributed to Dr Vera Rubin who coordinated a seminar on this theme in 1959. See V. Rubin et al. (1957), *Plantation Systems of the New World*, Pan American Union, Washington, D.C.

8. J. O'Connor (1976), 'What is political economy?', in D. Mermelstein (ed.), *Economics: Mainstream Readings and Radical Critiques*, Random House, New York, 3rd Edition, pp. 21-22.

SECTION 1

The Caribbean under Spanish Control: Sixteenth-century Patterns

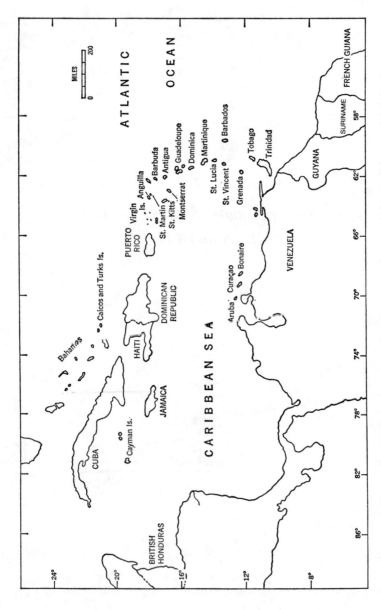

MAP OF THE REGION From *Peoples and Cultures of the Caribbean*, ed. Michael M. Horowitz. © 1971 by Michael M. Horowitz, reproduced by permission of Doubleday & Company, Inc.

1.0
Introduction to Section 1

On the eve of Columbus' fateful first voyage to the West Indies, the region itself was in a state of transition. The village settlers and sedentary peoples who inhabited the Greater Antilles (see Gorenstein's description in selection 1.2) were being forced from their sites by invasions of hostile Caribs, a group that apparently had originated in the Orinoco Basin. The upheaval and fear engendered by the threat of Carib intrusion left the more peaceful Arawak and Taino inhabitants easy prey for Spanish conquerors who offered "protection". As the *Asiento con Pinzón* (see selection 1.3) so clearly demonstrates, the Spanish immediately took a proprietary view of the Indians, their land and possessions. *Conquistadores*, like Pinzón, were given quasi-seigneurial rights over the territories they were assigned; only the requirement of remitting set proportions of profits back to the Crown distinguished the system from the manorialism of the Feudal Ages.

It was in the Caribbean, after all, that the Spanish experimented with their New World format, and the patterns of administration formulated for colonial Santo Domingo (see Selection 1.4) or Havana were transplanted along with waves of settlers to the continental territories of Nueva España (Mexico) and Nueva Castilla (Peru). The Spanish Conquest was ultimately a legalistic tour-de-force; what could not be justified on a religious or humanistic basis could be felicitously dealt with in legalistic *pronunciamentos*. Thus, the need for qualified scribes and notaries was self-evident; from the records of meticulous *escribanos* we can learn much about the mentality of the conquerors. The mere existence of four different notarial positions in Havana (see selection 1.5) suggests that the Spanish were frequently at loggerheads among themselves

3

over mining jurisdictions, urban allotments and the government's appropriate share of revenue.

Notwithstanding internal dissension, however, the Spanish apparently acted in concert ultimately to destroy Indian villages and culture. While the indigenous peoples were not without protectors (chiefly churchmen), the thrust of Spanish protectionist legislation for the Indian was to maintain the Crown's sovereignty (through its Indian subjects) against the increasingly wealthy and powerful *conquistador-encomendero* class (the individuals to whom Indian labor was 'entrusted').

In any event, the application of such protectionist measures was for all practical purposes impossible. When Fray Bartolemé de Las Casas left Santo Domingo permanently to write his fiery disclosure of Spanish atrocities committed against the the Indians (see selection 1.6), much of the indigenous population of the Caribbean had already been decimated or had perished by disease. Although there are descendants of Carib Indians living on the island of Dominica today, their numbers are but a fraction of the original population; only the continental portion of the Caribbean (the Guianas) have substantial autochthonous populations remaining (and their existence as separate cultures has recently been jeopardized, as well). Las Casas' indictment of the Spaniard's treatment of the Indians ultimately had more political value than humanitarian effect in its time; it provided competitive European nations with tempting grounds for rationalizing their entrance into the Spanish Caribbean, a process which was beginning as the sixteenth century drew to a close. The resulting multiple invasions and successive takeovers eventually led to the unique cultural diversity of the modern Caribbean, which Mintz describes in selection 1.1.

There is a substantial literature on the Spanish takeover of the Caribbean and several of the 'classic' classroom texts in Latin American history provide insight into the mentality and processes of the time period. These include C. Gibson, *Spain in America**; C.H. Haring, *The Spanish Empire in*

* The full citation for this and other suggested readings will be found in the Bibliography at the end of the text.

America; F.A. Kirkpatrick, *The Spanish Conquistadores.* Demographic profiles are provided in S.F. Cook and W. Borah, *Essays in Population History Vol. 1: Mexico and the Caribbean.* In Spanish, the well-known histories are S. Brau, *La Colonización de Puerto Rico* and T.A. Saco, *Historia de la esclavitud de los indios en el nuevo mundo, seguida de las historias de los repartimientos y encomiendas.*

The Caribbean Region   Sidney W. Mintz

In this introductory selection, Sidney Mintz comments on the diversity on the one hand, and the common denominators on the other, which characterize the Caribbean today. He concludes that the region is unique and does not easily fit into popular geopolitical categories. This excerpt is reprinted by permission of Daedalus: Journal of the American Academy of Arts and Sciences, *Boston, Massachussetts (Spring 1974 pp. 45–49 and 52–43) and the author.*

The despair of classifiers, area studies programs, kremlino-logists in ill-fitting sombreros, North American race relations experts, ambulent East European commissars and the CIA, the Caribbean region goes its own way, richly researched but poorly understood. Too black to be purely European, too North European to be simply Latin, too modern to be primitive, too "overdeveloped" to be accurately labeled "underdeveloped," its diversities seem contradictory, its unities artificial or obvious. "These Caribbean territories," V.S. Naipaul tells us sourly,

are not like those in Africa and Asia, with their own internal reverences, that have been returned to themselves after a period of colonial rule. They are manufactured societies, labor camps, creations of empire; and for long they were dependent on empire for law, language, institutions, culture, even officials. Nothing was generated locally: dependence became a habit. How, without empire, do such societies govern themselves? What is now the source of power? The ballot box, the mob, the regiment? When, as in Haiti, the slave-owners leave, and there are only slaves, what are the sanctions?[1]

Behold a patchwork quilt of societies, each one a patch-work itself, the whole a foreign invention, informed with reality and a scant integrity only by the lengthy presence of of the oppressors. "It is the brevity of the [British] West Indian's history," asserts George Lamming,

and the fragmentary nature of the different cultures which have fused to make something new; it is the absolute dependence on the values implicit in that language of his coloniser which has given him a special relation to the word, colonialism. It is not merely a political definition; it is not merely the result of certain economic arrangements. It started as these and grew somewhat deeper. Colonialism is the very basis of the West Indian's cultural awareness . . . A foreign or absent Mother culture has always cradled his judgement.[2]

That Naipaul and Lamming should appear to agree epito-mizes the Caribbean condition, for they must surely agree on nothing else. Naipaul, the child of Indian contract laborers from Uttar Pradesh who migrated to Trinidad in the nine-teenth century, is regarded as one of the most gifted — surely the most sardonic — of Anglo-Caribbean writers. The sym-pathy he manifests for Caribbean folk is always diluted by his — and, he contends, their — alienation. Lamming, a black Barbadian, hopes for more; his anger is less with the tawdri-ness of Antillean life than with the forces he feels have made it so. But that these two sensitive writers, so different in their perspectives, should find common ground in their conviction that an utter emptiness typifies the Caribbean scene makes the question they raise all the more urgent.

Naipaul wonders what sanctions to govern by, once the masters have gone away. On balance, however, Caribbean self-rule has surely turned out to be no more disastrous than national experiments in self-government elsewhere. At the same time, the Caribbean region has produced a quite stagger-ing number of political critics and activist leaders, given its size and its relatively brief trajectory within Western history. No need to go back to the first warriors of Haitian indepen-dence, or to the leaders of the antislavery struggle elsewhere in the islands. It should be enough to mention the names of the twentieth-century figures — Marcus Garvey, Frantz Fanon, Aimé Césaire, Eric Williams, George Padmore, C.L.R.

James, Eugene Chen and Fidel Castro. The truth is probably that this coruscating if ideologically heterogeneous array has been as much the *product* of colonialism and a disjunct past, as a measure of achievement in the face of such obstacles.

For Eric Hobsbawm, the Caribbean region is

a curious terrestrial space-station from which the fragments of various races, torn from the worlds of their ancestors and aware both of their origins and of the impossibility of returning to them, can watch the remainder of the globe with unaccustomed detachment.[3]

Indeed, if enslavement disjoined once-free men from a past they would have preferred to cling to, then renewed freedom — freedom from slavery — must prove a very different state from preslavery. The special enigma of Caribbean peoples may well lie in their never having settled for a vision of history as something that must or should repeat itself.

The "Caribbean" is a region of perhaps fifty insular societies scattered over more than two thousand miles of sea, as well as certain mainland subregions — the Guianas in particular — which all passed through broadly similar historical experiences. These societies range in scale from a few square miles and populations of a few hundred or a few thousand inhabitants, up to the 44,000 square miles and nearly ten million inhabitants of contemporary Cuba.[4] Whether one examines the region from a racial, a demographic, or a sociocultural perspective, it is as differentiated as it is complex. Any attempt to evaluate the experience of Afro-Caribbean peoples must lead the generalizer to despair.

The moment Columbus decided to build a settlement on the north coast of Española (today's Santo Domingo and Haiti), and to leave there a reputed thirty-nine crewmen from the sunken *Santa Maria*, the conquest, settlement, and "development" — the word is used advisedly — of the Caribbean region began. No part of the so-called Third World was hammered so thoroughly or at such length into a colonial amalgam of European design. Almost from the very first, the Caribbean was a key region in the growth of European overseas capitalism. The German historian Richard Konetzke has pointed out that, before Columbus, there were no *planetary* empires; the Antillean islands were Europe's first economic bridgehead outside itself.[5] Nor were these islands mere ports of entry, ports of trade, or ports of call; in fact they were Europe's first overseas *colonies*. As keystones in ultramarine economic "development," they required labor in large quantities. For a long time, that labor was African and enslaved; free men do not willingly work for agricultural entrepreneurs when land is almost a free good. Philip Curtin estimates that 28 percent of the total number of enslaved Africans who reached the New World ended up in the islands alone — something more than two and one-half million — between the first decades of the sixteenth century and the latter decades of the nineteenth.[6] Before and after slavery, however, other groups supplied labor — before slavery: indentured servants, convicts, whores, petty thieves, labor organizers, the pariahs of Britain and France,[7] as well as countless native Americans from the islands themselves and from the New World mainland; after slavery: contract laborers from India, China, Java, Africa, the Iberian Peninsula and elsewhere. Nor have such movements of people ever really ceased. They help to explain the unusual ethnic and physical heterogeneity of the Caribbean region; but they also reveal the economically motivated intents of distant rulers. It would be fair to say that almost no one who was not European ever migrated to the Caribbean region freely; and surely no non-European born in the region was ever consulted about the advisability of additional migration.[8]

This demography by fiat was remarkable, first of all, because it represented the *replacement* of indigenous populations by outsiders — unlike events in most of Africa, Asia, and even mainland Latin America;[9] and secondly, because it was, in the context of the time, always massive. More than half a million Indians, both Moslem and Hindu, were shipped to the Caribbean region, most going to Trinidad and Guyana (erstwhile British Guiana), with smaller numbers to Dutch Guiana, Jamaica and Martinique; about 150,000 Chinese were imported, principally to Cuba; more than 30,000 Javanese, entirely to Surinam (Dutch Guiana); even a few Indo-Chinese ended up in the canefields. Whatever their biases in other regards the European planters of the Antilles were apparently quite free of prejudice when it came to brute labor — even fellow-Europeans would do. Spaniards and Portuguese, in particular, reached the Caribbean colonies in large numbers in the nineteenth century, proving — as if it had to be proved — that Europeans, too, could cut cane beneath a broiling tropical sun.

Such movements forged societies of a special sort, in which people became accustomed to jostling with strangers matter-of-factly, accustomed to the presence of different habits, different values, different ways of dressing and of looking, accustomed to anonymity itself, as an expected part of life. That such goings and comings have been occurring for nearly 500 years — as long, that is, as the colonial domination they express — says much about the particularity of the region. The principal motive for such movements was the provision of unskilled labor in quantities sufficient to make European investment in plantation agriculture profitable. Hence the most advanced, the most "developed" enterprises in the islands for a long time — in many places, to this day — were rural, so that the rainbow-hued spectrum of Caribbean peoples and cultures is spelled out in the shacks and canefields of the countryside, as much as in the alleyways of the cities. That these societies are ethnically, culturally and racially various is just as important in understanding their true nature as that they are agrarian, rural, and poor. By putting these two axes of description together, we begin to see that, whatever the so-called Third World really is, the Caribbean region can only be part of it figuratively. Naipaul's assertion that the islands are merely the "Third World's third world"[10] is false; these lands were being force-fit into the First World, the European World, before the Third World even existed. It is being rural, agrarian and poor that makes Caribbean folk look like Third World peoples elsewhere; it is being so anciently heterogenized, enslaved, colonized, proletarianized — yes, and Westernized — that makes the Third World label inappropriate for them today.

ENDNOTES

1. V.S. Naipaul, *The Overcrowded Barracoon* (New York: Knopf, 1973), p. 254.
2. George Lamming, *The Pleasures of Exile* (London: M. Joseph, 1960), p. 35.
3. Eric Hobsbawm, review of *Frantz Fanon: A Critical Study*, by Irene L. Gendzier, *New York Review of Books*, Feb. 22, 1973, p. 8.
4. David Lowenthal, "The Range and Variation of Caribbean Societies," *Annals of the N.Y. Academy of Sciences*, 83 (1960), pp. 786-795.
5. Sidney W. Mintz, "The Caribbean as a Sociocultural Area," *Cahiers d'Histoire Mondiale*, 9 (1966), pp. 916-941.
6. Philip A. Curtin, *The Atlantic Slave Trade: A Census* (Madison: University of Wisconsin Press, 1969), p. 268.
7. Eric Williams, *Capitalism and Slavery* (Chapel Hill: University of North Carolina Press, 1944), pp. 9-19.
8. Sidney W. Mintz, "Groups, Group Boundaries and Perception of 'Race,' " *Comparative Studies in Society and History*, 13 (1971), pp. 437-443.
9. Sidney W. Mintz, "The Caribbean as a Sociocultural Area."
10. V.S. Naipaul, *The Overcrowded Barracoon*, p. 250.

The Indigenous Caribbean   Shirley Gorenstein

*The Caribbean had long been occupied before the advent of
the Europeans, and in this selection archaeologist Shirley
Gorenstein examines the cultures of these indigenous Antillean peoples. Of special significance for the student of the
region in more recent times is the fact that the Caribbean
was in a state of transition prior to the Spanish conquest.
The Arawaks' fear of hostile Carib groups, who were rapidly
penetrating the Greater Antilles by 1492, made the Spanish
invasion, under the guise of protection, that much easier to
facilitate. This selection is reprinted with permission of the
Author and Publisher from Shirley Gorenstein, et al., (1974),*
Prehispanic America, *pp. 101–103, St Martin's Press, New
York.*

The Caribbean area, as defined here, includes the islands of
the Caribbean Sea and the coast of central and eastern
Venezuela and the Guianas. The islands are logically included
in a consideration of eastern South American prehistory,
since there is ample evidence that almost all of their historic
Indian population came originally from South America,
displacing peoples who had moved into the area from Central
America and possibly Florida.

Conditions were much more favorable for hunting and
gathering peoples in the Caribbean area than in the tropical
forests of the mainland. This was especially true along the
coastlines of both the mainland and the islands, where the
ocean provided ample subsistence. At the same time, old
archaeological sites stand in little danger of being destroyed
and are fairly easy to find. Nor surprisingly, the archaeological record goes back further in time than that of Amazonia

and the Orinoco. As far as the islands are concerned, the earliest known archaeological sites are probably very close in time to the dates of first settlement — i.e., to the time when continental peoples developed canoes and moved out into the Caribbean Sea.

The central coast of Venezuela was occupied by food gatherers by about 4000 B.C., its eastern coast by about 3000 B.C. The most characteristic artifact of the Heneal complex of the central coast is an edge-ground stone also found in the preceramic of Panama. The Cubagua and Manicuare complexes of the eastern coast are known for their variety of bone and shell artifacts, including (in Manicuare) the shell gouges used to make dugout canoes. In both areas, the archaeological sites are deep, substantial shellmounds that suggest permanent and fairly sedentary village life on the shore. These eastern coastal cultures reached some of the offshore islands but did not penetrate into the Antilles.

Cuba and Hispaniola — the two largest islands — were occupied by the third millennium B.C. if not somewhat earlier. The Guayabo Blanco complex of Cuba includes shell gouges and other artifacts suggestive of Manicuare, but the same artifact types are known from the preceramic of Florida. The proximity of Cuba to the Florida coast, and the absence of similar artifacts on the islands between it and Venezuela, has led to the hypothesis that Cuba was first inhabited by Indians from Florida some time during the third millennium B.C. On Hispaniola, the Casimira and Mordan complexes are characterized by flint blades of types that suggest Central American ancestry. On other islands, such as Trinidad and Puerto Rico, there is no evidence of human occupation until nearly the time of Christ. As elsewhere in the area, the earliest sites here are coastal shellmounds without evidence of farming. Except for the edge-grinders characteristic of Heneal, they show no special affinities to continental South American cultures.

It thus appears that the entire Caribbean area was first occupied by food gatherers who lived on the shore and ate primarily fish and shellfish. They filtered out onto the islands at different times and from different places in North,

Central, and South America, bringing with them very different material cultures.

Early in the Christian era, pottery of the Saladoid tradition spread along the eastern coast of Venezuela and out into the Caribbean as far as Puerto Rico. Abundant clay griddles give evidence that the cultivation of bitter manioc spread along with the pottery. There is every reason to believe that this phenomenon represents the migration of manioc farmers out of the Orinoco Basin, and that these new immigrants displaced or killed off resident gathering peoples. They were almost certainly speakers of the Arawakan languages that ultimately spread throughout the Caribbean area, because there is no other time in the area's prehistory when South American cultures penetrated beyond Trinidad.

The subsequent culture history of the Caribbean area is varied. Along most of the Venezuelan and Guianan coasts the pattern of manioc-based village life, without marked evidence of ceremonialism, remained constant. At Cerro Machado on the central coast, however, there was a brief intrusion of Andean influences about the time of Christ. The pottery was decorated in a style derived from the Venezuelan Andes, and the lack of manioc griddles suggests that maize had temporarily become the staple crop. At Lake Valencia, again in north-central Venezuela, the appearance, about A.D. 1000, of urn burials and of artificial mounds as substructures for houses suggests influences from the Upper Orinoco.

In the Antilles, three strongly marked tendencies are to be seen. One is the continued spread of ceramics, manioc farming, and (presumably) Arawakan languages at the expense of the older food-gathering, aceramic way of life. The farming peoples gradually moved westward to Hispaniola. Jamaica, and Cuba. They did not, however, completely replace the food gatherers, some of whom (the Ciboney) still occupied unfavorable parts of Cuba and Hispaniola when the Spaniards arrived in 1492. A second trend, clearly related to the spread of agriculture, was the gradual filling up of the interiors of the larger islands by people moving in from the coast.

The third major development seems to have been the result of contact with the peoples of Mesoamerica. Starting shortly before A.D. 1000, the Taino peoples of Puerto Rico, Hispaniola, and eastern Cuba developed an elaborate ceremonial life centered on certain deities called *zemis*. The material remains of these ceremonies include ball courts and dance plazas with stone walls, large stone idols, and a variety of special small stone artifacts. The ball courts and plazas are so characteristic of Mesoamerica that they must have diffused from there. These islands, however, were never part of the Mesoamerican empires, nor were they invaded or occupied by people from Mesoamerica.

One final development in Caribbean prehistory is not obvious in the archaeological record. By the time Europeans arrived, the lesser Antilles were in the hands of the ferocious and rapidly expanding Caribs. As we have seen, these people seem not to have left the material remains of a unified cultural tradition, but their presence is attested by the writings of the early European conquerors.

Pinzón's Contract to Settle Puerto Rico

The contract (Asiento) awarded to Pinzón to conquer and settle the island of San Juan (Puerto Rico) is a carefully worded exercise in reciprocity. In return for colonizing the territory (and receiving what amounted to seigneurial rights), Pinzón was obliged to acknowledge the sovereignty of the Spanish monarch and to remit portions of his profits on a regular basis. It is this mixture of medieval feudalism and renaissance capitalism which makes this such a fascinating document; the student's attention should be drawn to this ambiguity. This translation is provided by the Editor.

1505

AGREEMENT WITH VINCENTE YAÑEZ PINZÓN TO SETTLE THE ISLAND OF SAN JUAN (PUERTO RICO)

1. In recognition of your services especially in the conquest of the [island of] Hispañola and in [the] discoveries, I am naming you my captain and magistrate of the island of San Juan to which you shall proceed within the space of one year with the necessary settlers.
2. You will designate sites for one, two, three or four settlements, of fifty or more households each, and subdivide the surrounding land, as was done on Hispañola, where they [the settlers] are to reside for five years.
3. You will construct a fortification at your own cost and retain hereditary rights to it for two generations.
4. On everything that is grown and cultivated they will pay me a ten percent tax and the first fruits, and nothing else for

a period of five years. We reserve the sovereignty for ourselves to mineral deposits, salt deposits, etc.

5. From all the gold which is collected they will give a fifth
of the net, but they may not extract it from the Indians.

6. They may not collect any Brazilwood.[1]

7. From the cotton and other things possessed by the Indians
living outside the limits of the settlements, they will give one
fourth.

8. If anyone discovers mineral deposits, he will be obliged to
give a fifth of the metal, while the mine [itself] will remain
the property of the King.

9. They may proceed to discover and recover [treasures]
from other islands and discovered lands, where there is no
Governor, but not from the coast[2] where Cristobal Guerra
and Pedro Alonso Niño have taken pearls, nor that [coast][3]
where Ojeda is going, and from everything of value one fifth
will be paid, and from everything else a sixth.

10. The same will be paid on everything recorded from newly
discovered lands, and they will not be able to return to them
without the permission of the King.

11. If mines are discovered on the island of San Juan, the
Crown will appoint overseers.

12. Those who are already in Hispañola or other parts of the
Indies will not be permitted to go to San Juan, nor will
Moors, nor Jews, etc.

13. The Governor of the Indies will be obeyed.

14. Those who do not adhere to the letter of this agreement,
among other penalties, will forfeit all of the provisions contained in this contract.

I order you to adhere to all of the above, etc. Given in
Toro 24 of April 1505- Grizio- Licenciado Zapata [for the
Crown].

ENDNOTES

1. A type of wood found along the Brazilian coast (and the source of
   that nation's name), which was commercially important because of
   the red dye it yielded.
2. The Spanish Main (i.e. the coast of Venezuela).
3. The Guiana — Brazilian coast.

An Englishman's View
of Santo Domingo   Robert Tomson

Although foreigners were officially proscribed from entering Spanish colonies in the West Indies, nonetheless the region was visited by outsiders. One such visitor, Robert Tomson, has left us an account of Santo Domingo in the 1550s which attests to the commercial diversity of this first important Caribbean city. The Caribbean served as a springboard for the explorations of continental Latin American and the capital in Hispañola frequently outfitted both conquistadores *and* settlers. *From R. Tomson,* Voyage to the West Indies . . ., *in R. Hakluyt,* Principal Navigations, Voyages . . . *(1589; modernization C.R. Beazley).*

. . . So that we departed from the islands of the Canaries in the month of October, that aforesaid year [1555], eight ships in our company, and so directed our course towards the Bay of New Spain, and, by the way, towards the island of Santo Domingo, otherwise called Hispañiola; so that, within forty-two days after we departed from the islands of Canaries, we arrived with our ship at the port of Santo Domingo; and went in over the bar, where our ship knocked her keel at her entry. There our ship [rode] before the town; where we went on land, and refreshed ourselves sixteen days.

There we found no bread made of wheat, but biscuit brought out of Spain, and out of the Bay of Mexico. For the country itself doth yield no kind of grain to make bread withal; but the bread they make there is certain cakes made of roots called cassava; which is something substantial, but it hath an unsavoury taste in the eating thereof. Flesh of beef and mutton, they have great store; for there are men that have 10,000 head of cattle, of oxen, bulls and kine, which they do keep only for the hides; for the quantity of flesh is so great, that they are not able to spend the hundredth part. Of hog's flesh there is good store, very sweet and savoury; and so wholesome that they give it to sick folks to eat, instead of hens and capons: although they have good store of poultry of that sort, as also of guinea cocks and guinea hens.

At the time of our being there the city of Santo Domingo was not of above 500 households of Spaniards; but of the Indians dwelling in the suburbs, there were more. The country is, most part of the year, very hot; and very full of a kind of flies or gnats with long bills, which do prick and molest people very much in the night when they are asleep, in pricking their faces and hands and other parts of their bodies that lie uncovered, and make them to swell wonderfully. Also there is another kind of small worm, which creepeth into the soles of men's feet, and especially of the Indians and children which use to go barefoot, and maketh their feet grow as big as a man's head, and doth so ache that it would make one run mad. They have no remedy for the same, but to open the flesh, sometimes three or four inches, and so dig them out.

The country yieldeth great store of sugar, hides of oxen, bulls and kine, ginger, cañafistula, and salsaparilla. Mines of silver and gold there are none; but in some rivers, there is found some small quantity of gold. The principal coin that they do traffic withal in that place is black money, made of copper and brass; and this they say they do use, not for that they lack money of gold and silver to trade withal out of the other parts of [West] India, but because, if they should have good money, the merchants that deal with them in trade would carry away their gold and silver, and let the country commodities lie still. And thus much for Santo Domingo. So we were, coming from the Isles of Canaries to Santo Domingo, and staying there until the month of December, which was three months.

The Office of Notary in Havana   Jenaro Artiles

The escribano *(or notary) was an indispensable functionary in the new Caribbean polity created by the Spanish. In Havana, notaries affixed legal seals to transactions involving all aspects of colonial life. Since the notarial office evolved into a lifetime occupation, it followed that the* escribano *was frequently a powerful figure in Caribbean colonial society. This excerpt is reprinted by kind permission of Duke University Press, copyright © 1969. The article originally appeared as J. Artiles (1969), 'The Office of Escribano in 16th Century Havana',* Hispanic American Historical Review, *Volume XLIX, No. 3 (August) pp. 489–92.*

The colonial office of escribano evolved into four distinct and well-established notarial institutions, not counting the church notaries, who had the same functions in Cuba as in Castile. The four types were: 1) the royal escribano, also called del número or público; 2) the escribano of gobernación; 3) the escribano of registers, mines, and reports; and 4) the escribano of cabildo. All of them called themselves His Majesty's escribanos when, as was often the case, they did not exercise any specific notarial functions in a given locality. All four types of escribanos are found in Havana, and all of them appear in the extant documents.

In theory, according to the letter of appointment, the jurisdiction of the escribanos extended over the whole island and made it possible for them to exercise their functions anywhere in Cuba. But the established practice of presenting their titles to the local cabildo for swearing in limited the offices, practically speaking, to the locality to which the escribano had been assigned by the Crown. Regardless of the individual escribano who had authorized the notarial instruments, these were valid anywhere in the Spanish territories as well as in Castile itself. The notary's sign, a very complicated hand-drawn rubric that always preceded his personal signature, was described and included in the official document of appointment. This *signo notarial* is sometimes missing in documents issued for local use, but it never fails to appear when the document is intended for circulation elsewhere. Moreover, as in Castile, if the document was to be used outside the local community to which the notary had been assigned — i.e. beyond the jurisdiction of the local authorities — both the signature and the notarial sign had to be authenticated by two other local notaries.

In contrast, the escribanos of registry and mines, as well as those of the governorship, exercised jurisdiction throughout the territory to which they were accredited, but not beyond that of the governor or lieutenant governor. In other words, their acts were valid all over the territory of the provincial division and not merely in the villages. The instruments issued by the escribanos of Havana were effective all over the island if they came from the escribano of registry and mines or the escribano of the governorship. Documents emanating from the escribano of cabildo, however, were valid only locally in the transaction of municipal business. This latter notary was the one who kept the municipal records and issued certified copies of their content.

The other types of colonial notaries also showed parallels with modern offices. In Cuba both rural and urban properties, *corrales, hatos, ejidos*, and *realengos*, as well as city lots or *solares*, were assigned by the city and registered by the escribano de cabildo. Property titles remained in the city archives under his custody. The escribanos de gobernación were directly under the governor and his lieutenants. Sometimes we find other public officials with enough influence and power to have their own personal notary, also called escribano de gobernación. Such was the case with several alcaides of the fortress in Havana. Finally, the ecclesiatic notary registered baptisms, marriages, and burials.

As Ots Capdequí has correctly established,[1] public offices
in the Indies were considered Crown privileges, and the king
might fill them as he wished, unless it was otherwise indicated on the capitulaciones, the contracts of discovery,
conquest, or settlement. The Crown was jealous of this
prerogative, which dated from the first capitulaciones of
Granada, April 17, 1492.

When we examine the system in Havana, we find that here,
as everywhere else in the Indies, the middle of the sixteenth
century brought a definite change in the procedure of
appointing notaries. The dividing line is marked by a royal
cédula of Valladolid, dated June 17, 1559, which deals with
growth of existing offices, the creation of the new office of
alférez mayor in the American communities, and the sale of
all these offices.[2] "This decree," writes J.H. Parry, "was
the first general act authorizing the sale of offices in the
Indies."[3] The cédula began by admitting the lack of information in Castile about the importance and needs of the newly
founded cities. It directed the governor to determine how
many offices should be created in each, to sell such positions
at public auction, and to install the candidates. Also as a
result of this cédula, another office of notary public (del
número) was added to the one already existing, which had
been scived by the escribano of the Havana cabildo. Tomás
Guerra was appointed to take over this expanded office.

The traffic in offices became common practice after 1560,
when the first one was sold in Cuba. It was confirmed by
another royal cédula, issued in Lisbon on November 13,
1581. This established detailed rules for the renouncement
and transfer of offices *por otra vida más*, i.e. for the lifetime
of the recipient.[4] At his death the privileges reverted to the
Crown to be granted anew. This device of renouncement and
transfer was expanded early in the following century by a
decree of Madrid, dated December 14, 1606, which allowed
the officeholders themselves to transfer their offices freely.

Under the cédula of 1559 and its successors we see for
the first time the governor and the officers of the treasury
intervening personally, together with the cabildo, in the
selection of new escribanos. The auction was conducted by
the governor, who drew up the appropriate diploma after the

beneficiary had paid the legal fees to the treasury. Within three years the escribano thus appointed had to show the royal confirmation to the council. The cabildo then accepted the appointee as escribano.

All proceeds from the sale of the first office were credited to the royal treasury, but after this time it received only one-third of the selling price, a practice confirmed in the cédula of 1581. The actual delivery of the money to the treasury was often postponed or paid in two installments. It was also delayed by the appointment of guarantors. These were sworn before a notary public, or at times before the cabildo itself, and, like present-day cosignatories, they guaranteed payment in case the newly designated notary defaulted. If the office should be renounced, the proceedings always included the appraisers' report of its value. There are many peculiar examples of such appraisals in the records of the Havana cabildo.

These records also include depositions by leading citizens who knew the prospective candidate, his "partes y calidados," his honesty, the purity of his lineage (*limpieza de sangre*), the legitimacy of his birth, and his good reputation, as well as his cultural fitness for the office. Other conditions to be satisfied were age (twenty-five years or older) and lay status. Ecclesiastics were automatically excluded, and the candidate had to swear that he would resign the office in case he became an ordained priest. Moreover, he was liable to a heavy fine if he were to receive holy orders *de corona* at any time.

The candidate also had to appear before the royal audiencia of Santo Domingo, which drew up the preliminary document for his appointment. The records of the cabildo of Havana during the sixteenth century contain only one case of this procedure, that of Gaspar Pérez de Borroto who passed his examination in Hispañiola before the president and oidores of the audiencia on April 8, 1570. In 1607 Gaspar's son, Luis Pérez Costilla, also passed his examination in Santo Domingo. Luis was found able and fit for office, even though he had been dismissed as notary of the cabildo for being implicated in a case of smuggling.[5]

These were the official regulations. As often happened in the colonies, however, there were exceptions and abuses. In several instances the escribanos were under the influence and control of the governors and of the captains general who put personal interests above those of the Crown and exerted all the pressure at their command. But these higher officials were not always at fault. On December 7, 1582, for example, the governor of Cuba, Diego de Luxán, in a lengthy memorandum to the crown about the general situation of the administration in the island, complained that the alcaide of the fortress, Diego Fernàndez de Quiñones, had named "un moço de hasta diez y ocho años" as his escribano.[6]

ENDNOTES

1. José M. Ots Capdequí, *Estudios de la historia del derecho español en las Indias* (Bogotá, 1940), 10, 70.
2. This law, together with the *memoria*, or regulations for its application, was issued by the Infanta of Portugal with the avowed purpose of replenishing the public treasury, badly drained by "the war against the Turk." This law (AGI, Archivo General de Indias, Indiferente general, 532, 24, VI, 1559) is transcribed in Libros de acuerdos, I, fol. 294-296. It stems from a consultaìlon of the Council of the Indies of March 12, 1558 iecounted in Parry, *The Sale of Public Offices in the Spanish Indies Under the Hapsburgs* (Berkeley, 1953), 12.
3. Parry, *The Sale of Public Offices*, 12.
4. A copy of this cédula, sent to the governor of Havana, Gabriel de Luxán, on January 27, 1584, is transcribed with the minutes of the council of Havana of January 17, 1592 (Libros de acuerdos, III, fol. 362r-364v). José Torre Revello mentions another copy addressed to the viceroy of Perú, Martín Enríquez, whose original call number is AGI, Indiferente general, leg. 606, lib. I, fol. 4r-v; in "La nobleza colonial," *Boletin del Instituto de Investigaciones Históricas* (Buenos Aires, 1938), XXIII, 5-6.
5. Luis Pérez Costilla had become a public escribano in 1592 by renunciation to him by his father, Gaspar Pérez de Borroto, who was at the time "old, sick, and feeble." Libros de acuerdos, III, f. 357 r.
6. "Has appointed a lad barely 18 years old as his escribano." AGI 54-22: 1-15; Irene A. Wright, *Historia documental de San Cristobal de la Habana en el siglo XVI, basada en los documentos existentes en Archivo de Indias de Sevilla* (2 vols., La Habana, 1927), I, 297-310.

1.6

---

*Spanish Treatment
of the Indians*   Bartolomé de Las Casas

*Las Casas, a priest and humanist officially appointed by the
Crown as the Protector of the Indians, deplored the conditions
of servitude through which the Spanish in the Caribbean controlled the indigenous occupants. This selection is excerpted
from his classic mid-16th century account of Spanish atrocities committed against the Indians. As with similar accounts
of this time period, Las Casas' exposé served as ammunition
for other European nations eager to challenge Spain's right to
warm climate colonies.* The student should bear in mind
when reading this fiery rhetoric that Las Casas was writing to
draw the Spanish Crown's attention to a serious condition;
clearly he needed to be as emphatic as possible. This selection is reprinted, with permission of the publisher, from B. de
Las Casas, The Devastation of the Indies: A Brief Account,
copyright © 1974 by The Seabury Press, Inc.

Yet into this sheepfold, into this land of meek outcasts there
came some Spaniards who immediately behaved like ravening
wild beasts, wolves, tigers, or lions that had been starved for
many days. And Spaniards have behaved in no other way during the past forty years, down to the present time, for they
are still acting like ravening beasts, killing, terrorizing, afflict-
ing, torturing, and destroying the native peoples, doing all
this with the strangest and most varied new methods of
cruelty, never seen or heard of before, and to such a degree
that this Island of Hispaniola, once so populous (having a
population that I estimated to be more than three millions),
has now a population of barely two hundred persons.
   The island of Cuba is nearly as long as the distance between

25

Valladolid and Rome; it is now almost completely depopulated. San Juan and Jamaica are two of the largest, productive and attractive islands; both are now deserted and devastated. On the northern side of Cuba and Hispaniola lie the neighboring Lucayos comprising more than sixty islands including those called *Gigantes*, beside numerous other islands, some small some large. The least felicitous of them were more fertile and beautiful than the gardens of the King of Seville. They have the healthiest lands in the world, where lived more than five hundred thousand souls; they are now deserted, inhabited by not a single living creature. All the people were slain or died after being taken into captivity and brought to the Island of Hispaniola to be sold as slaves. When the Spaniards saw that some of these had escaped, they sent a ship to find them, and it voyaged for three years among the islands searching for those who had escaped being slaughtered, for a good Christian had helped them escape, taking pity on them and had won them over to Christ, of these there were eleven persons and these I saw.

More than thirty other islands in the vicinity of San Juan are for the most part and for the same reason depopulated, and the land laid waste. On these islands I estimate there are 2,100 leagues of land that have been ruined and depopulated, empty of people.

As for the vast mainland, which is ten times larger than all Spain, even including Aragon and Portugal, containing more land than the distance between Seville and Jerusalem, or more than two thousand leagues, we are sure that our Spaniards, with their cruel and abominable acts, have devastated the land and exterminated the rational people who fully inhabited it. We can estimate very surely and truthfully that in the forty years that have passed, with the infernal actions of the Christians, there have been unjustly slain more than twelve million men, women, and children. In truth, I believe without trying to deceive myself that the number of the slain is more like fifteen million.

The common way mainly employed by the Spaniards who call themselves Christian and who have gone there to extirpate those pitiful nations and wipe them off the earth is by unjustly waging cruel and bloody wars. Then, when they have slain all those who fought for their lives or to escape the tortures they would have to endure, that is to say, when they have slain all the native rulers and young men (since the Spaniards usually spare only the women and children, who are subjected to the hardest and bitterest servitude ever suffered by man or beast), they enslave any survivors. With these infernal methods of tyranny they debase and weaken countless numbers of those pitiful Indian nations.

Their reason for killing and destroying such an infinite number of souls is that the Christians have an ultimate aim, which is to acquire gold, and to swell themselves with riches in a very brief time and thus rise to a high estate disproportionate to their merits. It should be kept in mind that their insatiable greed and ambition, the greatest ever seen in the world, is the cause of their villainies. And also, those lands are so rich and felicitous, the native peoples so meek and patient, so easy to subject, and that our Spaniards have no more consideration for them than beasts. And I say this from my own knowledge of the acts I witnessed. But I should not say "than beasts" for, thanks be to God, they have treated beasts with some respect; I should say instead like excrement on the public squares. And thus they have deprived the Indians of their lives and souls, for the millions I mentioned have died without the Faith and without the benefit of the sacraments. This is a well-known and proven fact which even the tyrant Governors, themselves killers, know and admit. And never have the Indians in all the Indies committed any act against the Spanish Christians, until those Christians have first and many times committed countless cruel agressions against them or against neighboring nations. For in the beginning the Indians regarded the Spaniards as angels from Heaven. Only after the Spaniards had used violence against them, killing, robbing, torturing, did the Indians ever rise up against them.

SECTION 2

The Magnetism of the Caribbean:
The Arrival of Competitive European Powers

2.0
Introduction to Section 2

By the mid-sixteenth century it was apparent that nations other than Spain and Portugal were restive with the Papal decision of 1494, granting those two nations exclusive rights to overseas territories. In consequence, the latter part of the sixteenth century saw Spain's right to the Caribbean challenged by deed as well as polemic, pacing the way for Dutch, Danish, French and English explorations and settlement in the following century.

Although reasons for these intrusions into the Spanish domain touched on by such spokesmen as Richard Hakluyt included harrassment of Protestant sailors by Spanish Catholic seamen, these complaints were frequently just peevish echoes of the real issues at stake: the acquisition of wealth and territory. In his summary of the arguments which the English could raise to justify entrance into the West Indies, Hakluyt (selection 2.1) suggests that a foothold in the Caribbean would pave the way to reviving English trade globally, while additionally serving to diminish the stature of the Spanish Empire.

Hakluyt's arguments were heeded. Although the sixteenth-century clergyman had in mind an expansion of the lucrative Asian trade, in fact (as Richard Sheridan demonstrates in selection 2.3) the British actually created their own global economy in which the West Indies became a vital part. In addition to exploiting the slave trade–sugar production connection, the English held temperate climate colonies, which supplied the sugar islands with staples and provided a consumer market for tropical products and by-products. Once contact with Spanish colonies in the Caribbean had been made through contraband smuggling (in payment for which the settlers provided specie), and the labor supply

31

guaranteed from Africa, the stability of the English position in the West Indies was assured.

The economic basis for non-Spanish expansion in the region, however, was provided by Holland. Dutch West India Company representatives successfully took over the Northeast of Brazil by 1630 and there familiarized themselves with the techniques of sugar production and refining. By bringing this knowledge, along with cane slips, to the Caribbean (even before the Dutch were expelled from Brazil in 1654), they proved how easily the crop might be grown on Antillean soil. Coincidentally, the expulsion of the Dutch West India Company from Brazil, and the destruction wrought by the struggle, crippled Brazil's sugar productive capacity at a critical juncture in Caribbean history. After the mid-seventeenth century, Brazil no longer held a monopoly on the world production of sugar (selection 2.2); Caribbean planters might now reap windfall profits by selling sugar to metropolitan middlemen for redistribution throughout Europe.

The early years of English colonization in the Caribbean are explored in R. Dunn, *Sugar and Slaves: The Rise of the Planter Class in the English West Indies, 1624–1713.* Insights into the economic development of the English Caribbean are found in R.B. Sheridan, *Sugar and Slavery: An Economic History of the British West Indies, 1623–1775* and R. Pares, *War and Trade in the West Indies, 1739–1763.* C.C. Goslinga, *The Dutch in the Caribbean and on the Wild Coast, 1580–1680* and N.M. Crouse, *The French Struggle for the West Indies, 1665–1713* are standard works (in English) on the history of European campaigns for territory in the Caribbean.

2.1

English Rationalizations for
Caribbean Expansion   Richard Hakluyt

This brief selection (reproduced with the spelling of the sixteenth century) is a summary of the arguments raised by Hakluyt to stimulate British exploration and penetration of the Caribbean region. Although the thrust of his line of reasoning is mainly economic, it is equally clear that Hakluyt was concerned with the overall prestige of the English nation vis à vis the Spanish Empire. The student should recall that the presentation of these arguments preceeded the defeat of the Spanish Armada by four years. This excerpt originally appeared in the Discourse of Western Planting, *1584.*

A particular discourse concerninge the greate necessitie and manifolde comodyties that are like to growe to this Realme of Englande by the Westerne discoveries lately attempted, Written in the yere 1584. by Richarde Hackluyt of Oxforde at the requeste and direction of the righte worshipfull Mr. Walter Raghly nowe Knight, before the comynge home of his Twoo Barkes: and is devided into xxj chapters, the Titles whereof followe in the nexte leafe.

1. That this westerne discoverie will be greately for thinlargement of the gospell of Christe whereunto the Princes of the refourmed relligion are chefely bounde amongest whome her ma^tie ys principall.

2. That all other englishe Trades are growen beggerly or daungerous, especially in all the kinge of Spayne his Domynions, where our men are dryven to flinge their Bibles and prayer Bokes into the sea, and to forsweare and renownce their relligion and conscience and consequently theyr obedience to her Matie.

33

3. That this westerne voyadge will yelde unto us all the commodities of Europe, Affrica, and Asia, as far as wee were wonte to travell, and supply the wantes of all our decayed trades.

4. That this enterprise will be for the manifolde imploy-mente of nombers of idle men, and for bredinge of many sufficient, and for utterance of the greate quantitie of the commodities of our Realme.

5. That this voyage will be a great bridle to the Indies of the kinge of Spaine and a meane that wee may arreste at our pleasure for the space of tenne weekes or three monethes every yere, one or twoo hundred saile of his subjectes shippes at the fysshinge in Newfounde lande.

6. That the mischefe that the Indian Threasure wrought in time of Charles the later Emperor father to the Spanishe kinge, is to be had in consideration of the Q. moste excellent Ma[tie], leaste the contynuall commynge of the like threasure from thence to his sonne, worke the unrecoverable annoye of this Realme, whereof already wee have had very dangerous experience.

7. What speciall meanes may bringe kinge Phillippe from his high Throne, and make him equal to the Princes his neigh-bours, wherew[th] all is shewed his weakenes in the west Indies.

8. That the lymites of the kinge of Spaines domynions in the west Indies be nothinge so large as ys generally ymagined and surmised, neither those partes w[ch] he holdeth be of any such forces as ys falsly geven oute by the popishe Clergye and others his fautors, to terrifie the Princes of the Relligion and to abuse and blynde them.

9. The Names of the riche Townes lienge alonge the sea coaste on the northe side from the equinoctialle of the mayne lande of America under the kinge of Spayne.

10. A Brefe declaracion of the chefe Ilands in the Bay of Mexico beinge under the kinge of Spaine, wth their havens and fortes, and what commodities they yelde.

11. That the Spaniardes have executed most outragious and more then Turkishe cruelties in all the west Indies, whereby they are every where there, become moste odious unto them, whoe woulde joyne wth us or any other moste willingly to shake of their moste intollerable yoke, and have

begonne to doo it already in dyvers places where they were Lordes heretofore.

12. That the passage in this voyadge is easie and shorte, that it cutteth not nere the trade of any other mightie Princes, nor nere their Contries, that it is to be perfourmed at all tymes of the yere, and nedeth but one kinde of winde, that Ireland beinge full of goodd havens on the southe and west sides, is the nerest parte of Europe to yt, wch by this trade shall be in more securitie, and the sooner drawen to more Civilitie.

13. That hereby the Revenewes and customes of her Matie bothe outwardes and inwardes shall mightely be inlarged by the toll, excises, and other dueties wch wth oute oppression may be raised.

14. That this action will be greately for thincrease, mayneteynaunce and safetie of our Navye, and especially of greate shippinge wch is the strengthe of our Realme, and for the supportation of all those occupacious that depende upon the same.

15. That spedie plantinge in divers fitt places is moste necessarie upon these luckye westerne discoveries for feare of the daunger of being prevented by other nations wch have the like intentions, wth the order thereof and other reasons therwth all alleaged.

16. Meanes to kepe this enterprise from overthrowe and the enterprisers from shame and dishono^r.

17. That by these Colonies the Northwest passage to Cathaio and China may easely quickly and perfectly be searched oute aswell by river and overlande, as by sea, for proofe whereof here are quoted and alleaged divers rare Testymonies oute of the three volumes of voyadges gathered by Ramusius and other grave authors.

18. That the Queene of Englande title to all the west Indies, or at the leaste to as moche as is from Floride to the Circle articke, is more lawfull and righte then the Spaniardes or any other Christian Princes.

19. An aunswer to the Bull of the Donacion of all the west Indies graunted to the kinges of Spaine by Pope Alexander the vith whoe was himselfe a Spaniarde borne.

20. A brefe collection of certaine reasons to induce her

Matie and the state to take in hande the westerne voyadge and the plantinge there.

21. A note of some thinges to be prepared for the voyadge wch is sett downe rather to drawe the takers of the voyadge in hande to the presente consideracion then for any other reason for that divers thinges require preparation longe before the voyadge, wth oute wch the voyadge is maymed.

The Influence of Brazilian Sugar Production on the West Indian Economy   Matthew Edel

While the role of the Dutch in introducing cash crop sugar cultivation to the Lesser Antilles is well known, this selection examines the Dutch scheme for expanding the market by opening the Caribbean for production, while at the same time maintaining control over the sugar fields of Northeastern Brazil. Rejecting the hypothesis that the expulsion of the Dutch from Brazil in 1654 was the impetus for the transferral of sugar technology to Barbados, Edel here presents chronological evidence demonstrating that the Dutch had definitely succeeded in promoting sugar cultivation in the West Indies even before mid-century. This selection is excerpted from M. Edel (1969), 'The Brazilian Sugar Cycle of the Seventeenth Century and the Rise of West Indian Competition', Caribbean Studies 9, No. 1 (April), 26–33. Reprinted by permission of The Institute of Caribbean Studies and the Author. Copyright © 1969, by The Institute of Caribbean Studies, University of Puerto Rico.

The decline of Brazilian sugar's position on the world market is linked with the rise of Barbados, and later of the British, French and Dutch possessions in the West Indies, as competing sources of cane. Their development, in turn, followed on the decline of Spanish power and the struggle that ensued for the spoils. In the 1620's, England and France began to occupy West Indian islands, while the Dutch West India Company made several attempts to gain a foothold in Brazil, finally capturing Pernambuco in 1630. The occupation of Recife and the subsequent subjugation of the hinterland did not mean that sugar refining would be relocated in Europe. Most sugar was already reaching Amsterdam, although it had to be routed there by way of Lisbon or Oporto. According to Boxer, the Dutch already held between one-third and one-half of the carrying trade between Brazil and Europe, and much of the sugar shipped in Portuguese vessels was captured by Dutch West India Company vessels. Thus even the profits of the carrying trade were not necessarily to be transferred to new recipients in their entirety.[1] The lack of a restructuring of sugar trade as a result of the occupation lends some credence to the view that it was a political event, without necessary economic implications. The Brazilian-Dutch "monopoly" of sugar production, of which Furtado speaks, was neither created nor disturbed by the occupation.

The sugar economy of the northeast was, of course, disrupted by the military phases of conquest, but after 1635, and particularly under the regime of Johan Maurits (1637-1644), it recovered. Watjen gives the following figures for sugar exports (in arrobas, including both West India Company and private exports of all three grades of sugar).[2]

1635	85,352	1643	282,286
1636	144,207	1644	252,126
1637	65,972	1645	207,710
1638	198,097	1646	75,590
1639	273,090	1647	95,821
1640	265,788	1648	20,993
1641	447,561	1649	28,071
1642	298,913	1650	15,823

These statistics are undoubtedly underestimates of actual exportation, covering as they do only transactions which were recorded and for which records survived. But they do serve to indicate the changes over time of Dutch-controlled exports, and allow a chronological relation of the growth of West Indian sugar production to conditions in the Brazilian industry.

This chronology is essential to an understanding of the decline, and for an evaluation of the theory, noted at the outset, that the Portuguese expulsion of the Dutch led to the introduction of sugar into the West Indies, rebounding against the Brazilians. There is abundant evidence that the Dutch did play a role in the spread of sugar in the Caribbean. However, the chronology is not that normally implied.

Barbados, the most important of the new sugar islands, was settled in the sixteen-twenties. From the start it maintained contact with Dutch settlers on the mainland. The island had been surveyed by James Powell, a Dutch captain in the employ of Sir William Courteen, a London merchant of Flemish extraction, who was engaged in commerce in Amsterdam as well as in England. They planted a settlement in Barbados, introducing tropical crops from the Dutch settlement which was already functioning on the Essequibo River in Guiana. Title to the settlement was disputed in England, and it was granted to the Earl of Carlysle, who had no connections with the Dutch. In the 1630's, Barbados passed through a period of prosperity as a producer of tobacco, cotton and ginger. The island, at the time, was settled by British-born freeholders.[3]

Sugar was introduced in 1636 or 1637. Different accounts credit Pieter Brower, who may be identified as Dutch by the spelling of his name, or Sir James Drax, the first man to make his fortune by sugar growing on the island. The roller mill was in use by 1640 or 1642, introduced either by Drax or by Col. Holdip; and by 1645, Drax was already adjudged to have made a fortune. By 1645, slaves were already being introduced in large numbers. There were more than five thousand in Barbados in that year; most of the slaves, and considerable sugar equipment were sold by Dutch merchants.[4]

The later dating of the sugar boom often given is based on the account of Ligon who was in Barbados from 1647 to 1650. Ligon claims that "the secrets of the work being not well understood," the British settlers were getting poor yields from their cane at the time of his arrival, but that with practice, and particularly through visits to Dutch Pernambuco, better techniques were learned, including the right manner of planting canes, the correct date for cutting to get maximum sugar yields, the making of white "lump" sugar, and the correct placement of coppers in the boiling operation.[5] However, another planter, who arrived the year before

Ligon, wrote a letter in 1647, which indicates that it was already technically possible to produce commercial sugar, but that he could not grow it in the first year of his operations, for want of capital. He planted tobacco the first year, and with the profits of its sale, intended to purchase the equipment for sugar operations the next year.[6]

Dutch loans were undoubtedly important in financing the new industry, and may be credited with allowing it to grow as rapidly as it did. However, Ligon's account shows the industry might have been capable of growth by self-financing alone. Given an initial capital of £1000, he wrote, a man could invest in goods for trade to Barbados, triple his capital, and by continuing to accumulate the funds generated on the island through trade, soon acquire the £14,000 needed to open a plantation. If the Dutch were not the only possible source of capital, neither were they the only traders who could handle the island's commercial needs. Massachusetts captains provided another. In 1647, John Winthrop wrote in his journal.

As our means of returns for English commodities was grown very short, it pleased the Lord to open to us a trade with Barbados and other islands in the West Indies, which as it proved gainful so the commodities we had in exchange there for our cattle and provisions, as sugar, cotton, tobacco and indigo were a good help to discharge our engagements to England.[7]

The argument that the Dutch developed Barbados following their loss of Northeast Brazil would only be correct if their efforts in the island were concentrated after, at least, 1645, when the rebellion in Pernambuco cut off much of the hinterland from their control, and their shipments of sugar declined. While the Dutch supply of credit and slaves and technology to Barbados seem to have intensified after 1645, they had before that year already provided enough so that the industry of Barbados could have survived even without this intensification of assistance. Why the Dutch would have had incentive to introduce sugar to Barbados, even during the period of their secure control of Pernambuco, and why Barbados had at least a temporary comparative advantage which would have enabled it to compete successfully with

Brazil even had the latter's trade ties to Holland not been interrupted, will be argued in the final section of this paper. One other factor, the physical damage done to plantations by the battles and raids of the Portuguese and Dutch during the expulsion of the latter, may be discounted. These ravages were probably no more severe than those of the battles between cavaliers and roundheads in Barbados at the same time.

This early dating of the introduction of sugar to Barbados also serves to refute the theory, first popularized by Sombart, that the Jews introduced the new crop. Merrill and Canabrava cite a number of instances of Jewish participation in the Caribbean sugar industry, although Wiznitzer disputes Merrill's conclusion that, "The vast majority . . . gained entrance into English speaking lands".[8] Furthermore, all of these evidences of Jewish entry into the Caribbean, except for a small group at Cayenne, follow later than 1656. By 1652, sugar was important enough in Barbados that it had replaced tobacco and cotton as the media for collection of taxes.

Similar chronological evidence may be presented for the French islands. Daniel Trezel, a Dutch resident of Rouen, received land in Martinique and a monopoly on sugar exports in 1639, and attempted to introduce cane cultivation. A lack of capital seems to have held the attempt back. Trezel asked permission to use some of the land to grow tobacco to raise the funds; when this was refused, the plantation was sold. Charles Houel, governor of Guadeloupe for the French Compagnie des Isles d'Amérique, carried on the effort and was soon producing sugar. "Trezel, too, was soon back on his feet, and we presently find him the chief producer in Martinique".[9] This must have been in the early 1640's, for he was murdered before the end of the decade. The arrival of Brazilian Jews in Guadeloupe, most of whom did not go into sugar production, did not take place until 1654. St. Kitts also began sugar production in the early 1640's. Here the secret of making white sugar by claying was reportedly learned without Dutch help; it was extorted from a captured Portuguese *mestre du acucar*, who taught the technique to save his neck.[10]

Once established in the Caribbean, sugar production expanded rapidly. Dutch capital, and the disruption of trade between Brazil and Amsterdam undoubtedly helped the industry to grow as rapidly as it did. But even without this help, growth would have probably been rapid once Britain and France themselves began to take an interest in the mercantilist development of their colonies in the 1660's. As it was, Barbados exported close to 7,000 tons in 1655, and by 1700, was exporting 12,000 in a good year. Guadeloupe exported more than 2,000 tons in 1674; by the early 1700's it and Martinique had expanded output to some 10,000 tons; and Jamaica and Surinam, later entrants into the sugar market, had surpassed 4,000 tons each. Brazil's production declined slightly over the second half of the century, from 28,500 tons in 1650, to 21,800 tons in 1710.[11] Brazil was the largest producer of sugar, still, but it no longer controlled the market.

ENDNOTES

1. C.R. Boxer. *The Dutch in Brazil, 1624-1654*, Oxford; Clarendon Press, 1957, p. 20.
2. H. Watjen. *O Dominiu Colonial Holandez no Brasil*. Translated by P.C. Uchoa Cavalcanti. São Paulo: Editora Nacional, 1938, pp. 494-509.
3. D. Davis. *The Cavaliers and Roundheads of Barbados, 1650-1652*. Georgetown: Argosy Press, 1887; R. Ligon. *A True and Exact History of the Island of Barbadoes*, ed. by P. Sherlock. Mona: University College of the West Indies, 1957. (Written 1653.); O.P. Starkey. *The Economic Geography of Barbados*. New York: Columbia University Press, 1939.
4. Anon. *Memoirs of the First Settlement of the Island of Barbados*. London: E. Owen, 1743; V.T. Harlow. *A History of Barbados*. Oxford: Clarendon, 1926; H.H. Parry and P.M. Sherlock. *A Short History of the West Indies*. London: Macmillan Co., 1957.
5. R. Ligon. *A True and Exact History* . . .
6. D. Davis. *The Cavaliers* . . .
7. V.T. Harlow. *A History of Barbados*, p. 272.
8. A.P. Canabrava. "A influencia do Brasil na technica do fabrico de açucar nas Antilhas francesas e inglesas no meado de seculo XVII." *Anuario da Facultade de Ciencias Economias e Administrativas*, São Paulo, 1946-47, pp. 63-76; G. Merrill. "The Role of Sephardic Jews in the British Caribbean Area During the Seventeenth Cen-

tury," *Caribbean Studies*, IV, 3 (1964), pp. 32–49; A. Wiznitzer. *Jews in Colonial Brazil*. New York: Columbia University Press, 1960.

9. N.M. Crouse. *French Pioneers in the West Indies, 1624-1664.* New York: Columbia University Press, 1940, p. 78.
10. A.P. Canabrava. "A influencia do Brasil . . ."
11. N. Deerr. *The History of Sugar*. London: Chapman and Hall, 1949. 2 vols.

The Plantation Revolution and the Industrial Revolution
Richard B. Sheridan

The direction of economic exchange in the Caribbean was not solely European-bound. In this concise discussion, Sheridan highlights the trade networks established in the British West Indies and indicates how important the markets in the North American colonies would become to sugar interests. Similarly, the English colonies in the Caribbean provided a base of operations for entrepôt *trade with the Spanish West Indies, a lucrative, if often illegal, source of revenue. This selection originally appeared as R.B. Sheridan (1969), 'The Plantation Revolution and the Industrial Revolution', Caribbean Studies 9, No. 3 (October), 10–19. Reprinted by permission of The Institute of Caribbean Studies and the Author. Copyright © 1969, by The Institute of Caribbean Studies, University of Puerto Rico.*

The remarkable expansion of the plantation colonies was both cause and effect of the developing Atlantic trading area which had been the theatre of conflict between North Europe and the Iberian countries in the sixteenth and early seventeenth centuries, was followed by the long and eventually successful attempt by England and France to destroy the Dutch hold on Europe's overseas trade, and then gave way to the bitter and protracted fight between England and France for ascendancy in world trade and empire, the Second Hundred Years War from 1689 to 1815, from which England emerged as the leader.[1] From the vantage point of the Caribbean plantations this was a struggle to expand the area of tropical staple production, to augment supplies of manufactures and services from the metropolis, to control and develop outlying regions capable of supplying forced labour and intermediate products, to build sea power to keep open the lifelines of trade in the formal empire, and to expand trade with the informal empires. The development of the whole trading area of economic interactions thus involves brief consideration of the component elements, that is, the slave trade from West Africa; the supply of foodstuffs, building materials, and livestock from North America, Ireland, Bermuda, and the wine islands; the informal empire trade with the Spanish Main and Brazil; and, lastly, the impact of these trades on the metropolis.

The black population of Africa was the great reservoir of labour for the plantations of America. Negroes entering America far outnumbered European immigrants before the nineteenth century. Total importations of Negro slaves are conservatively estimated to have numbered 15,000,000, of which 900,000 came in the sixteenth century, 2,750,000 in the seventeenth, 7,000,000 in the eighteenth, and 4,000,000 in the nineteenth.[2] Slavery was not only necessary to the colonies of tropical staple production; it also contributed to the economic growth of the metropolis and the colonies to the north of Maryland. "The *Labour of Negroes* is the principal *Foundation* of our *Riches* from the Plantations," wrote William Wood in 1718; "The *African Trade* . . . is the *Spring* and *Parent* whence the others flow . . ."[3]

A viable Atlantic trading area depended in large measure on the performance of the slave triangle, whereby European and East Indian goods were exchanged for African slaves; slaves for bills of exchange, specie, and plantation produce; and plantation produce for manufactures, intermediate goods, and services. In the final analysis it was the high rate of return on capital invested in human chattels which gave strength to the plantations; the plantations, in turn, supporting numerous branches of trade, manufacture, and service activity. Though statistics are too meager to compute the rate of return on slave capital, a recent study by the writer shows that the median sugar estate in Jamaica yielded a net profit of nearly ten per cent in the period 1771-75.[4] In a well-known passage Adam Smith said: "The profits of a sugar plantation in any of our West Indian colonies are generally much greater than those of any other cultivation that is known either in Europe or America: And the profits of a tobacco plantation, though inferior to those of sugar, are superior to those of corn, as has already been observed."[5]

The plantations' requirements for slaves was a function of the growth rate of such establishments and the labour replacement rate. In other words, slaves were brought to the West Indies to form new plantations, to increase the labour force of existing plantations, and to replace workers who died or became superannuated. Allocation of newly imported slaves to these usages obviously varied in time and place, but it is evident that few plantations could remain productive for long without imports for replacement. It is paradoxical that high profits were not necessarily incompatible with high mortality. Not a few contemporaries pointed out, as did Lord Broughham, "that so long as a slave market exists, men find their profit in working out a certain number of their slaves, and supplying the blacks by purchase, rather than by breeding."[6]

Slavery, as a profitable institution, thus depended on the constant recruitment of cheap labour by importation from Africa. Africa's capacity to supply the growing demand of the plantations was a matter of concern to both defenders and critics of the peculiar institution. Antislavery leaders claimed that the slave trade fostered tribal warfare, drunkenness and other vices to such an extent that, together with forced emigration, West Africa was doomed to social disintegration and depopulation. Contrary opinions were expressed by Europeans in West Africa, as, for example, the French merchant on the Isle of Gambia who asserted in 1786 that "this Continent is capable of supporting far more numerous exportations, without its population experiencing any sensible effects."[7] No doubt the slave trade retarded orderly progress and development in West Africa and made serious inroads into the population at certain times and places. Yet it is the contention of one modern historian that the average loss of population to West Africa as a result of the slave trade was less than one per cent a year of the total population, and that "such a rate of loss need not necessarily have been a crippling one for a healthy society."[8]

Given the labour requirements of the plantations and West Africa's capacity to supply slaves, the trade in human chattels might be expected to come under the domination of the European nation which was capable of supplying trading goods most cheaply. Moreover, this cost advantage would depend in large measure upon the nation's ability to dominate other branches of Atlantic trade. No doubt these were the controlling factors in the economic history of the slave trade, but they were so intertwined with the strategems of war and diplomacy, with innovations in trading methods and finance, that the path to dominance might be very devious indeed. The strategems of war and diplomacy are much too complex to recount here. In broad outline they led to Portugal's virtual monopoly of the slave trade from 1442 to about 1625; Dutch dominance during the greater part of the seventeenth century; French and English efforts to gain a foothold, especially after 1650 when West Africa was a theatre of action in three Anglo-Dutch wars; followed by Anglo-French rivalry and the emergence of Great Britain as the leading slave trader during the greater part of the eighteenth century.

On 19 July, 1647, Richard Vines of Barbados wrote to Governor John Winthrop of Massachusetts: "This gentleman, Mr. John Mainford, merchant, is coming to your porte to trade for provisions for the belly, which at present is very scarce . . . men are so intent upon planting sugar that they had rather buy foode at very dearc rates than produce it by labour, soe infinite is the profitt of sugar workes after once accomplished."[9] It is significant that the sugar revolution occurred at a time of economic crisis in New England. Before its virtual cessation in 1641, the "great migration" of Puritans to New England had encouraged the inhabitants to produce an agricultural surplus to exchange for the cash and metropolitan wares of the newcomers. The sudden collapse of the immigrant market so threatened the very existence of the settlers that their leaders considered relocating the colony in a more congenial environment. Fortunately, an alternative was at hand, for Boston had an active mercantile and

shipping community with capital resources to exploit the
agricultural surplus. At first, markets for pipe staves, grain,
fish and other products were sought out in Spain and the
Atlantic islands. But large-scale trading began in 1647, when
John Winthrop recorded in his diary: "it pleased the Lord to
open to us a trade with Barbados and the other Islands in
the West Indies . . ." Grain, beef, bread, fish, live cattle and
horses were exchanged for sugar, cotton, tobacco and indigo
"which were a good help to discharge our engagements in
England."[10]

If, at the outset, intercolonial trade was more vital to the
New Englanders than their tropical brethren, the dependency
relationship was subsequently reversed. Plantations which
were virtually self sufficient in foodstuffs, building materials,
and livestock began to concentrate more labour and capital
on cash crops. Advantage was taken of the unique combination of soil, climate, trade winds, and other location features
to expand the cultivation and processing of tropical staples.
As cane lands on a given plantation encroached on provision
grounds, pasture, and woodland, the proprietor turned more
and more to imported supplies. In time the Caribbean islands
and the colonies along the Atlantic seaboard became "one
great population." England was virtually unique among the
European powers in having detached temperate-zone colonies
to supply products of the field, forest, and fishery and to
absorb such tropical goods as molasses, rum, and sugar.

In the British West Indies a regime of near-monoculture
spread from Barbados to the Leeward Islands. By 1672 the
governor of Barbados estimated that the island did not
furnish of its own growth "one quarter victualls sufficient
for its Inhabitants nor any other necessaries for Planting . . ."[11] The governor of the Leeward Islands appealed to
the Board of Trade in 1756 for a strong squadron of warships
to protect the incoming provision vessels, "these Islands
being incapable, consistent with the Cultivation of the Sugar
Cane, which renders them so valuable to the Crown and to
their Mother Country, of raising Provisions for the support
of the Negroes which Your Lordships will observe are
become very Numerous in the several Islands."[12] By comparison with the Lesser Antilles, the monoculture of Jamaica

was less pronounced owing to extensive savannas for pasturing livestock and marginal lands suitable for provision culture. Nevertheless, the comparative cost principle was operative in Jamaica. Planters in that island were "so intent upon making sugar" that they chose rather to purchase flour, bread, corn, beef, pork, butter, saltfish, rice, staves, lumber, and horses "from their Neighbours than to Employ their own Slaves in that work . . ."[13]

The near-monoculture economies not only demanded a wide range of commodities from North America; they also drew into their orbit the products of Scotland and Ireland. By the Act of Union of 1707 Scotland was accorded all the privileges of the colonial trade that had hitherto been reserved by the Navigation Acts to England. Glasgow and environs grew remarkably, owing chiefly to its trade with the Chesapeake Bay area and the West Indies.[14] Ireland was treated on a par with England by the Navigation Acts until 1663, when direct exports to the colonies were limited to servants, horses, and provisions. Four years later Parliament prohibited the importation of Irish cattle into England. Irishmen responded to the Cattle Act by turning their surplus cattle into salt beef, which along with salt pork and butter rapidly became a leading export to the colonies and to foreign ports. Moreover, after 1705 certain kinds of Irish linen cloth were permitted in the direct trade with the colonies. Most of Ireland's colonial exports went to the West Indies, where they complemented the imports from North America which consisted primarily of corn, flour, and bread rather than meat and butter. In a reverse direction, Ireland developed into an important market for colonial sugar, rum, indigo, tobacco, and flax seed.[15]

Moreover, the economies of Bermuda and the other Atlantic islands were transformed in response to the sugar revolution in the Caribbean. Tobacco was the leading staple of Bermuda until about 1658 when the feeding of Barbados became perhaps the island's chief business. Bermuda exported live cattle, salt beef, pork, and fish to the plantations; indeed, the demand for livestock was so great that much of the island's available acreage was converted from tobacco to pasture.[16] Madeira developed a special relationship with the

English colonies in 1663, when an act of Parliament permitted wines of the growth of that island and the Azores to be carried to the colonies in English vessels.[17]

Much more valuable than the informal empire trade of Madeira was that carried on between Jamaica and the Spanish colonies. The latter trade must be seen against the background of Cromwell's Western Design, an ambitious scheme to break through Spain's monopoly in the West Indies and to gain control of Spanish America. Though in many respects disappointing, Cromwell's expeditionary force of 1655 did succeed in the conquest of Jamaica.[18] Jamaica was large by comparison with the English possessions in the Lesser Antilles, its environment was suited to tropical agriculture, and it was admirably situated to conduct an *entrepot* trade with the Spanish West Indies. "Great are the advantages accruing to Britain from the trade between Jamaica and the Spaniards of Mexico, etc . . . ," declared a commercial annalist. He went on to say that this trade sprang from the Anglo-Spanish treaty of 1670, and continued down to the beginning of Queen Anne's War in 1702 "to the value of near £300,000 yearly, in various European merchandise, negroes, provisions, etc., for all which our people were paid in good pieces of eight."[19] Jamaica's informal empire trade was even greater in the eighteenth century, owing partly to the famous *Asiento* of 1713, whereby England secured the contract to supply 4,800 slaves to the Spanish colonies, and partly to the complementary relationship which developed between the sugar plantations and neighbouring colonies. Added to the *entrepot* trade in slaves and manufactures was rum of local distillation; in exchange came horses, mules, and horned cattle for the plantations, and cochineal, cocoa, indigo, dyewoods, drugs, and especially specie for re-export to Great Britain.

ENDNOTES

1. A.H. John, "War and the English Economy, 1700-1763," *Econ. Hist. Rev.*, 2nd ser., VII, 3 (April 1955), 329-44.
2. Robert R. Kuczynski, *Population Movements* (Oxford, 1936), 6-17.

3. William Wood, *A Survey of Trade* (London, 1718), 179-193; Eric Williams, *Capitalism and Slavery* (Chapel Hill, 1944), 1-84.
4. R.B. Sheridan, "The Wealth of Jamaica in the Eighteenth Century," *Econ. Hist. Rev.*, 2nd ser., XVIII, 2 (August 1965), 293-311. For a criticism and defense of this article see R.P. Thomas, "The Sugar Colonies of the Old Empire: Profit or Loss for Great Britain?" and R.B. Sheridan, "The Wealth of Jamaica in the Eighteenth Century: A Rejoinder," both in *Econ. Hist. Rev.*, 2nd ser., XXI, 1 (April 1968), 30-45 and 46-61.
5. Adam Smith, *The Wealth of Nations* (New York, 1937 [1776]) 366.
6. Henry Brougham, *An Inquiry into the Colonial Policy of the European Powers* (2 vols., Edinburgh, 1803), 11, 469.
7. Elizabeth Donna, *Documents Illustrative of the History of the Slave Trade to America* (4 vols. New York, 1965), II, 567.
8. J.D. Fage, *An Introduction to the History of West Africa* (Cambridge, 1961), 84-7.
9. Thomas Hutchinson (ed.), *A Collection of Original Papers Relating to the History of the Colony of Massachusetts-Bay* (Boston, 1769), 222.
10. James K. Hosmer, *Winthrop's Journal*, 1630-1649 (2 vols., New York, 1903), II, 328; Darrett B. Rutman, "Governor Winthrop's Garden Crop. The Significance of Agriculture in the Early Commerce of Massachusetts Bay," *William and Mary Quarterly*, 3rd ser. XX, 3 (July 1963), 396-415.
11. *B.M. Egerton MSS. 2395*, f. 477. Lord Willoughby's Proposals Concerning the West Indies, April 8, 1672.
12. Public Record Office, London, Colonial Office 152/28, Bb. Gov. Thomas to the Board of Trade, February 20, 1756.
13. *Ibid.* C.O. 137/19, f. 47. Gov Hunter to the Board of. Trade, December 24, 1730/1; Douglas Hall, *Free Jamaica 1838-1865 An Economic History* (New Haven, 1959), 13-18.
14. Henry Hamilton, *An Economic History of Scotland in the Eighteenth Century* (Oxford, 1963), 260-7, 270-1, 279-81, 419-20.
15. Francis G. James, "Irish Colonial Trade in the Eighteenth Century," *William and Mary Quarterly*, 3rd ser. XX, 4 (October 1963), 574-82.
16. Henry C. Wilkinson, *The Adventurers of Bermuda* (Oxford, 1958), 302-3.
17. 15 Car. II, cap. 7.
18. Frank Strong, "The Causes of Cromwell's West Indian Expedition," *American Historical Review*, IV, 2 (January 1899), 228-45.
19. David MacPherson, *Annals of Commerce* (4 vols., London, 1805) II, 162.

SECTION 3
Slavery and Plantation Systems: Theory and Reality

3.0
Introduction to Section 3

Certainly one of the most controversial areas of current research on the Caribbean centers on the development of slavery systems. While seventeenth- and eighteenth-century pedants frequently searched for justification of human enslavement in ancient Roman texts, we know that during the heyday of Antillean slavery there were many who questioned the sagacity and even the economic necessity of the institution.

Yet, even if we accept the existence of slavery without attempting to unravel the legalistic and avaristic reasons for its persistence, we would still be in controversial waters. In large part, the credit for the continuing polemic on slavery stems from the 1946 publication of *Slave and Citizen* by the Columbia University professor Frank Tannenbaum. Tannenbaum revealed qualitative differences in slavery systems as practiced in the Americas by European powers and, based on his understanding of religious and juridical safeguards, he arranged the systems on a continuum with the Spanish and Portuguese emerging as the most lenient, and the Dutch and English at the opposite end of the scale; the French were consigned to the middle ground. Harry Hoetink (selection 3.3) discusses the applicability of this 'Tannenbaum thesis' to modern day social relations in the Netherlands Antilles, and concludes that for Curaçao, at least, Tannenbaum's model had little predictive value. Knight warns us (selection 3.2) that there are many variables which must be taken into consideration before a metropolitan country's treatment of slaves can be analyzed or quantified with any accuracy. On the other hand, Beckford thoughtfully suggests that the basic elements of plantation society have had a profound and 'emasculating' effect on today's Caribbean culture, which was not confined to one colonial power. Thus, the plantation in his view (see selection 3.1) must be treated as a cross-cultural phenomenon because its implications are clearly pan-Caribbean.

The remaining selections of this unit are devoted to discussing individuals affected by slavery, although not necessarily slaves themselves. De Groot's study (selection 3.4) of 'maroons' (runaway slaves) in the Guianas interprets the Boni Maroons as pawns in a power struggle between the French and the Dutch. Handler's description of freedmen of color in Barbados (selection 3.5) suggests that individuals who were technically free (even if they had originally been born into slavery) were discriminated against despite legal guarantees. While many representatives of this group possessed light skin tones, they were not accepted in white society as equals. On the contrary, as Shepard shows in selection 3.6, economically depressed whites in Barbadian society tended to represent themselves as superior to the freedmen class, and often competed with the latter group for the limited artisan occupations which the colony supported.

In the last article, Hall (selection 3.7) presents a schedule of the slave's workday in nineteenth-century Cuba. The work demands corresponded to those facing a slave in eighteenth-century Jamaica or St Domingue (Haiti), or wherever there was maximum emphasis on sugar production. That intense working conditions hastened an early mortality was of limited concern in colonies with constantly replenished slave populations.

The literature on slavery and slave systems is enormous, and the beginning student in the field can only expect to sample a minor portion of the excellent output of the last few decades. A good starting point may be found in P. Curtin's *The Atlantic Slave Trade: A Census.* M. Moreno Fraginal's *The Sugar Mill: The Socio-Economic Complex of Sugar in Cuba 1760-1860* (translated from the Spanish original) provides a description of the vital connection between slavery and technological innovation. L. Diaz Soler, *La Historia de la Esclavitud Negra en Puerto Rico* is the the standard work for that island, as C.L.R. James, *The Black Jacobins: Toussaint L'Ouverture and the San*

Domingo Revolution is for Haiti. O. Patterson's interpretive *The Sociology of Slavery: An Analysis of the Origins, Development and Structure of Negro Slave Society in Jamaica* examines the institution in Jamaica, while R. Price (ed.), *Maroon Societies: Rebel Slave Communities in the Americas* has a pan-regional perspective.

The Continuing Influence of the Plantation

George Beckford

The plantations that dotted the Caribbean landscape shaped more than just economic systems. The organization of labor for the production of sugar profoundly affected the nature and quality of social relationships in colonial societies. In this selection, Beckford comments on the plantation social system and develops a model of society that has had pervasive and often insidious influence in the Caribbean even up to present times. Reprinted from G.L. Beckford (1971), 'Plantation Society: Toward a General Theory of Caribbean Society', Savacou, No. 5 (June), 7-8 and 11-15, with permission from Savacou Publications and the Author.

Every society is a product of the particular historical forces that give it shape and form. The thesis of this paper is that modern Caribbean society displays structural forms that are a direct legacy of the slave plantation system. This legacy provides the single most important clue for an understanding of contemporary Caribbean society.

The plantation was the chief instrument of European colonization and exploitation in the Caribbean, the U.S. South, the Guianas, and Northeast Brazil — an area described by Wagley as Plantation America;[1] in certain islands of the Indian and Pacific Oceans; and in Ceylon, Malaya, Indonesia and the Philippines. In all these places the structural characteristics of the plantation system have persisted and they define a particular social framework. "Plantation economy and society" is an appropriate general description of this social framework. Elsewhere, I have explored at length its economic dimension.[2] This paper briefly considers its social and political dimensions. Although the Caribbean is the main point of reference, the general conclusions apply as well to other plantation societies to which some consideration is given.

Typically, a plantation is a unit of agricultural production with a specific type of economic organization characterized by a large resident labour force of unskilled workers who are directed by a small supervisory staff. As well, the plantation is a community, its social structure and the pattern of inter-personal relations within it reflecting to a large extent the authority structure governing the pattern of economic organization. Historically, plantations came to be established in places where land was abundant relative to population. Labour was imported (to carry out production tasks) on a scale that irreversibly changed the demographic picture in most places. The terms on which such labour was incorporated into the new locations involved a high degree of coercion and control; and thereafter determined social and political relationships in very precise ways. So that wherever plantations came to engross most of the arable land in a particular country, the resulting society consisted of a series of plantation communities.

Whether or not the economic dominance of plantations has persisted to the present time, societies with this historical legacy continue to reflect the plantation influence. All types of plantations have certain features in common: they cover relatively large areas; numerous unskilled workers are involved; decision making is highly centralized; the pattern of management organization is authoritarian; and the workers are separated from the decision makers by social and cultural differences. Within the plantation community there exists a rigid pattern of social stratification based on a caste system that separates owners and managers (normally white people of European extract) from the workers (normally Africans or East Indians).

The traditional plantation is a total economic institution. It binds every one in its embrace to the one task of executing the will of its owner or owners. And because it is omnipotent and omnipresent in the lives of those living within its confines, it is also a total social institution. Social relations within the plantation community are determined by the economic organization that governs production. Now imagine an economy composed of only plantation producing units. In such a case, the social structure and distribution of political power in the country as a whole would merely be a larger reproduction of that existing on the individual plantation. No country is purely an aggregation of plantations, in fact. But, as the discussion in this paper indicates, the plantation economies and sub-economies of the world reveal social and political characteristics almost identical to those found within the individual plantation community. Thus we can appropriately define plantation society as a particular class of society with distinguishing characteristics of social structure and political organization, and laws of motion governing social change. The rest of this paper develops this point.

SOCIAL ORGANIZATION AND STRUCTURE IN PLANTATION SOCIETY

The plantation influence can be traced almost directly in every important aspect of social life in the plantation societies of the world. As with plantation community, plantation society derives an ordering of social status of different groups and individuals within a country which is directly correlated with occupational status and rank in the authority structure of the plantation itself. Of course, correlation alone does not establish causality. To establish this we need to explore the historical legacy somewhat to determine what forces have moulded the pattern of social organization which we find today in these societies. The New World experience perhaps provides the clearest illustration of plantation influence on social structure. Since this area has the longest history of continuous plantation influence, the experience there should provide useful insights into the general phenomenon.

The slave plantations of the New World brought together a few white people from Europe as owners, and large numbers of black people from Africa as forced labourers.

The latter came from different parts of the west coast of Africa and were generally an odd mixture of people from different tribal and cultural backgrounds who, most often, did not speak the same language; the slave groups were mixed in terms of sex but men usually outnumbered the women, as more of them were required for the arduous task of sugar and cotton plantation work. On the other hand, the white Europeans who came were chiefly plantation owners, managers and skilled labourers; and these were mostly males who viewed their association with the plantation as a temporary affair. The two groups were thrown together with one single purpose — production of the plantation crop. This meant, therefore, that the structure of authority established for this exercise would influence the entire social order on the plantation. We have already noted that the slave plantation had the character of a total economic and social institution. Raymond Smith describes such institutions in the following way:

'Total institutions' are organised groups with well-defined boundaries and with a marked internal hierarchical structure approaching an internal caste system. Examples would be asylum inmates and staff, prisoners and wardens, officers and men on board a ship at sea, slaves and masters . . .

It is characteristic of total institutions that people enter them as already socially formed human beings with a culture and a set of attitudes which need to be reformed so that the inmate can be 'handled' as a lunatic, a monk, a prisoner, a slave or whatever it might be. Mechanisms arc brought into play designed to effect a clean break with the past and a destruction of the inmate's old self so that a new set of attitudes — a new 'identity' — can be imposed.[3]

The slaves were put through a process known as "seasoning" to adjust them for work on the plantation. And since then, right up to the present, the black experience in the New World has been a continuous process of acculturation and socialization to the norms of the plantation system.

The social structure of the slave plantation took shape from the social organization necessary for production. White European planters and administrators stood at the top; and were separated by a system of caste which placed the black slaves firmly at the bottom. An intermediate group of skilled white people also existed. And among the black people there emerged a group of racial and cultural halfcastes resulting from the exploits of white males with black females. This group was generally more privileged than the pure blacks and frequently made up the staff of house servants whose tasks were less arduous than those of other blacks.[4] Slave plantation society as a whole was simply made up of individual plantation communities. As Smith suggested, "one may say that this was a segmentary society with the plantations constituting a simple linear series of segments having little or no organic inter-relation."[5] The society as a whole was therefore rigidly stratified by race and colour directly correlated with occupational status on the plantation; and without any kind of social mobility whatever.

On each plantation, the white owner or administrator was lord and master; and his mansion was the centre of social life for all within the community. All decisions affecting the lives of the black people emanated from there. No church, state or other social institution had direct access to the slaves. Church facilities were provided on the plantation by the master who also exercised juridicial and state functions. The political order was despotic with commands issued by the master to the slaves through an overseer. Slaves were herded together as an undifferentiated mass in compounds that had a kind of village character. Because the slaves were drawn from different cultures, they had to develop a language on the plantation in order to communicate with each other. And a common language was also necessary to facilitate the chain of command from master to slave. In the circumstances what emerged was the language which was a simplification and modification of the tongue of the masters. These are the so-called "creole" languages of the plantation societies today. This pattern of acculturation was to have a lasting effect on the lives of black people. For, as Thompson points out,

Language is bound up with the system of social control. With its acquisition there tends to develop at the same time an acceptance of the situation. The meanings of the terms of the language develop in the general atmosphere of authority and against the background of co-operative activity involved in agricultural production. As this takes place, authority and obedience are determined more by moral and less by material factors.[6]

In the process, black people were increasingly emasculated culturally and socialized toward the culture of the planter class. However, they did succeed in retaining some of their original culture; and this was blended with the other to create what is now a clearly distinct and separate culture within plantation society today. Slave plantation society, therefore had certain distinctive features: a caste system based on race, rigidly stratified social structure based on occupational status on the plantation and divided along race and colour lines, and cultural plurality with integrative elements deriving from the common destiny to production of the crop for everyone in the plantation community. This last feature of the system is one which has largely escaped the notice of most plantation scholars. Yet it is one that is of great importance in explaining certain aspects of plantation societies today. The different groups on the slave plantation interacted with each other in one main area of activity — production of the crop; and from day to day, season by season, year in and year out, this was the chief bond between them. Because production of the crop was the only reason why these groups were brought together, it is not surprising that this dominated their lives. For the white masters who owned the slaves and governed the plantations, the pattern of tolerable social organization was one that would maximize profits on production. Rigid control of the labour supply was critical and this involved control over the movement of slaves in space and status.

ENDNOTES

1. Charles Wagley, "Plantation America — A Culture Sphere," Caribbean Studies — A Symposium ed. Vera Rubin (Institute of Social and Economic Research, University College of the West Indies, hereafter I.S.E.R., 1957).
2. George L. Beckford. Plantations and Poverty in the Third World (I.S.E.R.) published as *Persistent Poverty: Underdevelopment in*

Plantation Economies of the Third World (New York, Oxford University Press, 1972).

2. George L. Beckford, Plantations and Poverty in the Third World (I.S.E.R./O.U.P., forthcoming).

3. R.T. Smith, "Social Stratification, Cultural Pluralism and Integration in West Indian Societies," in S. Lewis and T.G. Matthews (eds.), Caribbean Integration (Río Piedras, Puerto Rico, 1967), p. 230.

4. The structure described here is a simplification of what obtained in fact. But the abstraction is fairly representative of the situation in most cases. For a detailed exposition on the social structure of the slave plantation, see H. Orlando Patterson, The Sociology of Slavery (London, 1967). For modification of the general pattern described here, see, for example, W.E. Moore and R.M. Williams, "Stratification in the Ante-Bellum South," American Sociological Review, June 1942.

5. R.T. Smith, op. cit., p. 229.

6. Edgar Thompson, "The Plantation: The Physical Basis of Traditional Race Relations," Race Relations and the Race Problem (ed. Edgar Thompson, Durham, N.C., 1939), p. 211.

How to Compare Slavery Systems   Franklin W. Knight

Although Beckford is undoubtedly correct in suggesting that *all plantation societies share certain economic and social* *features, there is a danger in generalizing about the nature of* *slavery and its application in colonial settings. Knight's essay* *alerts the reader to the necessity of distinguishing between* *urban and rural slavery, slaves held in plantation systems* *vs. slaves working in mining contexts, etc. Differences in* *environmental and political factors thus must be taken into* *consideration before the common denominators can be* *accurately assessed. Reprinted from F.W. Knight,* The African Dimension in Latin American Societies, *Macmillan Publishing Co., Inc. New York, with permission of the publishers; copyright © 1974 by Franklin W. Knight.*

How do we compare slave societies in the New World? Before we can do this, we must know what conditions were typical for any given slave society in any area of America. This is not an easy task. The quality of slave life and the conditions of slavery varied considerably throughout the New World. There is no doubt about this assertion, and historians have been debating the variations for a very long time. But while it is easy to arrive at some idea of the general conditions of slavery, it is less easy to determine the general quality of slave life from place to place and from century to century.

Most people who have tried to compare slavery in the Americas have done so according to the imperial systems and national boundaries of the slaveholding groups. This is especially true of North American historians. The general consensus classified slavery along a continuum that had the

Anglo-Saxons, that is, the United States and the British Islanders, as the most cruel and inhumane slaveowners, and the Iberians — the Spanish Americans and the Brazilians — as the most humane. And somewhere in the middle fell the French, the Dutch, and the Danes.

These thinkers on slavery and slave societies make useful contributions to our understanding of the subject. The difficulty is that they all use a "rigid" theory to explain a dynamic and changing social phenomenon. Slave societies, like all other societies, were never static. In all slave societies, therefore, there were stages, or even a single stage, when slavery was more important, socially, politically, and economically, than at other times. Barbados was a mature slave society in 1660; but by 1780 slavery had been in decline, and by 1838 it was abolished. The most important phase of slavery in the United States came only after the abolition of the English transatlantic slave trade in 1808. The majority of the slaves in the United States, therefore, was produced locally, not imported from Africa, which was a truly American phenomenon. About 75 percent of all Cuban slaves came during the nineteenth century, at a time when very few countries still engaged in slavery and the slave trade. Brazil, on the other hand, was a consistently high importer of slaves between the sixteenth and the nineteenth centuries.

One significant problem in comparing and categorizing American slave societies is simply timing. Except for Brazil, there was no uniform participation in the slave trade and slavery. Some countries were early starters, others late starters; some remained always important participants, such as Brazil or Jamaica, while Peru and Ecuador were quite unimportant. Cuba, Trinidad, and Venezuela developed significant slave components only during the very last days of slavery in the Americas.

Another problem is the internal diversity of slave societies. Within each society, slaves did a very wide variety of work. The view held by the society as a whole seems to be related to the numbers and jobs that they did. In any case, the conditions of slave life and the general attitudes toward slavery by the free society sprung from the role of slavery.

Two patterns existed in American slaveholding societies. One was the individual-ownership pattern, in which a master had from one to four slaves. These slaves were usually domestic slaves, or personal assistants in towns, but also included slaves who were engaged in such activities as piracy, ranching, and fishing. The other was the group-ownership pattern, where the masters owned slaves in large numbers for plantation or mining work.

Individually owned slaves had advantages and opportunities that group-owned slaves lacked. The most important aspect of the individual-ownership pattern was the absence of coercion and regimentation in their occupations. This is especially true of the largest group of such slaves, the urban slaves. Urban slaves had a wide range of social and sexual contacts with fellow slaves, with the free nonwhite community, with the free white community. Urban slaves had some social and legal resources — the intervention of the minister or employer in the southern United States; or the priest and government-appointed "Protector of Slave Rights" in Cuba during the nineteenth century — which for all practical purposes did not exist for the nonurban slaves.

Most writers on slavery generally concede that urban slaves, regardless of their occupations, established an understanding and a relationship with free society — and with their masters — which was not duplicated elsewhere. Having access to more money, urban slaves fed and dressed themselves better and certainly enjoyed themselves more, drinking, dancing, and entertaining openly where it was legal, or clandestinely where it was not. Since the day-to-day life of these slaves was less regimented than in the mines and on the plantations, these slaves tended to escape from slavery either through self-purchase or outright desertion. Moreover, their established connections with the free community also facilitated their way out of slavery.

With greater mobility, a greater range of contacts, and probably a greater degree of literacy, urban slaves tended to be more aware of their individual rights. The physical restraints and punishment of the rural areas had no place in the towns. Masters with troublesome slaves sent them off to the country or sold them.

Slaveholders disliked the urban setting for slaves. A Louisiana planter declared during the nineteenth century that slavery did not thrive "when transplanted to the cities," for the slaves became "corrupted," "dissipated," and "acquire the worst habits." Perhaps for this reason the general conditions and the number of urban slaves tended to decrease in both Cuba and the United States during the nineteenth century. Between 1820 and 1860, the percentage of urban slaves in the southern states fell from 22 percent to 10 percent. Between 1855 and 1870 the number of urban slaves decreased by nearly 20,000 in Cuba. Brazil had nearly four times as many rural slaves as there were urban and domestic. The urban-industrial complex was disastrous to slavery.

Rural domestic slaves also tended to share the opportunities of the urban slaves. In parts of the South, Cuba, St. Domingue, Martinique, Guadeloupe, Venezuela, and Brazil, the ostentatious luxury of the *Casa Grande* (the Great House), as the Brazilian Gilberto Freyre called it, required a number of domestic servants. And just as in the urban setting, these slaves tended to have a broader and freer system of social relations. Many were literate — deliberately taught by their masters or surrepticiously self-instructed. A number tended to be emancipated as a reward for faithful service, and some females derived special favors from the close relationship they developed with white males. But while domestic slavery extended the cosmopolitanism of the slave, it hardly facilitated any greater reconciliation to the system. Indeed, rural domestic slaves often were key figures in slave revolts; and the most successful slave rebel, Toussaint L'Ouverture, the "Father of Haiti" (even though he did not declare its independence), came from the ranks of the privileged domestics.

Slaves who were engaged in such activities as piracy, cattle herding, or fishing were virtually free men. But piracy, cattle herding, and fishing did not employ a large number of slaves anywhere, and so these occupations did not significantly affect the general nature of slavery in any particular country.

The worst conditions by far existed for group-held slaves in mines, in small, poor, rural communities, and on plantations.

Slaves on plantations and in mines formed a class unto themselves. For not only were the physical requirements of the mines and plantations more demanding, but the daily routine of the slaves was far more circumscribed. Part of the reason for the regimentation of slavery on plantations, in mines, and in the rural areas generally came from the method of production. Slaves did the repetitious, boring, and unskilled jobs. But their jobs had to fit into certain production deadlines, whether they were picking cotton, casing tobacco, or producing sugar. In any case, profit depended on a crude efficiency, and efficiency depended on careful organization and coordination.

Another reason for regimenting the lives of these slaves was for better control. Rural shareholders usually had many more slaves than urban slaveholders. In the American South, for example, urban slaveowners averaged less than 5 slaves. Indeed, in 1860 nearly 60 percent of all slaveowners had less than 5 slaves each. In plantation-tidewater Virginia the median holdings were between 24 and 28. The differences are even apparent on an island like Cuba, which had a tradition of urban living. The Cuban census for 1857 had an overall island ratio of 1 slaveowner to 8 slaves. In the towns, however, the mean holding was roughly 3 slaves per owner, while the rural owners had a mean of 12 slaves. The 483 largest Cuban slaveholders averaged 197 slaves each. This pattern of slaveholding in Cuba and the United States was also similar to that in Brazil.

The rural slaves lacked the numerous avenues of mobility that their urban counterparts enjoyed. But this did not mean that they were entirely without some degree of mobility. A male rural slave with special skills could be sent off to work in the towns or in some industrial enterprise. Such a slave could then accumulate sufficient money to purchase his freedom. Likewise, an attractive female slave could win the affection of her master and be promoted to domestic service in the Great House. With some luck she might even be granted her freedom on the deathbed of her master, for the practice of manumission in last wills was not infrequent throughout the slave societies of the Americas.

A Critique of the Tannenbaum Thesis   Harry Hoetink

This excerpt considers the applicability of Frank Tannen-baum's view that present day racial relations are determined by the experience of slavery in the colonial past. Using Suriname and Curaçao as examples to test out this premise, Hoetink finds that present situations contradict Tannen-baum's ideas, just as recent historical research has tended to reject much of Tannenbaum's original characterization of slavery systems. From H. Hoetink (1973), Slavery and Race Relations in the Americas: An Inquiry into the Nature and Nexus *Harper and Row, New York, pp. 3–9. Copyright © 1973 by H. Hoetink. Reprinted by permission of Harper and Row, Publishers, Inc.*

Since the publication of Frank Tannenbaum's *Slave and Citizen*,[1] much, maybe too much, has been written about the supposed differences among the slavery systems of the Western Hemisphere. However, less critical attention has been given to Tannenbaum's underlying hypothesis — the character of a society's race relations outside the system of slavery and its abolition is determined by the peculiarities of that system of slavery. Those systems of slavery that both permitted the slaves to preserve their moral personality and facilitated their integration into society through frequent manumissions produced conditions after abolition under which the chances of freemen to be accepted as social equals would be enhanced.

This postulate, which directly and even causally connects the conditions of slavery with the present-day socioracial structure and relations, has gained more popularity in recent years. The growing literature and number of conferences, especially in the United States, on comparative slave systems are not only the result of a legitimate need for further insight into the contributions and experiences of the black population in North American history but also the product of the belief that the present tragic racial situation in the United States can be explained by studying the tragic history of slavery. Thus, not only historians but also sociologists, who usually adhere to the ahistoricism so deeply embedded in North American culture, surprisingly genuflect before a methodology that in my view is unacceptable.

The phenomenon is not limited to the United States, nor to adepts of conservative ideologies. The Brazilian sociologist Florestan Fernándes thinks that the still-observable racial prejudices in Brazil have their origins in slavery; therefore, these prejudices are "anachronisms," and will gradually disappear. While he ably analyzes recent developments in Brazilian social structure, he prefers not to functionally dissect racial prejudice and explains its presence by referring to the past. In *The Growth of the Modern West Indies*, Gordon K. Lewis writes with some irritation about present-day Guianese who, like Barbadians or Jamaicans, "continue to refer to a slave past abolished over a century ago as if it were a continuing factor in their present discontents; as if, in Dr. Raymond Smith's apt phrase, one were to attribute Britain's balance-of-payments problems to the Napoleonic Wars."[2]

Tannenbaum's postulate may be simply stated as follows: Where master-slave relations were "good," race relations outside and after slavery would be "good"; on the other hand, where slavery developed in an unfavorable "moral and legal setting," there "the very nature of the institution of slavery . . . in turn shaped the political and ethical biases," which in Tannenbaum's view "manifestly separated the United States from other parts of the New World in this respect."[3]

Eric Williams, Sidney Mintz, and others who criticized Tannenbaum's ideas did not explicitly attack his postulate that links the conditions of slavery with race relations. Rather, they proposed to show that slavery in the plantation colonies of the Western Hemisphere was also, and possibly more than anything else, an economic institution. Therefore, the character of master-slave relations and the frequency of manumission directly responded to such factors as the supply and demand for tropical products on the world market. Where the economy was predominantly autarchic, as in Cuba and Puerto Rico in the early eighteenth century, slavery tended to be more benign than in a later period in the same territories when sugar became the main agricultural product. Similar observations can be made about Jamaica, Trinidad, or the United States in different periods of their economic history.[4]

This economic critique significantly undermined — correctly in my view — two other assumptions of Tannenbaum: First, that for noneconomic reasons, slavery in the United States (and by extension in the Anglo-Saxon colonies of the Western Hemisphere) was more cruel and damaging to the personality of the slave than in Brazil (and by extension in Latin America); second, that the benign or harsh character of master-slave relations was a permanent factor in any plantation colony in the Western Hemisphere. More recent research in which Brazilians also participated has generally confirmed this criticism.[5]

However, although the inconstancy of master-slave relations may hamper the empirical verification of Tannenbaum's postulate, its theoretical plausibility has not yet been questioned. Did not the future development of race relations have to profit from a generally benign system of slavery where manumission was frequent?

Before answering this question directly, it will be helpful to compare two different slave systems.[6] By comparing two colonies controlled by the same metropolitan power, the Dutch slave colonies of Curaçao and Surinam, several complicating cultural and political variables are eliminated.

During a long period preceding the abolition of slavery in 1863, Curaçao, a tiny island off the Venezuelan coast, was a society in which the relations between master and slave were decidedly "mild." Economic and demographic conditions caused such relative "mildness." The island was not a conventional plantation colony, but a commercial center; the small number of slaves per master did not inspire fear;

and the small size of the island made slaveholders susceptible to whatever social control emanated from the local political and religious representatives of the metropolitan power.

During the same period, however, Surinam, a real plantation colony, had very severe master-slave relations, so severe, in fact, that they gave the Dutch throughout the Western Hemisphere a reputation as harsh and oppressive slaveholders.[7]

The economic and demographic conditions in Surinam were antithetical to those in Curaçao. The large number of slaves per master induced a permanent fear and led to sadistic punishments; the large size of the country and its sparse settlement sufficiently isolated many plantations from the corrective social control of the capital. The geography of the country that enabled rebellious slaves to withdraw as Maroons into the jungle plus the difficult communication among plantations may explain why, in spite of the generally cruel conditions of slavery, Surinam did not witness a general slave rebellion, whereas such a rebellion arose in Curaçao in 1795 — showing that the causes of rebellions were neither exclusively economic nor always due to the severe treatment of slaves. In Curaçao, the ideological influences of the Haitian Revolution, which stretched far into South America, were clearly discernible. In turn, the Curaçao revolt inspired a slave rebellion in the nearby Spanish American Coro area.[8]

According to Tannenbaum's postulate, the experience of slavery in each of the Dutch colonies would result in the following: In Curaçao, with mild relations between slave and master as well as early and frequent manumissions. Negroes and coloreds (two social categories that outside the United States must be carefully distinguished) both outside of and after slavery would have been socially accepted by the rest of society and would have achieved increased mobility toward higher social strata. However, in Surinam, unfavorable master-slave relations and the small number of manumissions (excepting those immediately preceding abolition) would have produced very tense relations between whites and Negroid groups, and the latter hardly would have penetrated the more prestigious occupational strata of society.

Yet, precisely the reverse took place! In Curaçao, the appointment of nonwhite civil servants to high-ranking positions only hesitantly started in the second quarter of the twentieth century, and today the different racial groups maintain a certain social exclusiveness. The highest prestige and power remained in the hands of white groups, even though already in the eighteenth century a small nucleus of "respectable" coloreds, mostly merchants, had been formed. But, in Surinam already in the early nineteenth century, there existed a group of prestigious coloreds, several of them academically trained, who served in a number of the highest posts both in government and in plantation agriculture. Some of them had close social contacts with the upper stratum of white families. This nonwhite professional elite preserved and strengthened its dominant role after abolition and Negroes were gradually integrated into it.

This brief comparison at least seems to deny the general validity of Tannenbaum's postulate and even suggests its very antithesis: During a prolonged period where master-slave relations were "good" and manumission frequent, white attitudes would be more unfavorable toward the manumitted than toward the slaves; consequently, the chances for the manumitted's social acceptance and mobility would be less than in a slave society where master-slave relations were unfavorable and the number of manumitted and their descendants small.

The logic of this antithesis is clear: Where a master's relations with his slaves are "good," he need not fear them; where there are simultaneously too many freemen both whose social behavior is unregulated and whose subsistence is uncertain, the master's fear will be directed more toward them; and, if some of these freemen acquire a certain prosperity, the whites, especially the poorer among them, will perceive this as a social threat and rationalize it in racial terms and prejudices. Conversely, where the masters severely treat their slaves and perceive them as menacing, the whites will form a favorable opinion of freemen, as long as their number is small, and try to involve them in a social alliance against the slaves.

Historical reality in Curaçao and Surinam corresponded

to these alternatives. Observers from the early nineteenth century, comparing both societies, concluded that in Curaçao the colored (freeman) was more despised and feared than the Negro (slave), while in Surinam the situation was the reverse. Here at the end of the eighteenth century, when the number of freemen was minimal, white opinion about them was predominantly favorable. When the number of urban poor gradually increased, this general opinion took a turn for the worse, although it was always more favorable toward the colored elite in Surinam than it was in Curaçao.

Yet, general validity cannot be attributed to this counterpostulate, for that would again suggest a causal link between slavery and race relations, albeit in a sense opposite to Tannenbaum's. The exceptions to this counterpostulate are easily discernible: In the Spanish and Portuguese colonies, frequent manumissions and "good" master-slave relations over a long period of time coincided with a remarkable degree of social acceptance of the free colored, thus contradicting the Curaçao alternative; in the French colony of Saint Domingue, however, unfavorable master-slave relations accompanied the phenomenon of a considerable and prosperous group of freemen, who were often slaveholders themselves, but the initial alliance between this group and the whites was substituted in the course of the eighteenth century by an ever more virulent discrimination against the properous free colored, thus contradicting the Surinam alternative.

ENDNOTES

1. Frank Tannenbaum, *Slave and Citizen* (New York: Alfred Knopf, 1947).
2. Gordon K. Lewis, *The Growth of the Modern West Indies* (London: MacGibbon and Kee, 1968), p. 259.
3. Tannenbaum, *Slave and Citizen*, p. 42.
4. Eric Williams, *Capitalism and Slavery* (Chapel Hill, N.C.: University of North Carolina Press, 1944); Sidney W. Mintz, "Labor and Sugar in Puerto Rico and in Jamaica, 1800-1850," *Comparative Studies in Society and History* 1, no. 3 (March 1959). "In the mid-nineteenth century, Cuban slavery dehumanized the slaves as viciously as had Jamaican or North American slavery" (S.W. Mintz

in his review of Stanley M. Elkins, *Slavery: A Problem in American Institutional and Intellectual Life* [Chicago: University of Chicago Press, 1959], *American Anthropologist* 63, no. 3 [1961]).

5. See Octavio Ianni, *As Metamorfoses do Escravo* (São Paulo, Brazil: Difusão Europeia do Livro, 1962). See also David Brian Davis, *The Problem of Slavery in Western Culture* (Ithaca, N.Y.: Cornell University Press, 1966).

6. H. Hoetink, "The Free Black and Mulatto in the Slave Societies of the Netherlands West Indies," in *Neither Slave Nor Free: The Freedman of African Descent in the Slave Societies of the New World*, eds. J. Greene and D. Cohen (Baltimore: The Johns Hopkins Press, 1972).

7. See J.G. Stedman, *A Narrative of a Five-Years Expedition Against the Revolted Negroes of Surinam*, 2 vols. (London, 1813); see also Tannenbaum, *Slave and Citizen*, p. 65.

8. See Pedro M. Arcaya, *Insurreción de los Negros de la Serranía de Coro* (Caracas: Instituto Panamericano de Geografa e Historía, 1949); and Miguel Acosta Saignes, *Vida de los Esclavos Negros en Venezuela* (Caracas: Hespérides, 1967), pp. 277 ff. Compare further the causes of Jamaican slave revolts in H. Orlando Patterson, *The Sociology of Slavery* (London: MacGibbon and Kee, 1967), pp. 273-283.

The Boni Maroon War   Silvia W. de Groot

*Were maroons always a threat to colonial administrators or,
given certain conditions, might European powers utilize uprisings to their own advantage? In de Groot's analysis, the
Boni Maroons are shown to have been manipulated by both
French and Dutch interests in a continuing power struggle
along the Guiana Highlands. The success of the Boni Maroon
suppression suggests that traditional advantages of maroonage
may not always have been operative. This selection originally
appeared as S.W. de Groot (1975), 'The Boni Maroon War
1765-1793, Surinam and French Guyana', Boletin de Estudios Latino Americanos, 18 (June). Reprinted by permission
of the Author and Publisher.*

After crossing the Marowyne river at Akoli creek, the Boni
settled on the Siparuini creek. Alarmed, the small French
military post near the mouth of the Marowyne sent out a
reconnaissance party to investigate. They found nothing, and
the commander was reprimanded for his audacity. At the
time the French thought the Boni to number in the region of
8-10,000.[1] An intensive correspondence ensued between the
French Governor Fiedmond and Nepveu in Surinam. The
French complained bitterly that the Dutch military post
opposite the French one did not even know about the Boni's
crossing into French Guyana, and must hear it from the
French forces.

Governor Fiedmond visited the French post personally in
October, 1776, and considered launching an expedition.
But as long as the Boni kept quiet, he decided against this
course.[2]

The French colony had been an impoverished area since its inception in the beginning of the seventeenth century. Efforts were made to render the region profitable by recruiting waves of new colonists and "engagés" (contract labourers) in Europe to populate the region. But mortality among these new arrivals was high due to hard tropical conditions. One of the most notorious among repeated demographic catastrophes was the colonization of Kuru starting in 1764 with about 14,000 emigrants, of whom not more than 1,000 were still living after a year.[3] Meanwhile the colony began employing captured Indians as slaves, a policy which here as elsewhere proved a failure. The importation of black slaves from West Africa did not get underway until the eighteenth century, and then it was difficult to procure slaves: slave ships were reluctant to call at Cayenne. It was unfavorably situated with respect to access to the port and the marine currents, and the slave merchants were not satisfied with the profits they received. It was a vicious circle: poor, the plantation owners could not afford the prices asked for slaves; hence they missed the necessary labour to cultivate the land, and . . . they remained poor. The ratio of white to black population was about one to six during the eighteenth century; most of the colonists had less than six slaves, and only a few several dozen. Surinam's relative success, as a plantation enterprise and as a slave colony, was viewed with envious eyes by the French. The reclamation of marshy coastal areas, by means of which the Dutch created rich arable soil, demanded techniques in which the French colonists were not proficient.

The retreat of the Boni Maroons to the French side of the Marowyne gave rise to mixed emotions. On the one hand it was feared that the obstreperous defeated Boni would become a nuisance to the colony, and that in the event of a new conflict between them and the Surinam military forces, it was possible that the latter might pursue the Maroons onto French territory, with all the political consequences such action would bring with it. On the other hand the arrival of a large number of potential labourers gave rise to the hope that the Boni might eventually be a means of easing the shortage of hands in the French colony. These ambivalent feelings

influenced the political contact between French and Dutch
Guyana for many years. A bulky report by Baron Bessner,[4]
ex-commander of Cayenne (1773), written in 1775 (that is,
about the time the Boni crossed the Marowyne) contains a
detailed project to persuade the Surinam Maroons to move to
Cayenne and to throw in their lot with that of the French
colony. It was a well-meant, "enlightened", but impracticable
and utopian plan founded on many erroneous data. Well-
meant because it was designed to give the Maroons an opportunity to congregate in villages in an allotted area, make a life
for themselves and become a sort of "province" within the
colony. "Enlightened": Bessner believed it mistaken to
assume that "l'espèce nègre est une espèce maudite dont on
ne doit espérer aucun bien. Ceux qui pensent confondent
les dispositions avec les effets de l'esclavage." Utopian: the
plan assumed that the Djuka and Saramacca could be lured
away from their hard-won way of life to migrate to an unknown, undeveloped region along the coast in order to begin
an entirely different sort of existence there. Moreover,
Bessner estimated the population involved to be on the order
of 40,000 whereas the real figure was closer to 6,000. The
skilful economist P.V. Malouet, sent out by the French
government in 1777 to conduct an investigation in Surinam,
estimated their number at no more than 3,000.[5] In the same
way, the number of Boni who had crossed the Marowyne had
been grossly overestimated. While Bessner had presumed that
there were 8-10,000 Malouet was informed that there were in
reality no more than 2-300![6]

As for the Boni, it was difficult to know what to do with
them. Driving them back did not seem to be a possibility.
Surinam did not want them. To accept them as residents of
the colony offered few advantages, and might, in view of
their recalcitrance, entail certain dangers. Consequently
the government opted for a middle course: scouts, missionaries, geographers and soldiers were dispatched with vague
promises and some gifts for the Boni, and in 1786 a delegation from the Boni was received in the capital and sent back
with other vague promises and gifts. A result of French
vagueness and ambiguity was that the Surinam government
was unable to form a clear idea of the intentions of the

French Guyanese, with whom their contacts were scarce enough already. The Boni believed — or pretended to believe — the promises the French made over and over again. The chief of these were French governmental protection, the supply of essential utensils, and — this was important — the French would supply them with arms. The Djuka passed word of this on through their postholder (the Surinam government's representative among the free Maroons) to the authorities in Paramaribo. Neither the Djuka nor the government seems to have really known what was going on, and ignorance about the motives, reactions, and intentions of the parties involved resulted in a general atmosphere of uncertainty on the part of everyone concerned.

The Boni, unwanted by both the Dutch and the French, kept moving slowly along the Marowyne. Along the same river, however, lived the Djuka, who were by no means pleased with the intrusion of a new group of inhabitants with whom the colony was still on hostile terms. The Djuka regarded the Marowyne river as their domain. After the peace of 1760 they had moved from the Djuka creek to settle in villages higher up along the river. The Boni conglomerated along the lower reaches of the river, and were in a position to hamper the Djuka's free access via the river to the coast. This free access was important. Contact with the coast was essential for trade (even on a small scale) in order to procure necessities, and especially to supplement their food stores during the fairly regularly recurring periods of shortage. In October 1777 the Djuka launched an attack against the Boni, seizing 22 prisoners and killing 7. To the dismay of the colony, however, the Djuka and the Boni arrived at a pact at the end of the same year. The Djuka sent reassuring messages to Paramaribo: they would never help the Boni if they attacked the whites again, and Boni, himself, the Grand Chief, had declared never to undertake further action if he were now left unmolested.

As a matter of fact, the peace with the Boni was preserved until 1788 when the Boni again, and unexpectedly, invaded the colony, raiding the plantation Clarenbeek on the Upper Commewyne, situated outside the Cordon, and four other plantations on the Upper Surinam river simultaneously. The

Maroons killed the white inhabitants and carried off a large number of slaves. When Colonel Friderici arrived at the scene of the disaster with his Black Chasseurs, the attackers had already fled too far to be pursued. In 1789 the Boni attacked the military post of Armina on the Marowyne river. Conductor Stoelman repulsed the attack, and the Boni fell back.

Wolber's supposition[7] that the Boni launched their unexpected attack in 1788 from a strong base, aided by French arms, was founded on misinterpreted reports. On the contrary: the poverty and internal difficulties resulting from their position of isolation drove them to make a desperate attempt to procure arms, men and tools once again as before.

In 1790, with the help of information offered by Ascaan, a Boni deserter, a patrol advanced from the military posts on the Marowyne with a large contingent of Black Chasseurs, under command of lieutenant Stoelman, to launch an attack on Aluku, the village of Grand Chief Boni. Boni escaped, but a number of important chiefs were killed or captured.

Apparently Boni's strength was now broken, and he sent his oldest son and two chiefs to Paramaribo to arrange a peace settlement. Friderici, now Acting Governor, conducted the negotiations for the government. Little headway was made, however: the colonists were reluctant to legitimize this hardly reliable Maroon group in the bush while they were not even sure of the loyalty of the already existing pacified groups. The fact that the Boni had settled in French territory made a decision even more difficult. The colonists still feared an alliance of the Boni with the Djuka, or even with the Saramacca to undertake a large-scale offensive against the colony. Although the Boni declared that the Djuka no longer supported, but indeed had turned against them, and that given arms they would even gladly fight them, information given by the postholder could not confirm that this was true.[8] So Friderici limited himself to demanding the return of all deserters and captives by the Boni before negotiating further. Grand Chief Boni returned only a few captives and asked for more arms. He declared that, under pressure from his chiefs, he could not do otherwise. Hostilities were resumed in July, 1791, and the Boni suffered fresh losses.

The Boni (but also the Djuka) retreated further up the river in the face of the attacks: about this time they had settled in villages along the Lawa, the upper course of the Marowyne, and the Djuka along the Tapahoni, the largest western branch of the Marowyne. Meanwhile Friderici let the Djuka know that the aid they had given the Boni was deeply resented and was regarded as a breach of the peace treaty. He added a threat to attack them. In October, 1791 the Djuka sent a delegation to apologize and make amends with the colonists, agreeing to surrender all the Boni in their midst. The government promised the Djuka protection in the event of a Boni attack (no doubt Friderici had assured the delegation that this was what the Boni were planning to do).

Eventually the efforts to play the two groups off against each other were successful: in 1793 the indignant Boni raided and destroyed the Djuka headquarters at Animauw (called Ankerblauw by the Dutch). A counterattack was mounted by a small combined force of Chasseurs and enraged Djuka. On February 19, 1793 a party of seventy Djuka, led by the newly appointed supreme chief Bambi, surprised Grand Chief Boni and killed him. Eight days later Cormantin Cojo, another head chief, met with the same fate. Agossu, a son of Boni, escaped, "et comme les Français avaient déjà déclaré la guerre à la République, l'on n'était plus obligé à respecter les forêts de Cayenne, ce qui fit qu'on les chassa presque jusqu'aux frontières de la Guiana Portugaise"[9] — without success, however.

The struggle against a common foe reduced the mutual distrust between the Djuka and the white somewhat. A treaty signed in 1791 and renewed in 1809[10] placed the Boni under tutelage of the Djuka, who promised to keep them from moving freely on the rivers and in the territory of the colony.

ENDNOTES

1. Paris: Archives Nationales: Archives du ministère de la France d'Outre-Mer (hereafter A.C.-D.F.), Guyane 206, 1776.
2. Paris: Archives Nationales: Rue Oudinot Archives Coloniales, Séries Modernes, Guyane 281, 1776.

3. Mme. Marchand-Thébault, "L'esclavage en Guyane Française sous l'ancien régime," *Revue française d'Histoire d'Outre-Mer* XLVII (1960), pp. 5-75.
4. A.C.-D.F. Guyane 284, 1775.
5. A.C.-D.F. Guyane 285, 1778.
6. Paris: Archives Nationales: Palais Soubise, Archives Coloniales, Séries anciennes 45, 1777.
7. J. Wolbers, *Geschiedenis van Suriname* (Amsterdam: H. de Hoogh, 1861), p. 431.
8. The Hague: Algemeen Rijksarchief: Archives of the Political Council 172, January 17, 1791.
9. London/Kew Public Record Office, War Office Records 1/147, p. 361, 1801.
10. Silvia W. de Groot, "Black Revolt in Surinam, 1788-1809. The Aftermath of the Boni Wars and the Rebellion of the Black Chasseurs," *Caribbean Studies*, 1975.

3.5

Freedmen in Barbados   Jerome Handler

The historical position of the freed person of color within colonial societies has recently attracted much attention from social scientists. Here, anthropologist Jerome Handler examines the Barbadian freedman's often thwarted attempts to achieve full civil rights, despite legislative guarantees. The selection is extracted from J. Handler (1974), The Unappropriated People: Freedmen in the Slave Society of Barbados. *Johns Hopkins University Press. Reprinted with permission of the Publisher and Author.*

As a freeman, the freedman was a British subject and could theoretically lay claim to the legal rights held by white freemen; moreover, he shared with whites the obligations of citizenship, such as payment of taxes and service in the militia. Freedmen apparently neither doubted nor questioned their status as British subjects, nor was this status challenged by the Crown or uniformly denied by white colonial society. When, for example, a House of Assembly bill seriously threatened the freedman's property rights at the beginning of the nineteenth century, one Council member found the bill unconstitutional because it denied "free subjects . . . those rights and privileges legally and constitutionally incident to freedom"; another member doubted if the Crown would approve a colonial law that "destroy[ed] the rights of free subjects in their property already acquired."[1] The freedmen's status as "free subjects" was fundamental to the way in which they viewed their position in Barbadian society, and it provided the major moral underpinning of the reformist appeals they directed to legislative bodies. Their self-image

84

as British subjects was a positive one which, in their minds, legitimized their claims to civil rights. "We His Majesty's dutiful and loyal subjects," freedmen wrote in what was perhaps their earliest petition calling for a change in their legal status, "declare our unfeigned and inviolable attachment by principle and affection to our King and Constitution."[2] In 1823, they again petitioned: "There are certain parts of our Colonial Code which exempts us from participating with our white brethren in certain privileges and to which, as British subjects, we humbly conceive we have a claim."[3] Seven years later their requests for civil rights were, they emphasized, "claims which we conceive ourselves justly entitled to as British, Christian, faithful and loyal subjects."[4]

The absence of a legally defined position of intermediacy and the contradiction between their status as free British subjects, on the one hand, and the circumscription of that status by racial qualifiers associated with Negroid ancestry, on the other, resulted in the essential instability and ambiguity of the freedmen's position in the social system. The freedmen's struggle for civil rights can largely be viewed as a collective effort to resolve this ambiguity by maximizing their free status; they did not aim to establish a clearly defined position of permanent legal intermediacy between whites and slaves.

Freedmen were profoundly aware of their indefinite and subordinate status and were not reconciled to the limitations on their freedom. "Our words are inadequate to express," they wrote in 1799, "the due sense we have of our subordinate state," but "however humble our situation and condition may be," as freemen they felt themselves entitled to "the protection of the laws."[5] Most freedmen evidently shared a desire for such protection and the right of testimony. For a period of time, however, some *appeared* (as a matter of political expediency or genuine conviction) to rest satisfied with limited rights that served their most immediate interests and functioned to clearly distinguish them from the slaves. The group which in 1817 thanked the legislature for granting the right of testimony emphasized that this right "was all we wished for, having . . . obtained that we are perfectly satisfied and contented"; "where slavery exists," the group acknowledged, "there must necessarily be a distinction between the white and free coloured inhabitants, and . . . there are privileges which the latter do not expect to enjoy."[6] Although some of these men later participated in actions which contradicted these views, the freedmen community in general appears always to have had political divisions between conservative and progressive elements; however, these divisions increasingly came to hinge on disagreements over strategies and means by which to achieve complete civil equality with whites, rather than on disagreements over the desirability of this goal.

In any event, as the freedman community grew larger, became more organised, and achieved greater economic success, and as reformist pressures from Britain increased, the civil rights movement became less equivocal on the nature of rights sought and less hesitant in expressing the pace at which these rights should be achieved. Those freedmen who publicly expressed an acceptance of permanent sociolegal distinctions between white and freed became noticeably fewer; those, such as Samuel Prescod, who most forcefully challenged these distinctions and articulated a progressive concern with status maximization became leaders and were able to rally the greatest support from within the freedman community.

In the early phases of the civil rights struggle, freedmen concentrated on the security of their property and persons and the right of testimony, but as time went on they sought removal of other legal disabilities and the lessening of discrimination in various areas of social life. Ultimately their goals were defined not only in legal but also in social terms as they sought a level of parity with whites. In what was perhaps their final petition during the period of slavery, they expressed in no uncertain terms that it was "impossible for them, to rest satisfied until they . . . [were] placed on an equal footing with the present class of freeholders [that is, whites] in all respects"[7] − a public expression of status aspirations which would have been unthinkable a few decades earlier.

The subordinate position of the freedman was expressed in a wide variety of discriminatory practices, some of which derived their strength from the legal code and others from the force of social conventions based on the premise of white supremacy. Although the "brown privilege bill" of 1831 formally eliminated social prerequisites to the definition of a freeholder and extended to freedmen the political rights of voting and holding elective office — thus removing the final legal constraints on their free status — the legislature wrote the bill in such a way that it implicitly discriminated against freedmen. In general, the withdrawal of legal disabilities in the twilight of the slave period did not fundamentally alter the social status of freedmen, and they continued to experience the racial discrimination that white colonial society had consciously nurtured throughout Barbadian history. "As far as legislative enactments could remove the unnatural and impolitic distinctions between us and our white fellow-subjects," freedmen wrote in 1833, "those distinctions have been removed . . . [However,] the distinctions are, in reality, still kept up; and are now rendered, in consequence of that enactment [the "brown privilege bill"], more obviously invidious, and more galling to those whose prejudice they operate."[8]

The catalog of "unnatural and impolitic distinctions" was sizable, but not unusual for a society internally dominated and controlled by a white population imbued with an ideology of racial supremacy. Freedmen were excluded from positions of leadership, responsibility, and prestige in the Anglican church, an institution to which they were heavily committed; there were no freedman ministers throughout the slave period, and there is evidence of only one lay catechist. In addition, freedmen (as well as slaves) were prevented from taking communion at the same time as whites, and nonwhites were confined to special seating areas within the churches. Freedmen were neither encouraged to attend, nor admitted to, Codrington College, owned by the Church of England's Society for the Propagation of the Gospel.[9] Public schools and the vast majority of private schools were racially segregated, and racial distinctions were maintained among the teachers with respect to the pupils they taught and the salaries they received. Whites and freedmen were taxed by the parish vestries, but freedmen could not serve on these vestries, and the indigent among them could neither attend the publicly financed parochial schools nor receive pensions or other forms of relief provided by vestries from tax funds, as did the white poor.[10] Freedmen were obliged to serve in the militia, but were denied commissions and other important leadership positions within it; the militia units themselves were segregated, and freedmen were formed into their own companies led by white officers.

In the early nineteenth century the legislature attempted to curtail severely the freedmen's property rights, and the social conventions based on racism prevented freedmen from acquiring good agricultural land of consequential acreage; with few exceptions, wealthier freedmen were unable to become plantation owners. Freedmen "merchants of wealth were shut out of the merchants' exchange" in Bridgetown, and "colored gentlemen were not allowed to become members of literary associations, nor subscribers to town libraries."[11] There is suggestive evidence that whites reserved certain residential areas in the towns for their own use, and segregation was maintained in the Bridgetown jail.[12] From 1721 to 1830 most freedmen were legally prohibited from testifying in proceedings involving whites, although the testimony of whites could be used against freedmen. There is no indication — and it is highly unlikely — that freedmen served on juries prior to their legal debarment from doing so in 1721, and from that year until 1831 they could neither vote nor hold elective office; not until 1843 did Samuel Prescod take his seat as the first "colored" member in the House of Assembly's over two-hundred-year-old history, and it is doubtful that he would have been elected had it not been for the black and "colored" vote in the Bridgetown constituency from which he ran for office.

Eligible freedmen of wealth and education were also debarred from prestigious appointive positions in the civil-political structure and could not become justices of the peace or magistrates. Attaining positions such as magistracies became an important political issue to freedmen after they achieved legal equality in 1831, and they viewed their inability to gain these appointments as a symbol of their subordinate status; only in 1836, after considerable struggle, were two of their body appointed to magistracies.[13] "Parents, however wealthy," Thome and Kimball reported, "had no inducement to educate their sons for the learned professions, since no force of talent nor extent of acquirement could hope to break down the granite walls and iron bars which prejudice had erected round the pulpit, the bar, and the bench."[14]

ENDNOTES

1. Minutes of the Barbados Council, November 1, 1803, Lucas MSS, Barbados Public Library.
2. "The Humble Memorial and Remonstrance of the Free Coloured People . . . ," October 14, 1799, Minutes of the Barbados Council, October 15, 1799, *ibid.*
3. "The Humble Address of the Undersigned Free Coloured Inhabitants . . . ," December 17, 1823, printed in *Barbadian*, February 25, 1824.
4. "We . . . the Undersigned Free Coloured Inhabitants . . . ," July 15, 1830, printed in *ibid.*, April 22, 1831.
5. "The Humble Memorial and Remonstrance of the Free Coloured People . . . ," October 14, 1799, Minutes of the Barbados Council, October 15, 1799, Lucas MSS.
6. "To the Honorable John Beckles, Speaker of the House of Assembly and the Rest of the Honorable and Worshipful Members," March 4, 1817, Colonial Office Group, Public Record Office, Kew, England (hereafter CO) 28/86. See also "The Humble Petition of the Free Coloured People, Inhabitants of the Island," entered into the Minutes of the Barbados Council, November 1, 1803, Lucas MSS.
7. "Address of the Free Colored and Free Black Inhabitants of Bridgetown to the Council and Assembly," April 2, 1834, CO 28/113.
8. "The Humble Loyal Address of His Majesty's Free Coloured and Free Black Subjects . . . ," May 6, 1833, printed in *Barbadian*, May 15, 1833.
9. Between 1830 and 1900, 390 divinity students were educated at Codrington College, but only 10 percent were nonwhite, and all of them attended the college in the post-Apprenticeship period (see Jean Bullen and Helen E. Livingstone, "Of the State and Advancement of the College," in *Codrington Chronicle: An Experiment in Anglican Altruism on a Barbados Plantation, 1710-1834*, ed. Frank J. Klingberg, University of California Publications in History, vol. 37 [Berkeley and Los Angeles: University of California Press, 1949], p. 121).

10. See, for example, *Parliamentary Papers* (London) (hereafter *PP*), 1826, vol. 28, rept. 353: Combermere to Bathurst, January 18, 1819, CO 28/88; and Edward Eliot, *Christianity and Slavery; in a Course of Lectures Preached at the Cathedral and Parish Church of St. Michael, Barbados* (London, 1833), pp. 225-26.

11. Thome, J.A. and Kimbal, J.H., *Emancipation in the West Indies*, (New York: Anti-Slavery Society, 1838), p. 79.

12. "Humble Petition of the Debtors in the Prison," April 16, 1830, CO 28/106; see also Minutes of the House of Assembly, March 20, 1821, CO 31/49.

13. Joseph Sturge and Thomas Harvey, *The West Indies in 1837*, (London, 1838), app., p. xxxiv. Thome and Kimball reported that in 1837 one of the stipendiary magistrates was a "Mr. Galloway . . . a colored gentleman, highly respected for his talents" (*Emancipation in the West Indies*, p. 66). In actual fact, "Galloway" may have been Joseph Garraway, a stipendiary magistrate who assumed office in November 1836 (see "Papers . . . in Explanation of the Measures Adopted . . . for Giving Effect to the Act for the Abolition of Slavery . . .," pt. 4, *PP*, 1837, vol. 53, rept. 521-1, p. 403).

14. Thome and Kimball, *Emancipation in the West Indies*, p. 76.

Poor Whites in Barbados   Jill Shepard

As much attention as slavery systems have received, scant research has been carried out on the position of poor white groups within colonial Caribbean society. Jill Shepard has filled this lacuna with her study of the poor whites of Barbados, the so-called 'Redlegs', who often proved to be the object of derision and concern amongst their wealthier white planter brethren. The diminishing economic role of the poor whites is examined in this selection. Reprinted from J. Shepard (1977), The 'Redlegs' of Barbados: Their Origins and History, *pp. 46–51. Copyright © KTO Press 1977. By permission of KTO Press, U.S. Division of Kraus-Thomson Organization, Ltd (Millwood, New York).*

The poor whites, at this stage, were not only an embarrassment to the plantocracy and a burden to themselves, but they were also facing greater competition from the free coloureds. The latter were becoming an increasingly important section of the population and had reached over five thousand by 1829.[1] The Archdeacon of Barbados stated the position unambiguously in an appendix to the published sermons he had delivered at the Cathedral in 1833 on the subject of "Christianity and Slavery":

The free blacks have, by their superior industry, driven the lower order of whites from almost every trade requiring skill and continuing exertion. I believe that not one in twenty of the working shoemakers in Barbados is a white man. The working carpenters, masons, tailors, smiths etc. are for the most part men of colour; and this at a time when a large white population are in the lowest state of poverty and wretchedness.[2]

This was obviously not a situation making for a satisfactory relationship between the various classes of society. Indications have already been given of the disinclination of the planters to concern themselves with the welfare of the poor whites, to whom they naturally regarded themselves as immensely superior. The poor whites, in their turn, considered themselves to be far above the slaves and were thus determined to maintain this position by refusing to degrade themselves, as they saw it, by doing the same kinds of work as the slaves. But now they were confronted by a new breed of people, not white, but yet free, and evidently far more competent than they at doing very much the same types of jobs as those which they had long regarded as their prerogative. This, then, gave rise to considerable animosity between the two groups of poor whites and free coloureds.

Joshua Steele's friend and colleague, William Dickson, had drawn attention in no uncertain terms, and with the use of vivid examples, to the fundamental belief of the poor white that he was in every way the superior of the Negro;[3] the facts of their situation at the end of the eighteenth century ought to have made them question this belief, but their ignorance, being what it was, merely served to increase the resentment. Indeed, this reached such a point that, in 1799, in a memorial from the free coloureds to the Governor in connection with the discharge of a white man who had been indicted at the Court of Grand Sessions for the murder of a free coloured man, it was stated: "many profligate white persons have threatened to kill some of your Memorialists without the slightest provocation; and we not only walk abroad under apprehension of being assassinated, but we are continually in dread of being murdered in our houses."[4]

That this fear was not without justification was attested to a few years later by the Governor, Lord Seaforth, when he was in the process of conducting a campaign not only to bring about some improvement in the state of the police, but also to have legislation passed which would have made the murder of a slave a felony. He found that "to the greatest remissness in the execution of the Laws is joined the most barbarous and insulting oppression of the Blacks and coloured people by the refuse of the whites," and he cited three cases of "horrid murders" selected from a large number of similar ones. In all the three incidents poor whites — a Militia man, a plantation manager, and a butcher — had murdered slaves, two of them women and one a youth, in circumstances of extreme brutality.[5]

The comparative conditions of the poor white in relation to that of the black, whether slave or free, had been receiving attention in a number of quarters for some time. A physician, Richard Towne, was perhaps the first writer formally to draw the comparison to the attention of the public, though he did so perhaps inadvertently, in a treatise on local diseases published in 1726 after he had spent some seven years in the island. He noted, in a chapter on diarrhoea, that "fluxes" were common in the rainy season among "Negroes and the poorer sort of white People who in these seasons are much more afflicted with this Distemper than such whose condition of life does not subject them to such inconveniences." Dysentery was stated to rage "among the White Servants as well as the Negroes on the Plantations, which sort of people are much addicted to debauch in Spirits, and Punch made exceeding strong with new Rum, very acid with Juice of Limes, and very fermentative with coarse sugar." He also found that elephantiasis, which he claimed did not exist in Europe, nevertheless in Barbados affected "white people whose unhappy circumstances have reduced them to hardships but little inferior to what the Blacks are obliged to undergo."[6] These findings were later quoted by the Reverend Griffith Hughes in his *Natural History of Barbados* published in 1750.[7] The doctor and the parson were to a large extent responsible for sparking discussion and comment on the situation of the poor whites in relation to the blacks which, while throwing useful light on the position of the former, seems at the same time to have provoked much hostile comment.

The controversial question of the effect of a tropical climate on the European constitution was also one of the subjects that was batted back and forth during this debate; it even received some attention in official quarters in Barbados towards the end of the century when the future likely effects of the emancipation of the slaves were being discussed. A questionnaire, relating mainly to the conditions of slaves but including some items referring to poor whites, elicited the reply from members of the Council, in answer to one question dealing with the suitability of the European for field work on the plantation, that there had been "no single instance of a European dedicating himself to anything like hard labour in exposing himself to the sun who had been able to support the heat of this climate; nor do we think it possible."[8] The Governor, David Parry, was evidently not entirely satisfied with the results of this questionnaire and put further questions to Joshua Steele, who replied to a question on the effects of the climate thus: "although the climate is remarkably salutary, both to black and white, under equal treatment, the probability seems to be, that it should be more suitable to black workers in general; and yet white labourers are found to bear the hardest labour that is necessary, without any inconvenience, until they destroy their constitutions by rum-drinking and venery."[9] William Dickson commented to the same effect, noting that Barbados had originally been cultivated by whites and he saw no reason why "temperate, seasoned white men" should not work on the plantations in the same way that they cultivated their own private plots of land without any assistance from Negroes.[10]

The debate was continued by two early nineteenth-century visitors to Barbados. One of them considered that the physical appearance of the poor whites indicated that the climate was "irreconcilable with the condition of the race."[11] The other, a medical doctor, evidently agreed with Dickson's view that there was no reason why European labourers should no longer be able to withstand the climate and went on to imply that the reason for their apparent inability to do so was their general attitude toward work: "there is no lack of inhabitants in Barbados of the labouring classes — I beg their pardon, of the poorer classes, for labour is a disgrace for a white man in all slave countries, which the poorest wretch is ashamed to submit to."[12] Indeed, various comments made from the turn of the century suggest that the poor whites were in a state of serious physical and psychological deterioration. It was at this time that the term

"Redleg," or sometimes "Redshank," appears to have come generally into use. Dr. Williamson's reference to the "Redlegs" as gaunt in appearance, arrogant by nature and generally useless and degenerate, was earlier noted. The comments on the "Redshanks," made in the *Yarn of a Yankee Privateer* had also emphasized their arrogance, together with their idleness and degradation. J.B. Colthurst's remarks about the "Redshanks" in the Militia further confirmed these impressions.[13]

Indeed, the very appearance of these people was evidently such as to provoke a reaction not only from the foreigner describing his impressions of an unfamiliar country, but also from a Barbadian writing of his familiar native land. The poet H.J. Chapman enquired at the time:

> Who are those wretches of the lead-like hue,
> That seem some plague-ship's horror-haunted crew —
> Those nerveless children, woebegone and pale,
> Whose limbs seem wire-hung, and whose sinews fail?[14]

Commentators were again struck by the juxtaposition of the poor white and the black population. A doctor, who, as Deputy Inspector General of Hospitals to His Majesty's Forces, spent three months in Barbados in early 1796, referred to the existence of "a poorer order of white people . . . who obtain a scanty living by cultivating a small patch of earth . . . They are descended from European settlers, but from misfortune, or misconduct in some of the race, are reduced to a state far removed from independence; often, indeed, but little superior to the condition of the free negroes." Somewhat curiously for a man who presumably had had some scientific training, he also expressed surprise that, although they had been in Barbados for generations and had been exposed to the same life and work as the Negroes, they had remained entirely European in their physical characteristics.[15] Traveller H.N. Coleridge commented after his visit in 1825: "many of the wretched white creoles live on the charity of the slaves, and few people would institute a comparison on the respectability of the two classes. The lower whites of that island are without exception the most degraded, worthless, hopeless race

I have ever met with in my life. They are more pressing subjects for legislation than the slaves, were they ten times enslaved."[16]

Perhaps the clearest picture, though one marred, inevitably, by moral judgements, was provided by a young man of eighteen who was living in Barbados in the 1820s with his father, who was in the Army:

Of all the classes of people who inhabit Bridgetown, the poor whites are the lowest and most degraded: residing in the meanest hovels, they pay no attention either to neatness in their dwellings or cleanliness in their persons; and they subsist too often, to their shame let it be spoken, on the kindness and charity of slaves. I have never seen a more sallow, dirty, ill looking and unhappy race; the men lazy, the women disgusting; and the children neglected: all without any notion of principle, morality or religion; forming a melancholy picture of living misery; and a strong contrast with the general appearance of happiness depicted on the countenances of the free black, and coloured people, of the same class.[17]

ENDNOTES

1. E.B. Burley, *Memorandum summarising the returns of the census taken in the Island of Barbados in the year 1715* (Barbados, 1913); J. Handler and A. Sio in their contribution "Barbados" to David W. Cohen and Jack P. Greene, eds., *Neither Slave nor Free* (Baltimore: Johns Hopkins University Press, 1972), confirm this figure.
2. Edward Eliot, *Christianity and Slavery; in a course of lectures preached at the Cathedral and Parish Church of St. Michael, Barbados* (London, 1833), pp. 225-226.
3. William Dickson, *Letters on Slavery* (London, 1789), pp. 57-58.
4. Lucas Transcripts Barbados Public Library, *Minutes of Council*, vol. 32, pp. 116-117.
5. Colonial Office Group, Public Records Office, Kew, England 28/71, despatches 45 and 48 of 1 September and 13 November 1804.
6. Richard Towne, *Treatise of the diseases most frequent in the West Indies, and herein more particularly of those which occur in Barbados* (London, 1726), pp. 114-115, 188.
7. Rev. Griffith Hughes, *Natural History of Barbados* (London, 1750), pp. 35-36.
8. Lucas Transcripts, *Minutes of Council*, vol. 31, p. 83.
9. William Dickson, *Mitigation of Slavery* (London, 1814), p. 155.
10. Dickson, *Letters*, p. 41.

11. Daniel McKinnen, *Tour through the British West Indies in the Years 1802 and 1803* (London, 1805), pp. 30-31.

12. R.R. Madden, *Twelvemonth's Residence in the West Indies* (London, 1835), pp. 40-41.

13. See Introduction in Jill Shepard, *The 'Redlegs' of Barbados: Their Origin and History* (Millwood, New York: Kraus-Thomson Organization, Ltd., 1977).

14. H.J. Chapman, *Barbados and other Poems* (London, 1833), p. 27. F.A. Hoyos has an interesting note on Chapman in *Barbados Museum Historical Society Journal*, XVI nos. 1 & 2, (November 1948-February 1949): 14-20.

15. George Pinckard, *Notes on the West Indies* (London, 1806), pp. 132-139.

16. H.N. Coleridge, *Six Months in the West Indies in 1825* (London, 1832), p. 305.

17. F.W.N. Bayley, *Four Years' Residence in the West Indies* (London, 1830), p. 62.

The Slave's Life in Cuba   Gwendolyn M. Hall

There are many classic descriptions of the daily routine of the Caribbean slave, which are all too often obscured by the moralizing, patriarchal tone of the observers themselves. Gwendolyn Hall here presents a dispassionate account of the drudgery of field work in the slave economy of nineteenth-century Cuba and argues that slave overwork, to the point of exhaustion, was not only typical but accepted as an economic necessity by the sugar plantation owners. Reprinted from G.M. Hall (1971), Social Control in Slave Plantation Societies: A Comparison of St Domingue and Cuba, *Johns Hopkins Press, pp. 16-19, with permission of the Publisher and Author.*

The rapid using up of the work force was the rule rather than the exception, because the colonial officials and the metropolis were always greatly concerned that the work force on the sugar estates would disappear once the illegal African slave trade ended in practice as well as in law. Leopoldo O'Donnell, Captain-General of Cuba during the mid-1840s, after being instructed to find ways to reduce mortality among plantation slaves, laid great emphasis upon the impact of overwork.

. . . it is most important to reduce the number of work hours on the sugar plantations to rational proportions [*a un término racional*] to bring about the conservation of the robustness and life of the slaves for a longer time. These hours, which presently are distributed in a way that hardly leaves the operator the time necessary for food and for rest, should be arranged in a way that would allow prudent rest capable of avoiding his precipitous ruin.[1]

Overwork was undoubtedly a major factor in the high mortality rate among slaves in sugar colonies. The intensity of the labor demanded by sugar production was certainly crucial. Sugar stalks were heavy and bulky. The harvest season lasted from five to six months of the year. The cane had to be ground as soon as it was cut or the yield of juice would shrink, ferment, and spoil. The workers who did the cutting could not be the same as those who did the grinding of the stalks and the boiling of the syrup. The operations of cutting, hauling, grinding, clarification, filtration, evaporation, and crystalization had to be carried out in that order, without interruption, simultaneously, and at top speed. Although the grinding season lasted for months, the conversion of each stalk into sugar had to be completed within a few hours.[2] Because each plantation was a self-contained unit, and a limited supply of floating labor was available during the grinding season, excessive hours, including night and Sunday work, were an absolute necessity.[3] Slave labor was not spared, however, even outside of crop time. Slave manpower has been compared to plant equipment. The purchase price of the slave was the investment, and the maintenance of the slave was a fixed cost that had to be paid whether or not the slave was working. Just as the lost utilization of a machine that has to be discarded after a fixed number of years cannot be recovered, a lost hour of slave labor, economically speaking, was a waste, because the slave's labor was being paid for whether he worked or not. Out of crop season, the sugar plantation slaves did construction work, opened up new lands, and did fencing, ditching, other local improvements, and personal services.[4] But labor during the grinding season was particularly long and hard. Estimates from various sugar colonies in the Americas are on the order of eighteen to twenty hours a day. A description of the spell system enforced on estates in the British West Indies during the 1930s indicates one type of operation. All able-bodied workers were divided into two spells on small estates and three spells on large ones. Each spell was divided into two divisions. The first division worked from 8 p.m. to midnight; the second division from midnight to 6 p.m. For the first division, this labor was, of course, in addition to a full day's work in the fields, which began at 5 a.m. Thus each division worked from 5 a.m. to midnight one day, and from midnight until 6 p.m. the following day, alternating with each other on the night shift so that operations were uninterrupted.[5]

The workday during the grinding season on sugar estates in mid-nineteenth-century Cuba reached twenty hours. A traveler during the 1840s reported the incessant sound of the whip. "Indeed, it was necessary to keep the poor wretches awake."[6] Toward the end of the grinding season, even the oxen were reduced to "mere skeletons, many of them dying from overlabor; the negroes were allowed but five hours sleep."[7] Other reports indicate that four hours sleep was considered sufficient for a slave, and that twenty hours a day for five to seven months out of the year was the normal working day. Even on one well-run estate, which had a humane manager who had been with the family for thirty years, only three to four hours sleep was allowed during the grinding season. The manager explained apologetically that work could not be carried on with less labor. When the manager of another estate was asked whether the slaves' lives were shortened by lack of sleep during crop time, he replied "without doubt [*sin duda*]."[8] Keeping the slaves constantly occupied was also justified as a means of keeping them out of trouble. Cuban planters were amazed when informed of the amount of leisure that slaves in the United States enjoyed after their daily tasks were finished. They could not understand how the slaves remained disciplined with so much time on their hands.[9]

The nature of the crop was not, however, the only factor determining the intensity of labor. Fluctuations in the market for various crops encouraged planters to get in as big a crop as possible while prices were high. Slaves in the tobacco industry in the French West Indies during the seventeenth century were worked from early morning through most of the night and were allowed only three or four hours sleep. They often fell asleep standing up and were struck if they were found sleeping. From the time they were twelve years old, women and children were worked with the same intensity. The burden was lightened for women during the seventh or eighth month of pregnancy.[10] While labor on the coffee estates in mid-nineteenth-century Cuba was less intense (the workday was fifteen to sixteen hours) and the mortality rate was lower,[11] the coffee industry in Brazil maintained an extremely intense labor regime. With inadequate food, slaves worked from 3 a.m. until 9 or 10 p.m. Even during the rainy season, slaves had to pick coffee at night. One coffee planter calculated upon using a slave no longer than a year, "longer than which few could survive, but that he got enough work out of him not only to repay his initial investment, but even to show a good profit!"[12] What is unique about sugar production, however, it that even with the best intentions and the most humane management, the nature of the crop itself and the process involved in producing raw sugar, in the absence of an elastic labor supply, made intense utilization of the work force inevitable during the extended grinding season.

Moreno Fraginals, who has carefully researched nineteenth-century Cuban sugar estate records, concluded that conditions were the most barbaric in the entire world during certain periods of the last century. Contrary to the belief of some observers that mechanization of the sugar industry would improve working conditions for the slaves, the opposite result was produced. While the sugar mill was mechanized and railroads were used for transportation, field work remained unmechanized. Bottlenecks resulted, more slaves were needed, the length of the workday and the intensity of labor were increased. Little sentimentality crept into the calculations of management. Treatment of slaves was determined by the volume of manpower available, the price of the slave, techniques of production, and market conditions. Cuban estates operated under a highly rationalized system of time control. The slave's possibilities for survival depended upon the concepts of economy held by management at a particular time. If high productivity was chosen at the expense of a high mortality rate, slaves died in mass.[13]

ENDNOTES

1. Arquivo Histórico Nacional, Madrid, Ultramar Legajo 4655, Expediente 181, Raza Blanca y de Color, Carta de O'Donnell al Sec. de Estado, February 15, 1845; Informe de la Sección de Ultramar del Consejo Real, December 22, 1846.
2. Fernando Ortiz, *Cuban Counterpoint: Tobacco and Sugar*, trans. Harriet de Onis (New York: Alfred A. Knopf, 1947), p. 33.
3. Noel Deerr, *History of Sugar*, 2 vols. (London: Chapman and Hall, Ltd., 1950), 2: 354-55.
4. Celso Furtado, *The Economic Growth of Brazil: A Survey from Colonial to Modern Times*, trans. Ricardo W. DeAguiar and Eric C. Drysdale (Berkeley and Los Angeles: University of California Press, 1963), p. 53.
5. Deerr, *History of Sugar*, vol. 2, pp. 354-55. Testimony before a Parliamentary Commission in 1832, cited therein.
6. *Ibid.*, vol. 2, p. 359.
7. J.G.F. Wurdemann, *Notes on Cuba* (Boston: James Monroe and Co., 1844), p. 153-54.
8. Richard R. Madden, *Island of Cuba* (London, 1853), pp. 167-68.
9. Wurdemann, *Notes on Cuba*, p. 258.
10. Jean-Baptiste Dutertre, *Histoire général des antilles habitées par les français*, 4 vols. (Paris, 1667-71), 2, 523.
11. David Turnbull, *Travels in the West Indies* (London, 1840), p. 294.
12. Gilberto Freyre, *The Masters and the Slaves* (New York: Alfred A. Knopf, 1947), p. 131. See also Stanley J. Stein, *Vassouras: A Brazilian Coffee County, 1850-1900* (Cambridge, Mass.: Harvard University Press, 1957).
13. Manuel Moreno Fraginals, *El Ingenio: El complejo económico social Cubano del azucar* (Havana: Comisión Nacional Cubana de la UNESCO, 1964), pp. 155-62.

SECTION 4
Slave Emancipation and Changing
Economic Patterns of the British West Indies:
Emergence of the Peasantry

4.0

Introduction to Section 4

In 1807 the British called a halt to the invidious slave trade, which had played a catalytic role in the economic expansion of both the West Indian colonies and the mother country. The motivations for this act were numerous and controversial; were they primarily humanitarian or economic? Selection 4.1 examines the well-known figures of the early abolitionist movement, including Wilberforce and Clarkson, and presents evidence for strong conscience-stricken motivations for the ending of the trade. In selection 4.2 however, Craton posits the argument that the abolition of the slave trade was equally inspired by economic considerations, as the yearly loss of sailors in the merchant marine was high, and slaves, once transported to the West Indies, had limited possibilities as consumers of British manufactured goods.

Whichever argument is accepted, one fact remains indisputable; the end of the trade inevitably led to the abolition of slavery itself, an event which took place in the British West Indies in 1834. Amidst gloomy predictions of pending economic disaster, the former slaves, in that year, became "apprentices" to their masters. The purpose of the apprenticeship system was to avoid immediate loss of plantation labor, but the administration of the system was so difficult and abuses so rampant that the exodus from the estates was hastened, rather than achieving the desired effect. By 1838, apprenticeship was officially abandoned, and the former slaves were now legally independent.

The remainder of the nineteenth century saw fundamental changes in the traditional economic patterns of the English colonies. The newly liberated workers rapidly left plantations and moved onto small land parcels (some purchased, others possessed by squatter's rights), there to form the nuclei of peasant communities. Although the stigma of plantation labour must certainly have acted as a negative incentive for staying on the estates, recent evidence suggests that had planters offered reasonable wages and opportunities for cultivation of personal crops, the exodus might not have been as dramatic as it was. Not only did the pattern of land tenure change with the emancipation of the slaves, but the economic output did as well. Instead of concentrating on monocultural sugar production, the peasants grew ground provisions, citrus and banana crops, thus substantially modifying the traditional one-crop economy. We know a great deal about the peasantry at this early stage of organization through the superb scholarship of Woodville Marshall (see selection 4.3).

The success of the emerging peasantry in local market economies incited the planter class to redouble its complaints about inadequate labor for the monocultural export economy. The planters were convinced that there was a direct causality between the flight of workers from the estates and the bankruptcy which afflicted many formerly prosperous plantations. Lobdell (selection 4.4) examines this premise and finds that not all colonies suffered equally. Trinidad and British Guiana actually saw rises in the level of sugar production, a gain which is partly attributable to the active campaign in both these colonies for indentured emigré laborers. In selection 4.5, Boodhoo examines the circumstances under which East Indian indentured laborers toiled in Trinidad and suggests that they were not unlike the conditions under outright slavery. The demand for labor, however, continued to override more humanitarian considerations, and the exigencies of sugar cultivation reduced many of the new arrivals to abject misery.

The new student would do well to consult the classic work in this subject, L.J. Ragatz, *The Fall of the Planter Class in the British Caribbean, 1763–1833, a Study in Social and Economic History*. More recent monographs include W.A. Green, *British Slave Emancipation: The Sugar Colonies and the Great Experiment, 1830–1865*; B.W. Higman, *Slave Society and Economy in Jamaica, 1807–1833*; P. Curtin, *Two Jamaicas: The Role of Ideas in a Tropical Colony* and

D. Hall, *Five of the Leewards, 1834–1870*. K.O. Laurence, *Immigration in the West Indies in the 19th Century* is an account of East Indian, Chinese and Portuguese immigration into the Caribbean in this period.

The Humanitarian Influence in Abolition — Daniel P. Mannix

The influence of humanitarian idealism in the fight to undermine the slave trade, and ultimately slavery itself, is one of the most important themes of Caribbean history. The unlikely combination of Wilberforce and Clarkson, at a critical juncture in English history, provided the momentum for the abolitionist campaign. Although the smooth sailing of the anti-slave-trade bill was halted by the assumed association of British reformers with Jacobin France, the bill was finally carried successfully through Parliament. Britain's direct role in the slave trade thus ended in 1807.

This selection is taken from D.P. Mannix (1962), Black Cargoes: A History of the Atlantic Slave Trade. *Copyright © Daniel P. Mannix, 1962. Reprinted by permission of Viking Penguin, Inc. and Harold Matson Co., Inc.*

In 1765 a young Londoner named Granville Sharp came on a Negro slave lying at the point of death in Mincing Lane. His owner, David Lisle, a lawyer from Barbados, had beaten him, then thrown him into the street to die. Sharp took the slave home and nursed him back to health. Lisle, hearing that the man had recovered, kidnaped him and sold him to the West Indies. When Sharp protested, the Barbados lawyer brought suit against him for having stolen his property.

The case aroused so much indignation that Lisle withdrew his suit, to the great disappointment of Sharp, who had been studying the finer points of English law as it related to property in slaves. The law provided that "all men" should have certain rights. Would the court — Sharp asked in another case regarding a kidnaped slave — say that a Negro was not a man? This time the court evaded the main issue by freeing the Negro on the ground that his former owner had attempted to seize him without a warrant. Sharp then found still another fugitive slave, James Somerset, and brought a test case. In 1772 Lord Chief Justice Mansfield handed down the historic decision that "as soon as any slave sets foot on English ground he becomes free."

Although this judgment abolished slavery in Great Britain, it did not affect British possessions. Neither did it prohibit the trade itself, which might have continued indefinitely had it not been for the efforts of two remarkable men, Thomas Clarkson and William Wilberforce.

In 1785 Cambridge University offered a Latin prize for the best essay on the subject *Anne liceat invitos in servituten dare*: "Is it lawful to make slaves of others against their will?" A twenty-five-year-old student named Thomas Clarkson decided to compete for the prize. He knew nothing about the slave trade, but he procured a copy of Benezet's *Short Account* and set to work. Clarkson was the son of a clergyman in Cambridgeshire. His parents were reasonably well off, and the young man had a small private income. He was a quiet, unambitious, studious youngster whose only desire was to obtain a decent country parish and follow in the footsteps of his father. After reading Benezet's description of the trade, he was transformed into what the poet Coleridge would later call "a moral steam-engine," and what the pro-slavery element characterized as a "Jacobin white nigger."

Clarkson won the Latin prize. A few weeks later, while riding to London through Hertfordshire, he received what he considered to be a direct revelation from God, ordering him to devote his life to abolishing the slave trade. He dismounted, fell on his knees beside the road, and accepted his divinely appointed mission. Settling down in London, he began what at first seemed to be a one-man battle against the trade. He then discovered, however, that there was a Quaker committee which had been formed some years before to oppose the trade, and that there were a few men, notably Granville Sharp, more than willing to help in his fight. The Quaker committee had become inactive, but Clarkson reorganized it. With Sharp, Josiah Wedgwood the potter, and some other enthusiasts, he founded the Society for the Abolition of the Slave Trade in 1787. The seal of the Society was "An African . . . in chains in a supplicating posture, kneeling with one knee upon the ground, and with both hands lifted up to Heaven, and round the seal . . . the following motto . . . 'Am I not a Man and a Brother.' " Wedgwood copied the seal in china and turned out copies by the thousands.

In many respects Clarkson resembled the popular conception of a fanatical do-gooder. He was a humorless man, a poor talker, uncompromising, and a bore. Years later the artist Haydon said of him, "He is impatient, childish, simple, positive, hates contradiction [but is also] charitable and speaks affectionately of all." Physically he was a tall (six feet) and heavy man with a deeply furrowed face. He was an indefatigable worker. He visited Liverpool, Bristol, and the other slaving ports, gathering data on the trade from seamen, ships' doctors, merchants, and travelers. He started a collection of instruments used in the trade, such as leg shackles, handcuffs, thumbscrews, and the speculum oris, or mouth opener. Part of the collection is still in the museum at Wisbech, some thirty-five miles north of Cambridge. Also he made an English translation of his prize essay, which the Quakers published, and later he wrote many other pamphlets on his findings.

To interfere with the interests controlling the slave trade was a dangerous procedure. Once, in Liverpool, Clarkson was returning from his investigation of a slave ship when he saw a group of nine seamen walking down the pier toward him. One of the men had been previously pointed out to him as the murderer of a sailor who had dared to protest against a captain's brutality. Clarkson retreated, but the gang began to close in on him. There was no one else on the pier and the tide was running strong; a body thrown into the sea would never be found. Clarkson put his head down and charged like a bull. The sudden attack took the men by surprise. There were curses, a few blows, and then Clarkson broke through and escaped. The next day he was back again,

oblivious to the scowls and mutterings around him, gravely
jotting down fresh information.

Unlike many reformers, Clarkson realized his own limitations. He was not an orator or a national leader. His work
would have to consist in collecting evidence against the trade
and in performing the endless secretarial tasks that were
vital to the society. Someone else would have to be the
spokesman of the movement; a politician who could rouse
the public by trumpeting out Clarkson's painfully acquired
knowledge. But with the slave trade bringing in direct profits
of £300,000 a year to the Liverpool traders alone, and with
the merchants who supplied the "trade goods" used in
obtaining the slaves making another £140,000 — plus the
West Indian sugar trade valued at six millions — opposition
to slavery was political suicide. An utterly dedicated man had
to be found — eloquent, politically prominent, well connected, and wealthy enough to be independent of governmental favors. There was only one man who possessed these
qualifications: William Wilberforce.

Wilberforce was born in 1759 in Hull, Yorkshire, the son
of a rich merchant. He was a sickly child with bad eyes and
a puny frame, but he was brilliant and charming. His grand-
father left him a fortune, and the boy grew up to be a
prominent man about town. He was a member of the better
London clubs, a friend of George Selwyn, Sheridan, Charles
Fox, and William Pitt, and knew Benjamin Franklin. As was
fashionable among the young bucks of the time, he was a
gambler and a heavy drinker. His diary is interspersed with
such notes as "won 600 pounds this evening" or "lost 100
pounds at whist." In spite of his dissipation and his physical
handicaps, he impressed even casual acquaintances with his
capabilities. Boswell remarked, "I thought he was a shrimp
but the shrimp is a whale."

Bored with the fashionable world, Wilberforce decided at
the age of twenty-one to enter Parliament. The election cost
him £9000, as he paid two guineas to anyone who would
vote for him. Finding Parliament even more boring than the
coffeehouses, he decided to make a grand tour of the Continent, together with a Cambridge don named Isaac Milner.
Mr. Milner was an early exponent of what later became

known as "muscular Christianity." He was a big, powerful
man. cheerfully aggressive and the antithesis of his delicate,
intellectual charge. Milner converted him to Christianity of
the militant type that is more concerned with fighting evil
than with intoning pieties.

When Wilberforce returned to London, he resolved to
resign from Parliament and enter the ministry. Pitt persuaded
him to stay on, arguing that the brilliant young man could
accomplish more good as a politician than as a clergyman. So
Wilberforce retained his seat in Parliament, devoting much of
his time to writing religious treatises and pondering the state
of his soul. He also made several speeches denouncing both
slavery and the slave trade, but with little result, as he relied
on rhetoric more than facts to impress his listeners. Since he
was, however, almost the only member of Parliament who
had actively interested himself in the cause, the new Society
for the Abolition of the Slave Trade decided to ask him to
become its spokesman.

Clarkson was dispatched to ask Wilberforce for his help.
In the presence of a great London gentleman, the country
parson's son found himself tongue-tied; he mumbled a few
words and rushed out of the room. Another member had to
be selected as messenger, and Wilberforce gladly consented
to be the society's champion.

No one could resist his charm when he chose to exert it.
Wilberforce and Clarkson became close friends and worked
together as an effective team, each possessing the qualities
which the other lacked, and both dedicated to the same
principles. Together they devised a strategy for attacking
the trade. Clarkson had already collected figures showing
that more than one-fifth of the sailors on Guineamen died in
the course of a single voyage, and it was decided that the loss
of English seamen was more likely to rouse public animosity
toward the trade than the wholesale murder of any number
of African Negroes. Although this was the first point to
emphasize, the sufferings of the Negroes were not to be
neglected. Both Clarkson and Wilberforce intended to work
for the total abolition of slavery, but they agreed to confine
their attacks to the trade itself, meanwhile assuring West
Indian planters that domestic slavery would be untouched

and that they were interested only in preventing possible slave insurrections. They would assert that stopping the trade would double or even triple the value of the slaves then held in the British islands and would enable the British planters to monopolize the West Indian slave market.

Clarkson now set out systematically to collect so much detailed evidence against the slave trade that the pro-slavery forces would be unable to refute his facts. He rode more than three thousand miles during the next few months. He discovered evidence that a sailor named Peter Green had been flogged to death because he refused his captain's Negro mistress the keys to the wine locker. He found that another sailor, John Dean of the *Brothers*, had been chained face down to the deck and that the captain had made incisions in his bare back with red-hot tongs and then poured hot pitch over him. One man's brains had been beaten out with a double wall knot in the end of a rope. Clarkson was not content simply to accept the word of seamen who had witnessed these murders on slave ships; he double-checked the evidence, making sure that the murdered man had actually been part of the ship's complements, that they had not returned from the voyages, and that there were no records in the ships' logs of the manner of their deaths.

He soon found it increasingly difficult to obtain the kind of evidence he needed. Witnesses mysteriously disappeared or suddenly changed their minds. Tradesmen who were willing to cooperate with him had their shops boycotted. Ships' doctors who told him about the horrors of the Middle Passage were refused new berths on outgoing ships. The son of a West Indian planter who talked to Clarkson was promptly cut out of his father's will. On one occasion Clarkson traveled several hundred miles to interview a sailor who then refused to talk to him. Clarkson rode on, but received a message that the man had changed his mind. Clarkson rode back, traveling all night, only to find that although the sailor would talk, he would not allow his name to be used.

Some of the evidence uncovered was so patently incredible that Clarkson thought it had been deliberately arranged by the pro-slavery group as a trap for him. In Bristol he spoke to some sailors who told him that they were bound for Africa to pick up a cargo of seventy slaves. Clarkson obtained the dimensions of their vessel from the builder. It had been intended as a pleasure craft on the Severn and was designed for no more than six persons. The hold, where the slaves were to be stowed, was only thirty-one feet long and two feet, eight inches high. Obviously, Clarkson reasoned, the men had been instructed to tell him a ridiculous story in the hope that he would repeat it and make a fool of himself. Then, after checking with five other men, he discovered that the story was true. The slaves were to be piled on top of one another like sacks of merchandise.

Meanwhile the Abolition Society had started its public agitation against the trade. In its first 15 months it printed 26,526 reports and 51,432 books and pamphlets, many of which found eager readers. So many petitions for the abolition of the slave trade were submitted to Parliament in 1783 that the Crown appointed a committee of the Privy Council to hold hearings. Parliament itself took one legislative action. It passed a law limiting the number of slaves that a vessel could carry according to its tonnage: roughly five slaves for every three tons.

In 1789 Wilberforce, after an admirable speech, presented a series of resolutions as the basis for a future motion to abolish the trade. The resolutions led to the famous parliamentary hearings of 1790 and 1791, which examined every aspect of the purchase, transportation, sale, and treatment of Negro slaves. Abolition became a popular cause. At evening parties ladies refused to serve West Indian sugar and recited anti-slavery ballads, including Cowper's "The Negro's Complaint." Wedgwood's china seal of the Abolition Society appeared on snuff boxes, bracelets, and combs. Many grocers would not deal in rum or sugar, and Clarkson boasted that sugar revenue had fallen off by £200,000.

Already the excitement had spread to France, where a group of philosophers and liberal aristocrats had founded a Société des Amis du Noir. Clarkson set out for Paris in 1789, hoping to persuade the National Assembly to join with the British government in abolishing the trade. Having started with high anticipations, his visit ended with the first real setback to the cause. Although he enjoyed the support of Lafayette and Mirabeau, Clarkson was denounced as an English spy seeking to bankrupt French colonial possessions. The rumor circulated that he was planning to incite Negro slaves in the colonies to murder their masters.

A mulatto from Santo Domingo named Vincent Ogé was in Paris at the time. Ogé was demanding that all the slaves in the island be freed within fifteen years; if not, he threatened to lead a general uprising. Clarkson begged him to moderate his demands, but Ogé refused. "I begin not to care," he said, "whether the National Assembly will admit us or not. We will no longer continue to be held in a degraded light. We can produce as good soldiers as those of France. If we are once forced to desperate measures, it will be in vain that thousands are sent across the Atlantic to bring us back to our former states." Words like these infuriated the French. When Mirabeau introduced a bill to abolish the slave trade, the National Assembly refused to pass it — unless Parliament first abolished the trade. As not a few members of Parliament had already indicated that they would not vote to abolish the trade unless the French did, Clarkson was helpless.

Having returned to England, Clarkson was accused of being a Jacobin, the eighteenth-century equivalent of being called a Communist. In attacking the slave trade, his enemies said, he was upholding the claims of an inferior class against their masters and hence was supporting the French doctrine of the rights of man. He was also accused of bring a French spy.

In April 1791 a motion was finally made in the House of Commons to prohibit the importation of slaves into the British West Indies. Wilberforce shone in the debate that followed, but the ruling classes, disturbed by the French Revolution, had become less sympathetic to reforms. Also they were rendered fearful by signs of unrest in the sugar islands. Ogé had returned to Santo Domingo, had taken arms with a few followers, and, when he surrendered, had been broken on the wheel. There had been slave revolts in Martinique and in the British island of Dominica. After the long investigation of the slave trade, the motion against it was defeated by the discouraging vote of 163 to 88.

Clarkson and Wilberforce resumed their campaign. By this

time a new revolt had broken out in Santo Domingo, with
massacres of the planters, and the pro-slavery forces were
thoroughly aroused. Wilberforce was challenged to duels.
Gangs of thugs attempted to waylay him, and he was forced
to hire guards. The rumor circulated that he had a Negro
mistress. West Indian planters and Liverpool merchants
raised a campaign fund of £10,000 to fight the anti-slave-
trade bill in Parliament. Witnesses were rushed to London
from the West Indies and Africa prepared to swear that the
trade was a benevolent institution dedicated solely to civili-
zing the primitive Africans. The Abolition Society had lost
most of its wealthy supporters, but meanwhile it was gaining
new adherents among the industrial workers of the north and
among the Nonconformists, moved by the example of John
Wesley. When Wilberforce raised the motion for abolition a
second time, in 1792, it was supported by 312 petitions from
England, 187 from Scotland, and 20 from Wales.

In an impassioned speech Wilberforce urged his fellow
members to put moral responsibilities above economic considerations. A Mr. Henniker answered him by reading a letter
from the King of Dahomey to George I in which the Dahoman had boasted of ornamenting the pavement and walls of
his palace with the heads of his prisoners. Slave traders
testified to the notorious "customs" and to the wholesale sacrifice of captives. Wilberforce, however, was now
ready to answer this argument. Pretending great incredulity,
he insisted that primitive savages armed only with spears
and shields could not possibly overrun whole nations and
capture thousands of their fellow Africans. The slave traders
retorted that the Dahoman army was well equipped with
muskets and even cannon, adding that a sentimentalist who
had never been to Africa and obviously knew nothing of
the facts was presumptuous to propose laws concerning
the trade. Wilberforce then demanded to know from what
source the native kingdoms obtained their firearms.

The slave traders took refuge in describing the happy
life led by Negroes in the Middle Passage. The slaves had
abundant food, ample room, and plenty of air; when on
deck, they danced and made merry. The voyage was "one of
the happiest periods of a Negro's life." One witness added,

in the flush of his enthusiasm, "When the sailors are flogged, it is always done out of hearing of the Africans so as not to disturb them." With the blundering remarks of his opponents to help him, Wilberforce came somewhat nearer to success. This time Commons adopted an amendment to defer the abolition of the trade, but it then passed the emasculated bill. It was permitted to die in the House of Lords. Thus, after five years of desperate exertion by the Abolition Society, the only tangible result had been the law to limit the number of slaves that a vessel might carry, and this had been passed at the first session of Parliament that discussed the trade.

After 1792 political life in Great Britain entered a period of extreme conservatism. Revolutionary France was now the enemy, but British soldiers were also fighting the revolted slaves in Santo Domingo, where forty thousand of the soldiers died in four years, mostly of fever. Anyone demanding rights for Negroes was regarded in conservative circles as coming close to treason. Wilberforce did not flinch; he kept introducing his motions against the slave trade in each new session of Commons, where they were always defeated. The Abolition Society could find little money to carry on its work. Nevertheless it had created a lasting image of the slave trade in the public mind, and its work was meeting with a somewhat less violent opposition now that the West Indian planters were losing their influence in Parliament. As for the Liverpool merchants, they had become more interested in profits from wartime shipping and privateering than they were in the Guinea trade.

A new ministry, under Grenville and Fox, took office in 1806. Fox, easy-going as he was, had been a lifelong opponent of slavery. In June he brought forward a resolution "that effectual measures should be taken for the abolition of the African slave trade"; it was passed by a large majority. Fox died in September, but early the following spring Grenville presented to the House of Lords a bill providing that "all manner of dealing and trading in the Purchase, Sale, Barter or Transfer of Slaves . . . is hereby utterly abolished." It was passed by both houses, and Wilberforce collapsed weeping in his chair. He is said to have received the greatest ovation ever heard in Parliament.

*Economic Motivations
for Abolition*   Michael Craton

The relationship between free-trade advocates and anti-slave-trade proponents is just as critical to understanding the final demise of the slave trade as is interpreting the platform of humanitarian reformists. The perceived necessity of introducing 'free-grown' sugars, from foreign sources, to the home market, in order to satisfy the working classes' demands for cheap staples, aligned manufacturing interests to the doctrine of free trade and, ultimately, to the cause of abolition itself. This association is outlined in the following selection from M. Craton (1974), Sinews of Empire: A Short History of British Slavery. *Copyright © 1974 by Michael Craton. Reprinted by permission of Doubleday and Company, Inc.*

The legal reformers gained increasing support from economists as they, in turn, were increasingly supported by practical men. From the mid-eighteenth century onward, French physiocrats maintained that since law reflected the dictates of necessity as well as a more abstract natural law, rational utility could be used as an argument against slavery as long as slavery could be shown to be uneconomic. Physiocratic ideas were brilliantly developed by the Scottish economist Adam Smith (who had been feted by Turgot and his circle on a visit to France in the 1760s) in the form of arguments for the unimpeded operation of the principle of enlightened self-interest.

Although Adam Smith and his followers believed that the proper operation of enlightened self-interest and the removal of narrow protectionism would result in moral as well as

118

material improvement, their attack upon slavery was concentrated on its uneconomic aspects. The expense of slave labor placed it beyond the means of the producers of any but the most lucrative crops, so slavery encouraged the tendency to monocultural plantations in high-profit crops such as sugar, which nonetheless required protection to sustain their advantage. Moreover, slavery had disappeared from Europe (save Russia) because it was found more economic to provide workers with the incentive of a share in the produce. The continued existence of slavery in a nondespotic empire that protected property, meant that the masters' self-interest in subduing the slaves was tolerated although it was in conflict with the self-interest of the slaves not to work. Enlightened self-interest could only work to the public good if it were to the advantage of employers and employed alike that the workers advance in intelligence, usefulness, and the ownership of property. This could only be achieved by emancipation and the consequent decline of plantations based on slavery. Yet by condemning the old plantation system, emancipation might destroy the justification for mercantilist protection and release such energies that all sections in due course would be bound to benefit.

Adam Smith's arguments, particularly that which maintained that slavery was so manifestly inefficient that it was only sustained by the slave owners' lust for power, naturally never convinced slave traders or West Indian planters. But his arguments were deeply attractive to a growing body of practical men with countervailing interests. Chief among them were those whose interest it was to import sugar into England as cheaply as possible in order to satisfy the seemingly illimitable demand at home and in the rest of Europe. Sugar refiners, retailers, and re-exporters therefore argued for the removal of duties designed to protect the West Indian colonies, and the tapping of sugar plantations in the unprotected East or even outside the formal British Empire. The freeing of the sources of sugar, they claimed, would not only bring cheaper sugar to the masses but would have the additional merits of dooming slavery on British plantations while distributing sugar produced not by slaves but by "free" laborers. Accordingly, in setting afoot a campaign for "free sugar," disinterested abolitionists worked with capitalists who were far from altruistic, and together they had considerable success in convincing the ordinary people that in opting for unprotected sugar they would not only aid the slaves but also, in course of time, pay less. Apparently, philanthropy, *laissez faire*, and enlightened self-interest were neatly blended, at every level.

Although their campaign did not reach so wide an audience, the other "Easterners" who attacked the East India Company's monopoly in the hope of expanding Asian trade, and all those manufacturers who followed Adam Smith in believing that the Old Colonial System stifled their growing export potential, abetted the free sugar advocates. Among the East India Company's most cherished privileges was the re-exportation of Indian cottons to West Africa duty-free, while the expansion of the Lancashire cotton industry was hampered by duties designed to protect British Empire producers, including the few slave cotton plantations in the West Indies. The removal of these forms of protection would serve the purposes of encouraging English textile manufacturers and raw cotton importers, while discouraging the slave trade that had stimulated the old re-export trade and helped to supply the sugar plantations. It was acknowledged that the inefficient Indian cottage cotton industry might suffer as well as the slave traders, but it was argued that Indian raw cotton producers would benefit from increased demand, while Indians as a whole would benefit from the importation of cheaper English textiles. At the same time English workers would benefit from wider employment. As the free trade net spread to even wider areas and to other industries, so similar benefits would be brought to the people of the world, consumers and producers as well as capitalist entrepreneurs. The general good — to revert to Adam Smith's theme — would far outweigh the loss to the narrow interests dependent on slavery and protection.

These trends were not merely speculative; they were already discernible in British import and export figures in the last years of the eighteenth century, despite the prevalence of mercantilist policies. While sugar imports from the British West Indies between 1772 and 1807 barely doubled, the imports of raw cotton from all parts of the world went up by 1,000 percent. Over the same period the value of exported English cotton goods rose from an average of £240,000 a year in the five years after 1772, to £8,740,000 a year between 1802 and 1806. It is true that the proportion of British trade represented by the West Indies remained high until the ending of the slave trade, exports to the Antilles remaining roughly around 10 percent of the British total and imports around 20 percent from 1772 to 1793, and both actually rising during the subsequent war years to about 15 percent and 30 percent, respectively. Yet the very imbalance between exports and imports provided grist for the free traders, who maintained that drawing sugar and other West Indian products from a wider area while actively expanding exports would lead to Britain's general profit. Moreover, the wartime expansion of British West Indian trade was the result of the destruction or takeover of French, Dutch, and Spanish colonies, which as far as the colonists of the old-established British plantations were concerned, was tantamount to free trade anyway.

Certainly, the upsetting of the Caribbean and Latin American balance of power did much to promote the benefits of freer trade once the last French war was over, and this was highlighted by the adamant opposition to expansionism as well as by any move on the part of the embattled West India interest that undermined the Old Colonial System. Between the ending of the slave trade in 1807 and the ending of slavery itself in 1834, the index of British industrial output rose by 125 percent and total British exports by 133 percent; yet the amount of trade with the British West Indies (including new colonies) stayed practically stationary, and the percentage of total British exports destined for the West Indies fell from 15.1 to 4.8. The figures for capital investment in West Indian enterprises, if they were obtainable, would almost certainly show a similar relative if not absolute decline. Long before 1830 it should have been obvious that the increase in volume and the shifts of trade had already made the British sugar plantations based on slavery obsolete. Philanthropy was now a luxury that could be enjoyed by almost all.

To Eric Williams and his most ardent disciples, the degree to which the abolitionists and emancipists claiming to be motivated by religion or the rights of man subscribed to economic reform or were engaged in nonplantation trade made them no more philanthropic than the slave traders and slave holders themselves. This is almost certainly to understate the perverse power of disinterested idealism, as well as the value of engaging in good causes for dubious reasons, though not so absurd as to maintain that the philanthropists could ever have carried the day against unweakened vested interests. A more balanced summary might state that abolition and emancipation, while inevitable in the long run, occurred when they did because of a fortunate concatenation of interests, ideas, and extraneous events. To a certain extent the reforms were based upon misapprehensions. It was not long before it was apparent that unprotected sugar and cotton were by no means "freely" produced, coming in their largest quantities from the American slave states and slave-based Cuba and Brazil. Having destroyed Indian cotton manufacturing, free trade debilitated Indian raw cotton production as well. To some observers it was also ironically apparent that conditions for ex-slaves in the West Indies and English workers in textile and other "dark, satanic mills" alike, were in some ways worse than those for plantation slaves. Yet by that time the strange alliance, or *mésalliance*, of free traders and philanthropists had done its work.

West Indian Peasantry   Woodville Marshall

The abolition of slavery signaled the emergence of another class in West Indian society: the peasantry. The origins of this rural sector and the contributions of peasant farmers to the diversification of the West Indian economy are examined in this selection. The tenacity of peasant agriculturalists in the face of planter opposition is an important subtheme of the nineteenth century. Reprinted from W. Marshall (1972), 'Peasant Movements and Agrarian Problems in the West Indies, Part I, Aspects of the Development of the Peasantry', Caribbean Quarterly, *18, No. 1 (March), pp. 31-38 with kind permission of* Caribbean Quarterly *and the Author.*

The West Indian peasantry started its existence after the complete emancipation of the slaves in 1838. It was composed of those ex-slaves who started small farms on the periphery of the plantation areas, wherever they could find land, on abandoned estates, on Crown land and in the mountainous interior of the various territories. S.W. Mintz has noted the main features and implications of this development:

"They represented a reaction to the plantation economy, a negative reflex to enslavement, mass production, monocrop dependence and metropolitan control. Though these peasants often continued to work part-time on plantation for wages, to eke out their cash needs, their orientation was in fact antagonistic to the plantation rationale."[1]

This antagonism was basic to the situation, and it has rendered the growth of the peasantry difficult and made its existence marginal. The plantation, mainly the sugar plantation, had dominated the landscape and the society for

123

centuries. It engrossed nearly all the best land, monopolised the few technical skills available, controlled the sources of credit, and possessed a decisive voice on all questions of public policy. Emancipation of the slaves threatened a weakening of this control by creating a labour force which was no longer entirely dependent on the estates. For the planters, accustomed to a dependent and more than ample labour force, and habituated to the wasteful agricultural practices which this situation bred, the prospect was most alarming. They asserted that the loss of "steady and continuous labour" would endanger "the maintenance of the colonies as valuable and productive possessions of the Crown;"[2] and that the ex-slaves who left the estates would quickly and irrevocably decline in the scale of civilization.[3] What the planters wanted, as the Royal Commission of 1897 pointed out, "was a large supply of labourers, dependent on being able to find work on the estates and consequently subject to their control and willing to work for low wages."[4] The fact, therefore, of peasant land settlement would confirm their worst fears and disrupt their economy.

Consequently, planters sought from the beginning to obstruct peasant land settlement. They tried to bind the ex-slaves to the estates by a form of labour-rent tenancy and long labour contracts, and they attempted to limit opportunities for occupational differentiation by establishing a system of license fees for employment outside the estates. In addition, by means of another system of licenses and fees, they made it difficult for the ex-slaves to produce staple crops, or to employ themselves in the production of charcoal, firewood and arrowroot flour.[5] But above all else, they tried (and managed) to block extensive peasant settlement on the uncultivated land in the various territories.

Land suited to such development was available, to a varying extent, in all the territories. Most of it could be found in Trinidad and Guyana (British Guiana), Jamaica and the Windward Islands (St. Lucia, St. Vincent, Grenada, Tobago and Dominica). The first two territories had small populations and a relatively young sugar industry, while in Jamaica and the Windward Islands, the sugar industry had left undeveloped and unoccupied most of the mountainous interior.

Only in Barbados and the Leeward Islands (St. Kitts-Nevis-Anguilla, Montserrat and Antigua) was land scarce.[6] In those islands, a large population, and old sugar industry and small land area had left little land unalienated or unoccupied. In 1897, the Royal Commission found quantities of uncultivated arable land in all the territories. These quantities ranged from 10,000 acres in Barbados to more than one and a half million acres in Jamaica.[7]

Uncultivated land could be divided into two categories. First, there was Crown land, that is, the land which remained ungranted by the Crown to patentees. This area was extensive in many of the territories, particularly in Guyana, Trinidad, Jamaica and the Windward Islands,[8] but much of it was not suitable for settlement. For the most part, it consisted of the mountainous, forested, sometimes inaccessible, interior. Moreover, its extent and exact location were difficult to determine. The portion that was cultivable or, on other ways exploitable, was often appropriated illegally by squatters and charcoal burners and by neighbouring estates.[9]

The second category of surplus land was uncultivated estate land, the vacant successions, ruinate or abandoned land, often called Back Lands.[10] This was also an extensive area, and it comprised most of the usable land which was not being cultivated in the West Indies. The ease with which land was acquired by the early settlers, the vicissitudes of the sugar industry and wasteful agricultural practices were mainly responsible for a situation in which, as one governor said, estates usually had "more land out than in cultivation".[11]

F.L. Engledow found in 1939 "large parts of estates, not uncommonly up to half, and in some cases entire properties" in a ruinate condition.[12] Moreover, this area of land was being continually increased after Emancipation by the high incidence of misfortune in the staple production. Long depression in the sugar industry, disease in cocoa, coffee and banana cultivation, hurricanes and earthquakes forced contraction of plantation cultivation, abandonment of estates and, sometimes, a resumption of ownership by the Crown when the land became forfeit for the arrears of quit rent. It was estimated that in Jamaica at Emancipation some 815,000 acres of land were in arrears of payment of quit rent and other taxes,[13] and between 1871 and 1912 nearly a quarter of a million acres did, in fact, become forfeit to the Crown for the non-payment of taxes.[14] This was the type of land most desired by the potential peasants and when access to it was limited or denied, they squatted on portions of it, or surreptitiously exploited its timber and pasturage.[15]

The ex-slaves were allowed legal access to only a small portion of this land. Crown land was closed off almost completely by the various legislatures' actions and deliberate inaction. They refused either to finance surveys of the Crown land or to frame liberal regulations for its disposal. At the same time, they adopted stringent legislation against squatting and the "despoiling" of Crown land. It was not until 1895 that any of the territories modified this policy. In that year the Jamaican Government initiated small hold land settlement on liberal terms on the Crown land. But, despite strong metropolitan encouragement and local peasant demand for similar action, such a policy was not generally adopted until the late 1930's.[16,17]

Surplus estate land was almost as difficult to acquire by peasants and potential peasants. Some planters refused to sell or rent their surplus land; others agreed to rent but refused to sell; and most of those who did sell land exacted high prices for small portions of it. Prices after Emancipation ranged between £5 and £20 per acre, and sometimes reached as high as £100 and £200.[18] Moreover, the land sold was usually of marginal quality, land regarded as unsuitable for staple cultivation, located on "the interior mountain ridges",[19] often far from water and good roads, sometimes unsurveyed and uncleared and, in Guyana, almost certainly requiring drainage. This meant that the process of freehold land acquisition by the individual peasant tended to be a slow one. Often, he bought his land on an instalment plan, and could only afford a small lot. Therefore, it took him a long time both to acquire clear title and to build up a sizeable holding out of a number of small scattered lots.[20] Often, too, the potential peasant had to use various expedients on his way to freehold land acquisition. He might perform almost regular estate labour, accept a metayage agreement or a "contract", lease extensive portions of land, follow a trade, keep a shop, fish, etc.[21]

Some land was acquired by the ex-slaves partly because many had a burning land hunger, but mainly because the plantation and planters did not control the situation as completely as they had done during slavery. Immediately after Emancipation many observers remarked on the ex-slaves' "avidity" for land, "however limited in extent".[22] In 1897, a Royal Commission found evidence of the same land hunger: "both the Negro and the Coolie like to own small patches of land by which they make their livelihood, and take a pride in their position as landholders."[23]

This land hunger was satisfied in the extremely limited extent that it was, only because of the extent of the planters' difficulties. The sugar industry was already in decline at Emancipation because of massive indebtedness, a shortage of credit and capital, and falling sugar prices.[24] Its condition was aggravated after 1838 by the new capital and labour problems which Emancipation created, by British Free Trade policy, by a commercial depression in 1847 and finally, by a ruinous competition with beet sugar between 1876 and 1903.[25]

Depression became, therefore, the normal condition of the industry throughout the second half of the nineteenth century. As a consequence, the plantation system was continually being modified as the area of sugar cane cultivation contracted, and new staple crops were experimented with. More land became available for peasant settlement as a result either of the abandonment of estates or of the eagerness of some planters to seize cash returns wherever they could find them. Moreover, some planters recognised that they could win advantage in the labour market by selling land to their ex-slaves. Such action was likely to (and did) dispose these small holders to offer some of their labour to the planters who had sold them land. Finally, these same difficulties forced the planters in Trinidad and Guyana to promote actively the settlement on the land of their Indian indentured labourers who had been imported both to replace the Negro labourers on the sugar estates and to lower the rate of wages. Anxious to avoid the costs of repatriating these labourers and of importing new ones, the planters and legislatures, as Williams as pointed out, made land grants to these labourers as commutation of their return passages. In this way, 32,000 acres were allotted in free grants to Indians in Guyana between 1891 and 1913; and in Trinidad 23,000 acres were sold to Indians between 1885 and 1895, and a further 31,766 acres were similarly disposed of between 1902 and 1912.[26]

The ex-slaves took full advantage of these few opportunities for land acquisition. By practising thrift and industry, sometimes by pooling their savings in informal joint stock companies, by accepting the help of Baptist parsons in bargaining with planters; they accumulated the purchase money, or a portion of it, and established themselves as peasant farmers.[27] The success which attended these efforts can be judged by the following statistics for Jamaica.

Estimates of Small and Medium Sized Holdings, 1838-1902

(Compiled from Eisner's Jamaica 1830-1930, Hall's Free Jamaica, and the 1897 Royal Commission Report)

Holdings under 10 acres	Holdings under 40 & 50 acres
1845 19,397	1838 2,114
1882 43,707	1841 7,919
1896 81,924	1860 50,000
	1902 133,169

Similar development could be found in Guyana, Trinidad and the Windward Islands. By 1852, there were in Guyana, more than 11,000 new freehold properties worth about £1 million.[28] Trinidad possessed some 13,000 cane farmers by 1911.[29] In the Windward Islands there were about 10,000 new freeholders by 1861, and in Grenada alone, the number of peasants increased from 3,600 in 1860 to more than 6,000 in 1896.[30]

These new cultivators of the soil introduced elements of a new economy. They produced a great quantity and variety of ground provisions, vegetables and livestock; for instance, it is estimated that the value of Jamaican peasants' ground provisions was £2,601,200 in 1890 which represented about a three hundred per cent increase in a period of forty years.[31]

Even more important, the peasants indulged in cash crop production. They produced significant quantities of the existing staples (sugar, coffee and cotton) and, in addition, they introduced or reintroduced on a wide scale such crops as arrowroot, bananas, cocoa, spices, coconuts and citrus. This activity diversified the basic monocultural pattern of the economy and strengthened it by introducing some elements of self-sufficiency. In addition, the presence of a new class might have helped to soften some of the rigid divisions of class and race which were a feature of the plantation society.[32] By 1900, the peasantry had earned its commendation from a Royal Commission as "a source of both economic and political strength".[33]

Nevertheless, the peasantry was a marginal feature of West Indian life. In the first place, peasants occupied (and still occupy)[34] a small portion of the land. For instance, in 1930, Jamaican peasant holdings (holdings under 10 acres) totalled 171,683 and comprised 512,092 acres or about 20% of the land, while 1,391 large properties comprised 1,368,465 acres or about 56% of the land.[35] Much of the land was of poor quality. C.Y. Shepherd said in 1945 that many peasant holdings in the Windward and Leeward Islands were "Characterized by some such defect as low fertility, inaccessibility, or steep slopes; in instances these handicaps, either singly or in combination, preclude the peasant from attaining a reasonable standard of living".[36]

Secondly, the peasantry was almost completely neglected by government. Little or no provision was made for the construction and maintenance of roads into peasant districts; local markets, schools and hospitals were seldom constructed; no attempt was made to initiate schemes of land settlement or to increase and improve the agricultural skills of the peasant.[37] There were a few exceptions to this, notably in Jamaica after 1865, but generally the situation was what F.L. Engledow found in 1939: "British West Indian Governments as a whole have completely failed to take steps to understand peasants agriculture and its needs."[38] The plantation, on the other hand, was favoured by government. A large portion of the slender resources of the territories was often diverted to the support of the estate-based sugar industry. In particular, the importation of Indian, Chinese and African labourers into Guyana, Trinidad, Jamaica and the Windward Islands was heavily subsidized by governments, and, in addition, the planters were often relieved of a part or all of the export duties on staple produce.

Thirdly, the planters continued a damaging campaign through propaganda and legislation against the peasantry. They and their supporters ignored the social and economic potential of the new class. Rather, they castigated its members as squatters, possessing a "love of uncivilized ease"[39] and likely "to relapse into barbarism and the savage state".[40] In short, the peasants were described as individuals "too lazy to work on the sugar plantation."[41] Therefore, steps had to be taken to drive them to work on the estates. The main instruments of such policy were heavy indirect taxation on articles of mass consumption and mainly heavy discriminatory taxation on the peasants' land, houses and working animals. For instance, plantation working animals in Grenada and Tobago were either not taxed or taxed very lightly while those of the peasants were always taxed at fairly high rates.

Land taxation revealed most clearly the coercive edges of this policy. In St. Vincent, a tax was levied in 1844 on all farmers who did not raise taxable produce. In St. Lucia, land taxes were at first levied at the rate of £1-4-10 for all holdings under 100 acres in extent and £3-4-0 for all holdings over 100 acres in extent. In Tobago, a land tax of 8/- per acre was levied in 1843 on land not attached to the estates or leased to small holders. In both of the latter cases, the tax was modified mainly because of peasant opposition to it. It was first converted into a tax on cultivated land, and eventually into a property tax. Until this happened the basic inequality was plain for all to see. The Governor of St. Lucia pointed out in 1847 that "the hillsides" where the peasant usually had their holdings were taxed at the same rate as "the fertile bottom land tho' of course the former is much more difficult to clear and cultivate and yields much less than the latter".[42] A Stipendiary Magistrate in Tobago probably spoke for many peasants when he described the land tax in 1853 as "either robbery or confiscation" and "harder to bear inasmuch as no attempt seems to be made to extend the operation of the land tax to abandoned estates."[43] It was the deliberate refusal of government to enforce the provisions of forfeiture against estates which were in arrears of quit rent and land taxes that was partly responsible for the continuing increase of the Back Lands and ruinate estates in Jamaica and some of the other territories.

Peasant protest against taxation was frequent. The peasants complained through the Stipendiary Magistrates of the high rate of land taxation, particularly during and after the commercial depression of 1847 when cash was in even shorter supply than usual and the opportunities for employment in estate labour were being curtailed. As a result, they were less anxious to buy land, and more eager to evade tax collection. They were also upset by the whole process of taxation. It was new and strange to individuals who were probably ignorant both of measurement and of the amount of tax for which they were liable. Moreover, tax collection was inefficient and sometimes dishonest. A shortage of collectors aided evasion; some collectors were most arbitrary in their methods; and others, being planters, were suspected of manipulating the tax schedule in their own interest.

One of the strongest protests against land tax was registered in St. Lucia during March 1849.[44] This protest, which was first expressed through petitions to the governor and then through a demonstration near the headquarters of government, eventually escalated into a bloody riot in which eight of the rioters were killed and a number of sugar estates were extensively damaged by fire.[45] The governor claimed that the riot was instigated by refugees from Martinique who were infected with "communist and republican principles" and who wanted to test "the strength and firmness" of the government.[46] But it seems clear from the information which the governor himself supplied that the rioters were mainly peasants of the Northern District who had evaded payment of the land and other taxes for some time, and on whom attempts had recently been made to levy for the arrears of taxes. Some of these peasants had sent two deputations to the governor to express their grievances. They argued that because of the low prices of provisions and the high rent for land they could not pay the land tax which was "a very great imposition", and were not inclined to pay it "at all hazards". They pointed out that they were in a worse position than lease holders for whom the landlords paid the tax. Therefore, they wanted the tax repealed so that they could "earn a small living for themselves". When these petitions failed to bring favourable response, except for the promise that the proceeds of the tax would be devoted to the provision of educational facilities for their children, the peasants demonstrated in the capital. Violence erupted when attempts were made to arrest some of the tax defaulters. Parts of the town were evacuated, and the troops were called out to restore order. This was done on the same day after "savage fighting" and "determined resistance" from the rioters who were armed with cutlasses, sticks, stones and bottles. Disorder in the countryside continued longer; and the most significant aspect of it was that the estate owned by the tax collector of the Northern District suffered the most extensive damage.[47]

ENDNOTES

1. In Foreword to R. Guerra y Sanchez, Sugar and Society in the Caribbean, New Haven, 1964, pp. xx-xxi.
2. West India Committee Protest against the end of Apprenticeship 26th March 1838, in West India Committee Minute Books (London).
3. British Colonial Office Paper (C.O.) 253/61, The Humble Petition of the St. Lucia planters against the end of Apprenticeship. McGregor to Lord Glenelg, 5th June 1838.
4. Report of Royal Commission 1897, Cmd. 8655, London 1897, p. 18.
5. See W.G. Sewell, The Ordeal of Free Labour in the West Indies, New York, 1862; G. Eisner, Jamaica 1830-1930, Manchester 1961, p. 211; W.K. Marshall, "Social and Economic Problems in the Windward Islands, 1838-1865", in Andic and Matthews, The Caribbean in Transition, Rio Piedras, 1965, pp. 247-252. The tenancy regulations were part of the local Emancipation Acts. The acts allowed untroubled occupancy of "house and ground" on the estates provided the ex-slaves worked "truly and faithfully" on the estates for the wages the planters offered.
6. In 1838 Barbados (166 sq. mls.) had as large a slave population as Trinidad (1,864 sq. mls.), and Antigua (108 sq. mls.) had more slaves than Guyana (83,000 sq. mls.).

7. Appendix A. Report of D. Morris on Agricultural Resources, p. 82, Guyana had 20 million uncultivated arable acres.
8. Ibid pp. 96-136. Jamaica was estimated to possess 272,068 acres, and Trinidad 366,157 acres, while most of the mountainous areas in St. Lucia and St. Vincent, and nearly the whole interior of Guyana was declared to be Crown land.
9. See C.O. 260/65 (Grey's despatches to Lord Stanley on 8th May and 31st May 1845) for information on estate encroachment on Crown lands in St. Vincent.
10. See Lord Olivier, The Myth of Governor Eyre, London 1933, pp. 176-181; F.L. Engledow, Report on Agriculture, Fisheries, Forestry and Veterinary Matters (W.I. Royal Commission) Cmd. 6608, London HMSO, 1945, p. 32.
11. Col. Hay's description in C.O. 253/88 (Reid to Earl Grey, 25 Oct. 1847).
12. Report on Agriculture, etc. p. 32.
13. Olivier (1933), p. 177.
14. Eisner, p. 222.
15. See Olivier (1933) pp. 176-181; Eisner, pp. 214-216; R. Farley, "The Rise of the Peasantry in British Guiana", Social and Economic Studies Vol. 2 No. 4, pp. 93-95.
16. This was particularly true of the Windward Islands. For example, the St. Vincent legislature ignored the Colonial Officer's directive that squatters could not be evicted after more than one year's "quiet possession", and adopted legislation in 1844 to permit eviction after three years of occupancy. Eventually, the Colonial Office offered a compromise of no eviction after two years' occupancy.
17. The Trinidad legislature raised the price of Crown land from £1.10.0 per acre to £2.10.0 per acre in 1911 (E.E. Williams, Inward Hunger, London, 1969, p. 15).
18. See D.G. Hall, Free Jamaica, New Haven, 1959, p. 20; Farley, pp. 99-100, Eisner, pp. 210-11, 214.
19. Agriculture in the West Indies, Colonial No. 182 London HMSO 1942, p. 16.
20. See Engledow, pp. 34-35.
21. See M.J. and F.S. Herskovits, Trinidad Village, New York, 1947, pp. 53-55; W.K. Marshall — "Metayage Cultivation in the sugar industry of the British Windward Islands, 1838-1865", Jamaica Historical Review, Vol. V No. 1, pp. 51-53; W.A. Lewis, The Evolution of the Peasantry in the British West Indies, Colonial Office Pamphlet No. 656, pp. 15-17; M.G. Smith, Dark Puritan. U.W.I., Jamaica, 1963, pp. 41-65.
22. See, for instance, H.M. Grant's evidence before the 1842 Select Committee on West Indian Colonies, in British Parliamentary Papers (P.P.) 1842 Vol. XIII.
23. Cmd. 8655, 1897, p. 17.
24. See L.J. Ragatz, The Fall of the Planter Class in the British

Caribbean 1763-1833, London 1928.

25. See Hall; R.W. Beachey, The British West Indies Sugar Industry in the late 19th century. Oxford, 1957.

26. Eric Williams, "The Importance of Small Scale Farming in the Caribbean", Small Scale Farming in the Caribbean, Caribbean Commission, Trinidad, 1954, p. 4.

27. See Farley, pp. 98-101; H. Paget, "The Free Village System in Jamaica", in Caribbean Quarterly, Vol. 10, No. 1, pp. 38-51; P.D. Curtin, Two Jamaicas, Cambridge, U.S.A., 1955, pp. 114-116.

28. Farley, pp. 100-102 Depression in the sugar industry probably caused a slowing down of peasant development in Guyana during the 1850's.

29. Williams (1954), p. 4. These farmers produced in that year one-third of the sugar cane crop.

30. Marshall (1965), p. 252; W.K. Marshall, "Notes on Peasant Development in the West Indies since 1838", Social and Economic Studies, Vol. 17 No. 3, 1968, p. 257.

31. Eisner, pp. 53, 80.

32. Lewis (1936), pp. 14, 36-40.

33. Report of Royal Commission, 1897, p. 17.

34. The following table indicates the recent percentage distribution on the land of holdings of different sizes:

	Holdings under 5 acres	Holdings between 5-100 acres	Holdings over 100 acres
Jamaica	11.8	32.2	56
Trinidad & Tobago	12.5	40.1	47.4
Grenada	22.9	29.9	47.2
Antigua	26.9	14.0	59.1
Barbados	13.4	4.9	81.7
Dominica	12.7	32.0	55.3
Montserrat	16.1	15.5	68.4
St. Kitts-Nevis-Anguilla	12.5	8.7	78.8
St. Lucia	14.9	37.5	47.6
St. Vincent	22.5	28.0	49.5

(Source: A Digest of West Indian Agricultural Statistics, U.W.I. St. Augustine, Trinidad, 1965, p. 14.)

35. Lord Olivier, Jamaica, the Blessed Isle, London, 1936, p. 272; Agriculture in the West Indies, p. 15.

36. Peasant Agriculture in the Leeward and Windward Islands, Report to Colonial Office 58948-1, Trinidad, 1945, p. 14.

37. See Eisner, pp. 177, 318-371.

38. Report of Agriculture, etc., p. 45.

39. This was the opinion of Sir Henry Barkly, Governor of Guyana, quoted in Williams (1954), p. 4.

40. This opinion was expressed by the West India Committee in England, by some of the local legislatures and by historians and writers like Herman Merivale, Thomas Carlyle, J.A. Froude, Anthony Trollope. See E.V. Goveia, A Study on the Historiography of the British West Indies, Mexico, 1956, pp. 140-155.

41. Williams (1954), p. 4.

42. C.O. 253/88 (Reid to Earl Grey, 25th October 1847) Col. Hay's despatch on land tax.

43. C.O. 290/4 Child's Stipendiary Magistrate's Report, June 1853.

44. There was an earlier protest and riot against corvee in St. Lucia during 1844, and a protest riot against the Land Tax in Tobago in 1852.

45. Five estates were damaged. The cost of repairs on three of them was estimated at £7,322.

46. The only evidence for this conclusion was that one of the refugees did organize some Negroes for classes in adult education, that another of the refugees had been heard to assert "an equal right to the soil in all the children of God"; and that one officer heard the Revolutionary Song of France during the rioting.

47. C.O. 253/101 (Darling to Earl Grey 9th and 12th March, 1849); C.O. 253/98 (Colebrooke to Earl Grey, 4th April, 1849).

Credit Problems of West Indian Planters

Richard Lobdell

Did the end of slavery cause widespread depression in the economy of the British West Indies, or was bankruptcy limited to particular estates and locales? Presenting a substantially different interpretation of economic events from nineteenth-century planter assessments, Richard Lobdell, in this selection, suggests that estate owners were more hampered by a crisis in capital generation than in actual labor shortage. The lack of credit, rather than the withdrawal of labor to the peasant sector, explains the failure of planters to modernize the sugar industry and the ensuing financial difficulties of some areas of the sugar economy. Reprinted from R. Lobdell (1972), 'Patterns of Investment and Sources of Credit in the British West Indian Sugar Industry, 1838-1897', Journal of Caribbean History, 4, pp. 33-39 with permission of the Publisher and Author.

By 1840, therefore, most British West Indian planters were convinced that costs of production were rising as a result of emancipation and that some remedial action was urgently required if the sugar industry were to survive. Thus, when it began hearings in 1842, the Select Committee on the West India Colonies encountered a variety of proposals designed to check the declining fortunes of sugar. Without question the most frequently heard complaint dealt with the 'labour problem' and possible solutions to it. Mr Burnley, whose particular interests were in Trinidad, echoed the opinion of many when he declared that if only labourers could be induced to work regularly, then profits could still be made in spite of the high wage rates.[1]

The Committee of 1842 also considered the usefulness of capital investment in reducing overall costs of production. Of course, certain improvements in field operations had been made long before emancipation. In Grenada, for example, ploughs had been employed since 1815, although they were not extensively used until after 1838.[2] This wider use of field implements after emancipation seems to have been common in most of the West Indian colonies. Hence, in Barbados it appears that more extensive use of artificial fertilizers and better drainage systems were undertaken mainly after 1838.[3] Similarly, cultivation machinery is said to have become widespread in Trinidad by the mid-1840s,[4] and certain estates had clearly improved production through the use of ploughs and harrows in Jamaica after 1838, but capital needed to finance further improvements was very scarce.[5]

It was in British Guiana that cultivation techniques were most advanced before 1845. Although extensive use of ploughs was limited by the layout of estates and soil conditions, British Guiana could easily boast the best cultivation and transportation systems in all the British West Indies. Steam engines, cane carriers, and megass carriers were widely employed in the transportation of estate products, while new techniques of fertilization and irrigation were known and used before 1845.[6] Indeed, the only obstacle to even greater employment of machinery in field operations (e.g. relaying of fields to facilitate steam ploughs) was the acute shortage of finance capital.[7]

Capital investment was not limited to field operations during the period 1838-45. Indeed, it is not unlikely that most new capital was invested in factory equipment during those years. One obvious innovation was the introduction of steam-powered mills for the crushing of cane. Although they were expensive, a number of estates installed these new mills in order to reduce overall production costs. In St Kitts, for example, only one steam engine was to be found in 1833, but by 1847 some twenty-three were employed on the island.[8] Likewise in British Guiana a good number of steam mills were employed during the period 1838-45, though some planters seemed unwilling to risk capital on sugar's dubious future.[9] Barbadian planters ordered over £14,000 worth of factory equipment from one manufacturer alone in the two years ending 1846.[10] Steam mills were widely employed in Trinidad in 1842. In fact, Mr Burnley reported that while others might speak of a capital shortage, he was of the opinion that in Trinidad there was much more capital in relation to labour than prudence dictated.[11]

Nonetheless, steam mills remained the exception on most of the less prosperous sugar estates before 1845. In Antigua, for example, only six or seven steam mills were employed on more than 125 estates in 1842.[12] Virtually all sugar mills in Grenada were turned by water power in that same year,[13] and even in the previously most prosperous colony of Jamaica, investment in factory equipment was concentrated on a few estates, most notably at Worthy Park in St Catherine.[14]

These attempts to reduce the costs of sugar production were not dramatically successful before 1845. Planters generally found it difficult to economize on labour as it became virtually impossible to make substantial reduction in wage rates. On those estates where new factory and field machinery were introduced, the costs of transition, as well as inadequate accounting systems usually put an intolerable strain on finances. On the surface at least, costs of production continued to rise in spite of planters' efforts to rationalize production before 1845. And yet, there is some evidence that capital investment made during this period was useful in reducing costs of production in later years. Mr Greene of St Kitts, for example, reported that the previous introduction of machinery on certain local estates had led to a marked fall in production costs by 1848.[15] In 1850 Lord Stanley argued that Barbadian planters who had made capital improvements before 1846 were in a stronger financial position than their less adventurous neighbours.[16] Even the ultra-cautious Guianese planter Henry Barkly admitted that some neighbouring estates' cost of production had been reduced through the employment of new machinery during this period.[17] In short, those estates which made substantial capital investment in field and factory improvements before 1845 were generally in the best position to withstand subsequent crises.

A British West Indian planter interested in continuing the operation of his estate, or in making capital investments in the hope of future profits, might acquire financial support from a number of sources after 1838. He might try to continue previous credit arrangements with his agent in Britain. Under this system a planter acquired on credit from a British merchant the supplies necessary for the operation of his estate. The subsequent crop would automatically be consigned to the same merchant who would arrange its sale on the British market. Once the crop had been sold, deductions were made for supplies shipped to the estate on credit, commissions were subtracted, and the balance credited (or debited) to the estate's account. At the end of the Napoleonic Wars, however, many consignee creditors began to despair of such arrangements as the indebtedness of planters grew with declining sugar prices. Consequently, advances were limited to the barest necessities and following emancipation only the financially strongest plantations could safely rely on this traditional source of credit for investment funds.

A second possible source of investment funds was the £17 million voted by Parliament in 1834 as partial compensation to British West Indian planters for emancipation of slaves. Had this money been used for rational investment, the productivity of sugar estates would have undoubtedly improved. Although a few planters did invest their compensation payments in sugar estates,[18] the greatest share of the compensation money seems to have been used to reduce indebtedness previously contracted. In so far as these debt payments increased creditworthiness, they may be considered to have established a potential source of credit for future capital investment. But as suggested above, many consignee merchants had grown suspicious of West Indian plantations and viewed the compensation money as a last chance to make good an increasingly worthless planter indebtedness.[19]

Thirdly, planters might have financed capital improvements from savings accumulated during periods of past prosperity. Unfortunately, only estates free of debt in 1838 and in possession of sizeable savings could consider such an undertaking. Although not unheard of, this alternative was not a very real one for the vast majority of planters.[20]

Finally, sugar planters might turn to the newly established local banking system for help in financing estate operations. Of the local banks, by far the largest was the Colonial Bank of the West Indies which was granted a Royal Charter in May 1836. By the mid-1840s branches had been established in most of the British West Indies, as well as in Cuba and North America. Under its Charter, the Colonial Bank was empowered to carry on the normal operations of a commercial bank, including dealing in bills of exchange, accepting deposits, and advancing money on commercial paper and government securities. However, the bank was expressly forbidden 'to lend or advance money on the security of lands, houses, or tenements, or upon ships or to deal in general wares or merchandise of any nature or kind whatsoever.'[21] Consequently, the bank was legally forbidden to undertake substantial loans to sugar estates. It might advance money to meet some working expenses of the estates if owners were willing to sign a personal guarantee of liability. But long term capital improvements were quite impossible for the bank to finance. Hence, although it prospered throughout the 19th century, the Colonial Bank had little beneficial effect on investment in the British West Indian sugar industry. Indeed, through its excessively high discounting rates, the Colonial Bank may have seriously hindered the industry's development.[22]

Other local banks followed the practice of the influential Colonial Bank and refused to lend money on the security of sugar estates. By the mid-1840s there was only one rival to the Colonial Bank in British Guiana. Established sometime in 1836, the Bank of British Guiana was granted a Charter very similar to that of the Colonial Bank.[23] There is no evidence that this smaller bank lent money to finance capital investment in sugar during the years preceding 1846.

Jamaican local banks appear to have adopted the same policy towards estate financing as did their counterparts in British Guiana. For example, an institution known as the Jamaica Planters' Bank was formed in 1839, but was never given a charter. There is no evidence that it undertook estate financing, but instead seemed particularly interested in financing commercial activities. It is not surprising, therefore, that the Planters' Bank fell victim to the British financial crisis of 1848 and was forced to close its doors in Jamaica.[24]

A final example of the kind of banking institution which existed during these years is the Bank of Jamaica which was founded in 1837 and closed in 1865. Like the Planters' Bank, the Bank of Jamaica was refused a formal charter. But unlike other local banks, the Bank of Jamaica's Deed of Settlement hints at a more liberal policy towards advances and credit. According to the Deed, the Bank was allowed to

give credit or make advances to any person or persons whomsoever, to such amount, at such rate of interest, and upon such terms, as the Directors may think fit, and such credit may be given, and advances made, with or without security, at the discretion of the Director . . .[25]

Whether in fact the Bank of Jamaica did pursue such a liberal credit policy is not known. From the lack of planter comment and enthusiasm, however, it is probably safe to assume that the Bank of Jamaica did little to finance capital investment in that island's sugar industry.

In summary, those British West Indian planters interested in capital improvement before 1846 had either to rely upon their own meagre savings or upon consignee credit which was becoming increasingly restricted. Undoubtedly, many planters and merchants had lost confidence in the future of sugar in the West Indies. The steady decline of sugar prices, the mounting indebtedness of estates as profits diminished, and the alluring prospects for investment elsewhere all acted to divert capital away from the British West Indies between 1838 and 1845.

ENDNOTES

1. Evidence of Mr. Burnley in *Report of the Select Committee on the West India Colonies* (London: H.M.S.O., 1843), pp. 92 ff. Hereinafter referred to as *Report* (Committee of 1842).
2. Evidence of Mr Barkly, *Report* (Committee of 1842), p. 205.
3. Earl of Derby, *Further Facts Connected with the West Indies*

(London, 1851), pp. 28, 41.

4. Evidence of Mr Bushe, *Report* (Committee of 1842), pp. 287-8.

5. Evidence of Mr MacCornock, *Report* (Committee of 1842), p. 359. N.B. Alexander Geddes disagreed, believing that little machinery had been introduced in Jamaica and was of no value to those estates where it had been employed. See his evidence, ibid, p. 477.

6. Evidence of Mr Campbell, *Report* (Committee of 1842), pp. 152ff.

7. Evidence of Mr Barkly, ibid., pp. 187-8.

8. Evidence of Mr Greene in the *Report of the Select Committee on Sugar and Coffee Planting* (8 Reports, London, 1848), *Third Report*, p. 138.

9. Evidence of Mr Barkly, *The Sugar Question*, vol. 2, p. 86.

10. Evidence of Mr Moody, ibid., p. 121.

11. Evidence of Mr Burnley, *Report* (Committee of 1842), p. 76.

12. Evidence of Mr Nugent, ibid., p. 227.

13. Evidence of Mr Barkly, ibid., p. 205.

14. Evidence of Mr Price, *Second Report* (Committee of 1848), pp. 62-70.

15. Evidence of Mr Greene, *Third Report* (Committee of 1848), p. 138.

16. Earl of Derby, pp. 27-8, 41.

17. Evidence of Mr Barkly, *The Sugar Question*, vol. 2, p. 82. See also the evidence of Dr Rankin, ibid., pp. 74-6.

18. Evidence of Mr Barkly, *Report* (Committee of 1842), p. 188.

19. That most consignees viewed suspiciously the future of sugar in the B.W.I. during these years is beyond dispute. The evidence collected by the Committees of 1842 and 1848 is full of such suspicions. See for example the evidence of Mr Innes in *The Sugar Question*, vol. 2, p. 53, and that of Mr Hankey in the *Third Report* (Committee of 1848), p. 26.

20. Although the evidence is not conclusive, Mr Barkly seems to have been one of those who did so (*Report* (Committee of 1842), pp. 187-8). On the other hand, Mr Tollemache's estates in Antigua were debt free and reasonably profitable, but he flatly refused to invest in new equipment (*Third Report* (Committee of 1848), p. 247).

21. As quoted in R.M. Martin, *History of the Colonies of the British Empire* (6 vols., London, 1843), vol. 4, pp. 20, 21. See also, Barclays Bank, *A Banking Centenary: Barclays Bank, 1836-1936*. (Plymouth, England, 1938).

22. R.W. Beachey, *The British West Indian Sugar Industry in the Late Nineteenth Century* (London, 1957), p. 159. J.W. Root, *The British West Indies and the Sugar Industry* (Liverpool, 1899), pp. 12-14.

23. Martin, p. 134.

24. D.G. Hall, *Free Jamaica, 1838-1865* (New Haven, 1959), pp. 122-4. G. Eisner, *Jamaica, 1830-1930* (Manchester, 1961), pp. 196, 199.

25. Bank of Jamaica, *Deed of Settlement of the Bank of Jamaica* (Kingston, 1837), p. 15.

4.5

East Indian Laborers   Ken Boodhoo

When slave labor was no longer available, West Indian planters appealed to the home government for aid in transporting contractual labor from India and elsewhere to Caribbean sugar fields. In this selection Ken Boodhoo examines the plight of East Indian laborers in the colony of Trinidad and comments upon the often miserable work conditions in which such indentured servants found themselves. The similarities to the conditions of slavery, especially at the beginnings of the contract period, are evident. Reprinted from Caribbean Review, *5, No. 2, pp. 17-20, published at Florida International University, copyright © 1973,* Caribbean Review, *with permission of the Publisher and the Author.*

Writing on the question of East Indian indentureship just over one hundred years ago, Charles Kingsley described it as "this admirable system of satisfying the great need of the West Indies." One must clarify to what extend there was a "need" in the West Indies; who were satisfied by the fulfillment of this need; and what the consequences were of the need having been satisfied. Whereas the question of sugar preoccupied the minds and actions of the British throughout their Caribbean colonies, the focus of the East Indian indentureship system was towards Trinidad and Guyana.

Partly because Trinidad was underpopulated, agricultural development, particularly sugar, was generally neglected until the Cedula of 1783 facilitated the influx of large numbers of settlers of French origin. Desiring quick returns on their investment, these settlers immediately turned to the

143

development of a sugar industry, which was originally started in 1542 primarily as a subsistence crop. Thus when the British captured Trinidad in 1797, their primary preoccupation was the takeover and further development of the sugar industry. So much emphasis was placed on this industry that the history of Trinidad during the nineteenth century was largely the history of sugar. The political, economic and social life of the colony was geared to meet the needs of sugar — a condition which generally continued well into the twentieth century until the petroleum industry assumed primary position.

Trinidad, it should be noted, had developed an export trade in cocoa in 1680. In the early 18th century cocoa was the chief industry and soon after the British captured Trinidad, Governor Picton actually recommended to the British Secretary of State that the cocoa industry continue since it was most adaptable to local conditions. This advice was disregarded. British capital poured into the country to develop sugar.

One of the foremost reasons for disregarding this advice was the question of British tastes, and consequently, British markets. There was little demand for cocoa in Britain because it was not yet palatable to British tastes. Then too, the Van Houten process for the extraction of cocoa butter from the beans was not developed until 1828, and indeed, was not practiced in Britain until 1866. In 1840, a mere 1,562 tons of cocoa were imported into Britain and while almost half of this was consigned to the Navy, much of the remainder was re-exported to other cocoa-consuming countries. Another factor influencing the general disregard for cocoa was that in Trinidad it was "foreign" owned — primarily by Spanish and French peasants. And since the early history of British occupation was one of conflict with the Spanish and French settlers, this conflict spread to ownership of the cocoa estates.

With sugar gradually assuming the primary position, the chief preoccupation of the British planters was the attraction of labor. Trinidad never had a large number of slaves so that in order to develop the plantations the slaves' "free" days had to be reduced from 134 to 69 per annum and Trinidad soon earned the reputation of having both the greatest production of sugar per capita and the highest mortality rate in the British West Indies. With the passage of the Slave Trade Act in 1806 planters were required to seek a new source of labor, for the inter-colonial slave trade was not sufficient to meet their needs.

Attention turned to China as a possible source of labor and in 1806 some 192 Chinese workers were admitted into the colony. This scheme quickly failed, for not only did many of these workers petition to return home, but the Government, found the financial burden of maintaining the Chinese immigrants too much and agreed to their repatriation.

The planters began looking for more labor and between 1815-1816 a number of former slaves from the southern United States were settled as "free colored" in Trinidad, a reward for the help they had given the British forces during the War of 1812. Portuguese immigrants, too, were induced into the country, but soon they were begging to be sent home claiming that they were tricked into leaving their native land and were being decimated by the cruelties of the slavery system. The Emancipation Act of 1833 dealt the final blow to slavery. Yet the compulsory apprenticeship period which followed attempted to transform the slaves into loyal and paid workers. This attempt failed.

Since their primary concern was sugar, the planters, at emancipation had to utilize whatever means possible to keep the freed laborers on or near the estates. Thus this group brought all its weight to bear on the local Council, and in cooperation with their sugar lobbies operating in the metropolitan Parliament, were able to influence legislation suitable to their needs. In quick succession land ordinances and increased taxation on land, among other legislation, were passed which inhibited the independent establishment of freed workers, and conversely, made these workers dependent upon the estates for their income. An examination of the colonizer's land policy is revealing of the attitude to the laboring masses.

Even before emancipation, a "proper" land policy preoccupied the minds of the British. In 1832 Lord Howick,

Under Secretary of State for the Colonies, wrote that with emancipation it was necessary to devise some plan which would induce the (former) slaves to undergo the regular and continuous labor which was indispensable in carrying on the production of sugar. He thought that "it would be great for the real happiness of the Negroes themselves, if the facility of acquiring land could be so far restrained . . ." He continued, ". . . accordingly, it is to the imposition of a considerable tax upon land that I chiefly look for the means of enabling the planter to continue his business when emancipation shall have taken place."

The stage was thus set for implementing this policy in the post-emancipation period. The general attitude and philosophy being, that if the freed worker was prohibited, by one means or another, from obtaining land, then he would be forced to offer his labor to the sugar estate and accept the wages offered. Within a few years, the Secretary of State in a despatch to the West Indian colonies suggested that Crown lands, at emancipation, be sold at a minimum upset price of one pound per acre, but apparently left the minimum acreage for sale to be fixed by the local Councils. The Trinidad Council of Government promptly fixed this acreage at 320 acres. This was deliberately done to prevent the individual worker from purchasing land, simply because it was beyond his means. When a suggestion was made in 1841 that the minimum acreage be reduced to forty acres the local Council established a planter-dominated committee to examine the suggestion. This Committee and the Council not only disagreed with the suggestion stating that they "thought that such a small parcel of land would too easily come within the reach of persons who were required as laborers," but as importantly, while they held that the minimum size should be 320 acres they suggested that 640 acres should be considered minimum for a sugar estate! It was left to Governor Gordon, some twenty-five years later, to liberalize land policy.

In conjunction with a discriminatory land policy were other forms of inducements offered on the estates to encourage the now freed workers to maintain their former occupations. Free housing, small plots of land and some food and drink supplies were given to those who chose to remain on the estates, in effect, therefore, perpetuating a practice established during the days of slavery. Other planters rented or gave small patches of land on the periphery of their estates to workers to keep them at hand. Yet despite the inducements Sewell has commented that the freed workers left the estates to "better their circumstances and lead a more independent life," since "tenancy on the estates after emancipation was virtual slavery."

The biggest inducement to attract the freed laborer was, of course, the wages offered. At emancipation, wages in Trinidad were fixed at about 30 cents per task. A task was of flexible size and on the average required about five or six hours to complete. By 1840 wages had increased to 50 cents and in certain areas 80 cents per task. With the allowance for housing, food, and drink, a worker could clear over $1.20 per day for two tasks. With the increase in wages, workers were content to pursue their jobs for three or four days a week, thus accumulating sufficient income to meet their needs. Therefore, instead of having a regular and docile labor force with a low turnover as they had grown accustomed to, the planters were faced with a relatively mobile group who were unwilling to be bound by contracts, and who in general, worked only when necessary.

Alarmed at the shortage of a dependable labor supply the planters sought assistance from the metropolitan government, many of whose members were themselves absentee owners of local sugar estates. They pointed out that the sugar crop of 1840 was 13,288 tons, the lowest of the decade, compared to a production of 14,312 tons in 1838, the year of emancipation. Regardless of the planters' cries, they were yet making a huge profit. The Orange Grove estates for instance showed a net profit of £3,433 from proceeds of £10,463 in 1840.

The metropolitan Parliament gave in to the planters and on July 25, 1842 passed resolutions which have had significant implications for the eventual development of a number of Caribbean societies, particularly Trinidad. The resolutions stated that while emancipation "has been productive, as regards the character and condition of the Negro population," it has also contributed to "a very great diminution in the staple products of the West Indies." The resolutions considered that the principal cause of diminished production was due to "the great difficulty which has been experienced by the planters in obtaining steady and continuous labor . . . caused partly by the fact that some of the former slaves have betaken themselves to other occupations more profitable than field labor." A major recommendation of the British Parliament was that a "most desirable mode of endeavouring to compensate for this diminished supply of labour, is to promote the immigration of a fresh labouring population, to such an extent as to create competition for employment."

Thus were the conditions outlined. Even if it required the introduction of an entirely new group of people into the society, this would be done, since the needs of the sugar industry were most important. And so natives of India were introduced to Trinidad, purely to further the development of a plantation-type sugar industry which was controlled, directed and owned by British capital.

Subsequent to the entry of the East Indian immigrants a storm of protest arose in Trinidad. The system was rightly viewed as an attempt to flood the labour market, which would result in reduced wages. Since the scheme was to be financed partly out of public revenue, protestors charged that taxes would have to be increased. Therefore, not only would they suffer from the burden of increased taxes, but also, the protestors believed that they could possibly also lose their jobs to the East Indians, or at best, would have to work for reduced wages.

After the actual entry of the East Indians into Trinidad, one group in particular, the cocoa peasants, was required to shoulder a disproportionate share of the cost of the scheme. This was done by the local Council, even though the regulations outlined for the conditions of immigrants' work effectively excluded their employment on the cocoa estates, e.g. that a hospital be maintained on the estate. For instance, while 40 per cent of the indentured laborers were employed on sugar plantations and approximately 5 per cent on the cocoa and coconut estates, yet, states Eric Williams, between

1881 and 1885, the Legislative Council reduced the export duty which was levied to finance in part the cost of the immigration system from 80 to 60 per cent on sugar, whilst on cocoa it was raised from 20 to 37 per cent.

The regulations concerning the entry of the immigrants, their living and working conditions and salaries were outlined in an ordinance passed by the local Council after collaboration with the planter-organized Immigration and Agricultural Society. It is instructive to review some of these regulations to determine to what extent these indentured immigrants were "free" individuals.

The more important regulations are contained in Part VIII of the ordinance including such areas as labor and wages. The employer was required to provide every indentured laborer with sufficient work for a full day's labor except Sundays, Good Friday, Christmas and New Year's Day. The work day was fixed at nine hours, which included half an hour for eating and resting. The wage was originally fixed at $2.40 (B.W.I.) per month for male laborers and $1.45 for females. This amount was later amended to not less than 25 cents a day for an able-bodied adult immigrant. The immigrant was made liable to fines or imprisonment for a number of offenses related to his daily work. Such offenses included refusal or neglect of work, drunkenness in or about the plantation buildings, the use of abusive or insulting words or gestures to his employer.

Questions pertaining to leave and desertion were considered in Part IX of the ordinance. Every indentured immigrant was bound to reside on the plantation to which he was indentured. Any immigrant found on a public highway or on any land or in any house not the property of his owner, or in any ship or boat within the waters of the island could be stopped and arrested by the Protector of Immigrants or any person authorized by him, unless the immigrant was in possession of a suitable certificate of leave. In effect, therefore, no immigrant could leave his owner's property without the appropriate "pass" ticket. Such were the conditions outlined by the colonizers and which were termed "free" labor. Needless to say, the practical conditions under which the East Indians endured their period of indentureship, did not necessarily follow the theory of the system.

During the initial period the immigrants suffered greatly. Harsh treatment on certain plantations and sickness, influenced by unfamiliar conditions, culminated in the death of a large number of this group. The creation of the positions of Inspectors of Immigrants, and the actual "field" work by these officials somewhat alleviated the conditions under which the immigrants served their indentureship. One condition of indentureship was the right of the East Indian immigrant to return to India, free of cost to himself, at the termination of his contract. However, once the planter had the worker on his estate, he made the prospects for leaving rather difficult. Soon after the introduction of the indentureship system, the planters, through the Council, began placing restrictions upon the absolute right of the East Indian to a free return passage. Ordinance 24 of 1854 provided that immigrants introduced into the colony after that date were entitled to a return passage only after ten years of residence in the colony and only on payment of a sum of 7.5s ($35.00 B.W.I.) Succeeding years saw further similar restrictions. Two major reasons motivated this attitude of the planters. Firstly, this source of cheap controlled labor was necessary for high profits to be gained from the sugar industry. Secondly, the planters were required to meet part of the cost of the laborer's return passage.

Together with these restricting ordinances were some generous inducements to remain in Trinidad. These inducements generally took the form of small patches of land which were either sold at nominal cost, given or rented to the immigrant at the expiration of the contract. This land was usually situated on the periphery of the estate and not only did it induce the East Indian to remain in Trinidad, but it also kept him relatively close to the estate, so that his labor would be readily available, especially during the "crop" or harvest period. It was this granting of land by the planter, accompanied by the progressive land policy of Governor Gordon that ultimately resulted in the growth of the cane farming sector of the sugar industry.

The mere acquisition of land did not necessarily mean that the "freed" laborers, now peasants, had also acquired the "right" to grow sugar cane. For during the period 1860 to 1880 even though these individuals possessed some land they were effectively prevented from using it for the cultivation of cane because of the restriction indirectly imposed by the estates who had the monopoly over the factories. It was not until the late 1880's that a few small farmers in the Southern areas were able to start cane farming to any appreciable degree. This remarkable turn of events was influenced by the general depression in the plantation sugar industry.

As a consequence of competition from Cuban sugar, and European beet sugar, Trinidad, and indeed the other islands of the West Indies, faced a general depression in the sugar industry during the late nineteenth century. Ironically, the planters who formerly prevented farmers from cultivating sugar cane now encouraged them to do so. The reason was quite simple. While the farmer's cultivation of sugar cane was done at no cost to the planter, it was the planter-controlled factory that purchased these canes. The price to purchase the cane ensured a profit to the planter, at little cost to himself, but bore no resemblance to the actual costs incurred by the peasant farmer. The conflict over cane prices resulted in considerable friction between the farmer and the (planter) government. A second factor influenced the planters' encouragement of farmers' cultivation of canes. The advent of the sugar depression caused a number of estates to close down while others amalgamated. Those that continued processing were unable to provide sufficient canes to allow for efficient running of the factories. If only to meet the needs of the expanded mills, the planters encouraged the cane farmers.

A Royal Commission, established in 1896 to investigate the sugar industry situation in the West Indies, recommended the encouragement of the cane-farmer sector as a possible means for the reduction of the overall costs in the industry. The Commission recognized that the cane-farming system "would be attended by many advantages," since the immigrants prefer growing canes on their own plots to working on the estates, and "they are willing to sell their canes at a price below the cost at which the estates can produce them." Whereas the Commission emphasized the "willingness" of the farmer to dispose of his cane, it is undoubtedly more appropriate to stress the "necessity" of such action — since sugar cane is of little use without processing facilities.

It is quite ironic that this metropolitan government, called upon soon after emancipation to assist in the financing of the indentureship system to perpetuate the plantation sugar industry, and was again instrumental in the 1850's and the 1860's in restricting land ownership to the planters, was now being asked to encourage the small land owner to produce cane for the estates. The cane farming sector very quickly had a stimulating effect upon the industry. For while in 1895, 17,502 tons of farmers' cane was accepted by the factories, 62,629 tons were taken one year later.

Whereas the entry of natives from India into the Caribbean, specifically Trinidad, was determined by the need of cheap labor, when this need was no longer due to a general depression in the sugar industry, the indentureship system was terminated. That the immigrants contributed substantially to the prosperity of the industry is undoubted, whether the industry promoted the East Indians' welfare remains questionable.

SECTION 5
*Political and Economic Upheavals
of the non-British Caribbean:
The Nineteenth Century*

5.0
Introduction to Section 5

The non-British Caribbean took its cue in the nineteenth century from the political upheaval in St Domingue, the most prosperous of the French sugar islands in the preceding century. This revolt, which began in the 1790s, fanned by sensitive readings of liberal Enlightenment tracts, resulted in the 1804 creation of Haiti, the first independent nation in the Caribbean. The career of the man who engineered this feat (but did not bring it to fruition) is examined in selection 5.1. Toussaint L'Ouverture is here portrayed as a determined reconstructionist of his country, a strong leader pledged to inevitably controversial programs to set his country back to production.

Seventeen years after Haiti severed connections with France, her neighbor on the island of Hispañola Santo Domingo broke away from Spain. Freedom for this oldest Caribbean colony was short-lived, however; a year after independence was declared, the country was invaded by Haitian troops and remained occupied until 1844. In the wake of the Haitian takeover, and in view of the limited time span in which to reorganize economically, the Dominican Republic reluctantly petitioned Spain to reassume control in the 1860s. The failure of this experiment in voluntary colonialism is examined in selection 5.2.

Although the Dominican Republic wrested an early independence from Spain, her sister colonies of Cuba and Puerto Rico remained the last vestiges of Spanish authority in the New World. After the independence of the continental Latin American colonies had been assured by the Battle of Ayacucho (Peru) in 1824, Spain focussed all her colonial aspirations, and frustrations at the loss of empire, on her remaining Caribbean territories. Small wonder, then, that

155

the Spanish government acted to suppress the sporadic movements toward independence in these islands.

Despite vocal sentiment that viewed slavery as anachronistic for the nineteenth century, the Spanish government favored the planter class, sponsored the expansion of the slave trade and reorganized its Caribbean colonies to fill the gaps in sugar production caused by economic recession in the British West Indies. So successful was the sugar plantation system in Cuba, that the highly competitive tobacco industry — once under royal protection in the eighteenth century — was now relegated to a minor portion of the export production, and even coffee estates were gradually changed over to sugar. The cost in human suffering among the slave population, which provided most of the labor for sugar production, has already been examined in selection 3.7.

Harrassment of Spanish slave ships by the English encouraged Cuban planters to seek annexation to the United States South, but the failure of the Confederacy in the Civil War put an end to such scheming. In 1868, therefore, Puerto Rican and Cuban partisans jointly engineered a plan to liberate both islands from Spain. That the revolt at Lares (in Puerto Rico) lasted for two days, while the Cuban rebellion at Yara touched off a ten-year guerilla war can be explained by economic, political and geographic variables, as Maldonado-Denis demonstrates in selection 5.3.

In both situations, however, the 1868 revolts ultimately failed. Nonetheless, the machinery had been set in motion for the final independence strike, and a coordinated attack from bases in the United States and the Dominican Republic was eventually planned by Cuban and Puerto Rican representatives. Writing in 1895 (selection 5.4), the distinguished Cuban patriot, José Martí, described the independence campaign as a 'Caribbean struggle'.

Cuba's bid for independence, however, was lost after the entrance of the United States into the arena. The sinking of the U.S. battleship *Maine* in February, 1898, provided the grounds for transforming the Cuban War of Independence into the Spanish–American War. In the meantime, Puerto Rico had negotiated a separate treaty with Spain which gave her autonomy within the Spanish Kingdom. This 1897 arrangement was shortlived, as the following year the United States Army invaded the island and ' "liberated" it from Spanish control'. By the opening of the twentieth century, Cuba had been transformed into a United States protectorate, while Puerto Rico became an outright colony.

The classic work on the Haitian revolt is C.L.R. James, *The Black Jacobins: Toussaint L'Ouverture and the San Domingo Revolution*; H. Cole, *Christophe, King of Haiti* reviews the career of one of Toussaint's successors. Two works that cover the socio-economic background of Cuba in the nineteenth century are V. Martinez-Alier, *Marriage, Class and Colour in Nineteenth Century Cuba: A Study of Racial Attitudes and Sexual Values in a Slave Society*, and F.W. Knight, *Slave Society in Cuba during the 19th Century*; G.M. Hall's monograph excerpted in Section 3 is also recommended. An unusual, first-hand narrative of the slave experience in Cuba can be read in E. Montejo, *Diary of a Runaway Slave*. M. Maldonado-Denis, *Puerto Rico: A Socio-historic Interpretation* is an excellent introduction to the history of that island in the nineteenth century.

Toussaint's New Order   Thomas O. Ott

The peace-maker role of Toussaint L'Ouverture has not received as much consideration as his heroic achievements in the face of European military muscle. Yet, his reconstructionist period, in which he invited white planters back to Haiti (albeit with clearly defined restrictions), and endeavored to reorganize the sugar economy is certainly as important to Haitian history as are his earlier accomplishments. This selection provides an introduction to this brief creative period, and attempts to explain the reasons for the mounting controversies in which Toussaint found himself embroiled. First published as T.O. Ott (1973), 'Toussaint's New Order, 1797–1801', chapter seven in The Haitian Revolution, 1789–1804. *Reprinted by permission of the University of Tennessee Press. Copyright © 1973 by the University of Tennessee Press, Knoxville 37916.*

As early as 1794 Toussaint began to encourage the return of absentee planters. By providing that the returning plantation owners could regain the net profits from their lands, he attracted hundreds of whites to Saint-Domingue. Even Bayon de Libertad, former manager of Bréda plantation, returned. Moreover, Toussaint protected the whites regardless of whether their antagonists were Sonthonax or Hédouville or wrathful blacks, such as Moyse or Dessalines.[1]

Toussaint made it clear, however, that the old position of the planters had been radically altered. In several decrees and in the Constitution of 1801 he clarified the new duties of the planters. The proprietor would share the produce of his estate with the laborers; he had to tend to their needs; he

158

could not use the whip; and he was not to consider the workers as slaves, even though they were under rigid three-year contracts and needed the planter's permission to leave.[2] He further decreed that the proprietors "must on all occasions conduct themselves as good family men. They are to encourage the cultivators to form legitimate marriages by making them feel that it is the best means of assuring themselves the enjoyment of all the advantages of society."[3] Legitimate families, Toussaint felt, would encourage social stability.[4]

Another white group included in the plans of Toussaint was the Americans. That the black leader intended to use the United States as the bedrock of Saint-Domingue's independence was discussed in an earlier chapter; of equal importance were commercial relations. With France unable to supply the colony's needs and with England wavering in its fear for Jamaica, Toussaint desperately needed American trade, particularly because Saint-Domingue had mostly an export economy. So valuable did trade with the United States become that it was not uncommon to hear the blacks refer to Americans as "good whites."[5]

Although American shipping had been continuously active in Saint-Domingue since the beginning of the Haitian Revolution, Toussaint wanted to give it formal standing. This was partly the reason for sending Joseph Bunel as his representative to Philadelphia in mid-1798.[6] Many important Federalists were quite receptive to Bunel's offer of an alliance with Saint-Domingue because the United States would guarantee the blacks "their independence, furnish them with necessaries, and stipulate for the exclusive carriage of their produce."[7] On May 22, 1799, Toussaint signed a tripartite treaty with Great Britain and the United States, establishing formal trade relations with the United States. From 1799 to 1801 American trade became so active that it played no small role in promoting "the happiness and prosperity of St. Domingo."[8] On a single day early in July 1801 no less than thirty-two American vessels were counted at Le Cap François alone.[9]

After the end of the Quasi-War and the rise of Jefferson to the presidency, however, Toussaint found both his

economic and political relations with America in sharp
decline. The United States would no longer support the
independence of Saint-Domingue, and Toussaint sarcastically
asked if the change in administrations had destroyed all the
American ships.[10] For all practical purposes it had, for Jefferson could see the coming of Bonaparte to the colony as well
as could Toussaint.[11]

Without the regimentation of the blacks, even the temporary success of Toussaint's commercial alliance would have
been impossible. In several decrees culminating in the Constitution of 1801, Toussaint protected the plantation from
dismemberment, sentenced vagabonds and criminals to
forced labor, greatly curtailed worker migrations, and subjected the cultivators to military discipline. In return for his
regimentation, the black was guaranteed a quarter share of
the plantation's produce, given regulated and reasonable
working hours, and protected from abuse by the proprietors.[12] Undeniably, the system was effective because idle
blacks all through the colony were forcibly returned to the
plantations; soon Toussaint had "re-established the agricultural and economic pursuits of the colony."[13] Even the
ruined plantation of the Marquis de Beauharnais was restored
and its profits forwarded to its new owner, Josephine Bonaparte.[14]

Despite Saint-Domingue's return to economic prosperity,
Toussaint's labor program contained great evils.[15] One
problem that it bred was corruption among the black military. Instead of encouraging a wide distribution of plantation
proprietorships and acting only as policemen of the system,
the black commanders centralized land ownership in their
own hands. The desire for affluence caused many black
generals to be blinded by the gilded glare of self-interest:
Henri Christophe amassed a fortune of $250,000; Dessalines
controlled over thirty plantations; and there is evidence that
even Toussaint himself indulged in the race for personal
wealth. Eventually more than two-thirds of the land in Saint-
Domingue was state controlled.[16]

The corruption of the military was exceeded only by its
brutality to the worker. One observer noted that "great
attention is paid by the military and civil officers to keep the

cultivators employed and steady to their work, and in some cases not a little severity is used."[17] Dessalines became inspector general, a type of collective plantation overseer. Accompanied by mounted guards, he ranged vast areas to keep the blacks steady at their labors. For minor offenses, since the whip was outlawed, Dessalines administered lashes "with a strong knotted limb of the lemon tree upon the bare backs."[18] Sometimes he even buried victims alive and committed mass murder to force the blacks to remain on the plantations.[19] Such a heavy hand led Roume to the conclusion that "the cultivators were oppressed more under Toussaint than under their old masters."[20]

T. Lothrop Stoddard claimed that the blacks were now "slaves of the state."[21] Was he correct? Saint-Domingue was no different than most countries whose citizens are subject to martial law in times of great peril. Toussaint had no other choice because France was closing in from the outside and anarchy was threatening collapse from the inside. It was a question of priority, and order outweighed both corruption and brutality. Perhaps Toussaint grimaced at the furious efficiency of Dessalines and looked forward to the end of conditions which he considered temporary. The black masses must have sensed that this was Toussaint's policy, or they probably would have been more restive.[22] After all, Toussaint was trying to ensure that the blacks would never "again submit to the yoke of slavery."[23]

Any permanent social and economic achievements, however, depended upon political stabilization. Unless Toussaint could veil his dictatorial authority with a constitution, he would be faced with the growing independence and power of his generals. Bonaparte, moreover, might better accept Saint-Domingue's autonomy; at least he would clearly be faced with that decision. Thus on July 16, 1801, Toussaint uncovered his political order for everyone to see.[24]

All important powers belonged to Toussaint. He controlled major appointments, both civil and ecclesiastical, and each of the six departmental governors, as well as other chief administrators, communicated directly and only with him.[25] In this way he could isolate the members of his administration, lessening the chance of conspiracy. Even the

Central Assembly was only a façade for Toussaint's power:
it could not initiate legislation, and although it had the power
to reject legislation, no delegate dared to try.[26]

The system was not without weaknesses. By not including a
French agent in his plans, Toussaint was making his challenge
to Bonaparte obvious. It would have been less offensive to
France had he made provision for one with nominal powers.
The greatest weakness of the system, however, was the over-
centralization of power in the hands of one man,[27] for as
governor-general for life, Toussaint refused to delegate much
authority: "Everything at this time," U.S. consul Tobias
Lear explained, "is done by his special authority."[28] Perhaps
Toussaint felt that he could trust only himself, but such a
burden was overwhelming.

Yet the Saint-Domingue that emerged after ten years of
conflict was largely a tribute to the abilities of Toussaint.
He had brought the colony to the threshold of independence
and had placed it on the road to recovery. The problem of
race, furthermore, seemed solvable because all three castes
— black, mulatto, and white — showed signs of fusing. It
was because of these achievements that an American observer
enthusiastically proposed that Toussaint should be "considered as a phenomenon which every century does not
produce."[29] But the "phenomenon," at the pinnacle of his
political career, was about to fall from power.

ENDNOTES

1. Providence *Gazette and Country Journal*, June 28, 1800; Toussaint
   to Municipality and Military Commandant of Gros Morne, Dec. 13,
   1794, Etienne Lavaux Papers, Library of Congress, Washington,
   D.C.; *The Times* (London), March 11, 1802; Great Britain, *State
   Papers*, X, 146-47; Ralph Korngold, *Citizen Toussaint*, 2nd ed.
   (New York: Hill, 1965), 214-15.
2. Korngold, *Citizen Toussaint*, 207; Stephen Alexis, *Black Liberator:
   The Life of Toussaint L'Ouverture*, trans. W. Sterling (New York:
   Macmillan, 1949), 167; Law of July 24, 1798, Rochambeau
   Documents.
3. Law of July 24, 1798, Rochambeau Documents.
4. *Ibid*.
5. Richard Yates to Pickering, April 30, 1797, vol. 1; Toussaint to
   Lear, July 14, 1801, Consular Dispatches, Cap-Haitien, vol. 3;

Pickering to Stevens, March 7, 1799, King Papers; *Gazette Officielle de Saint-Domingue* (Le Cap François), Aug. 21, 1802.

6. Charleston *City Gazette*, June 3, 1799; DeConde, *Quasi-War*, 135; Hubert Cole, *Christophe: King of Haiti* (New York: Viking, 1967), 57.

7. Adams to William Vans Murray, July 14, 1798, in Worthington C. Ford, ed., *The Writings of John Quincy Adams*, 7 vols. (New York: Macmillan, 1913-17), II, 336.

8. Stevens to Marshall, Sept. 10, 1800, Consular Dispatches, Cap-Haitien, vol. 2.

9. Lear to Madison, July 7, 1801, *ibid.*

10. Jefferson's policy is more fully discussed in the next chapter.

11. Lear to Madison, Aug. 4 and Nov. 9, 1801, vol. 3; Madison to Lear, Feb. 28, 1802, Consular Dispatches, Cap-Haitien, vol. 4.

12. Lear to Madison, Oct. 22, 1801, vol. 3; Lear to Madison, Jan. 17, 1802, Consular Dispatches, Cap-Haitien, vol. 4; Peter S. Chazotte, *Sketches of the Revolution and the Foreign and Civil War in the Island of St. Domingo, with a Narrative of the Entire Massacre of the White Population of the Island: Eye Witness* (New York: William Applegate, 1840), 16; Alexis, *Black Liberator*, 167; Law of July 24, 1798, Rochambeau Documents; Henry Addington, *The Crisis of the Sugar Colonies, or an Inquiry into the Probable Effects of the French Expedition on the West Indies* (London: J. Hatchard, 1802), 16; Korngold, *Citizen Toussaint*, 206.

13. *Le Moniteur*, April 11, 1799.

14. Korngold, *Citizen Toussaint*, 234-35.

15. There are several statistics that indicate that prosperity returned. From 1796 to 1797 the value of Saint-Domingue's exports rose from $700,000 to $3,000,000, and from 1800 to 1801 Saint-Domingue's exports almost doubled. *The Times* (London), Oct. 10, 1797, and June 15, 1801.

16. Cole, *Christophe*, 67; Korngold, *Citizen Toussaint*, 205, 217; Alexis, *Black Liberator*, 169; Benjamin Dandridge to Madison, July 23, 1801, Consular Dispatches, Cap-Haitien, vol. 3.

17. Lear to Madison, July 20, 1801, Consular Dispatches, Cap-Haitien, vol. 3.

18. Chazotte, *Sketches of the Revolution*, 21.

19. Cole, *Christophe*, 67; W.L. Whitfield to Edward Corbett, June 13, 1801, Colonial Office (Great Britain), 137/50.

20. Roume to Minister of Marine Forfait, Sept. 25, 1801, Philippe Roume Papers, Library of Congress, Washington, D.C.

21. *San Domingo*, 292.

22. Letter extract from Le Cap François, Jan. 1, 1799, in Baltimore *Federal Gazette*, March 15, 1799; Charleston *City Gazette*, Aug. 20, 1801; Letter Extract from Jamaica, Dec. 6, 1801, in *The Times* (London), Jan. 26, 1802; New York *Evening Post*, March 22, 1802; Stevens to Marshall, Sept. 10, 1800, Consular Dispatches, Cap-Haitien, vol. 2.

23. Lear to Madison, Jan. 17, 1802, *ibid.*, vol. 4.
24. Stevens to Pickering, Dec. 2, 1799, *ibid.*; *The Times* (London), Oct. 21, 1801; Means Proposed to the French Government for the Reorganization of that Colony by its Agent to St. Domingue, June 12, 1800, Roume Papers; Charleston *City Gazette*, Jan. 18, 1802.
25. Charleston *City Gazette*, Nov. 27, 1801; Alexis, *Black Liberator*, 166; *Mirror of the Times and General Advertiser*, Nov. 21, 1801; James, *Black Jacobins*, 264.
26. James, *Black Jacobins*, 264; Chazotte, *Sketches of the Revolution*, 17-18.
27. Charleston *City Gazette*, Jan. 18, 1802; Lear to Madison, July 25, 1802, Consular Dispatches, Cap-Haitien, vol. 4.
28. Lear to Madison, July 25, 1802, Consular Dispatches, Cap-Haitien, vol. 4.
29. An American at Le Cap François to Gentleman in Providence, R.I., April 14, 1800, *ibid.*

5.2

Spanish Repossession of the Dominican Republic

John E. Fagg

The four-year period (1861-1865) in which the Spanish were invited to return to the Dominican Republic and reassume authority brought few benefits and many unanticipated difficulties to this Caribbean nation. The 'Restoration' was universally accepted as a failure by both the Spanish and Dominicans, and illustrates the precarious situation in which the few independent units of the Antilles found themselves in the nineteenth century. This selection originally appeared in J.E. Fagg (1965), Cuba, Haiti and the Dominican Republic, *Prentice-Hall, Englewood Cliffs, New Jersey, pp. 147-50. Copyright © 1965. Reprinted by permission of Prentice-Hall, Inc., Engelwood Cliffs, New Jersey.*

Juan Pablo Duarte and a few other Spanish-speaking creoles and mulattoes organized a secret society, *La Trinitaria*, in 1838 in the hope of recovering independence and promoting liberalism. Their opportunity came in 1844, after Boyer had been overthrown and Haiti had become disorganized. In February they proclaimed the independence of Santo Domingo. The liberal triumph was shortlived, for the Haitians invaded and were turned back by rustic bands led by caudillos who had little interest in ideology. Presently, the most successful of them, Pedro Santana, took over the capital and exiled Duarte and his allies. This uncouth warrior loved power for its own sake and felt the temptation to make public office profitable for himself. Yet he probably meant well and was, in a deep sense, patriotic. To him, patriotism meant keeping the country out of Haitian hands even if he

165

had to place it under European or United States control
in order to do so. Certainly there was little to build on: an
illiterate, demoralized population of impoverished mulattoes,
no commerce or industry, and only subsistence farming and
livestock-raising to support economic life. Memories of
gentler days were all but obliterated, and ideals had no meaning except for the few men like Duarte, who were expelled.

Santana was informed enough to issue a constitution for
the new nation, now called the Dominican Republic, and to
have himself named president. Rural leaders like him raised
bands and contested his power, and in 1848 he was bested
in a power play and resigned. He restored himself in 1849
as the principal military chieftain when the dreaded Negro
tyrant of Haiti, Faustin Soulouque, invaded the Dominican
Republic, and he defeated the attempted reconquest. Instead
of becoming president again, he allowed an ally, Buenaventura Baez — a mild-mannered gentleman who had acquired
some sophistication during a long residence in Europe — to
serve for four years in that capacity, while Santana remained
head of the military forces. The two leaders were preoccupied with fending off another invasion from Haiti. Nearly all
of their efforts went into maintaining enough forces to discourage one and in soliciting support from Spain, France,
England, and the United States, none of whom exhibited
much sympathy for the republic. Not even requests for the
establishment of a protectorate met with enthusiasm.

Baez offended Santana by bringing in foreign clergymen
to restore the Church, and Santana offended Baez by usurp-
ing his presidential prerogatives. In 1853 Santana took over
the presidency and declared his former partner a traitor.
There followed renewed efforts to interest foreign powers in
establishing a protectorate, but none wanted it badly enough
to risk antagonizing the others, with the result that, in 1855,
Haiti made another effort at reconquest. Soulouque, now the
imperial Faustin I, led 30,000 soliders into the Dominican
Republic, vowing to kill everyone, even the chickens. Again,
Pedro Santana turned back the offensive and saved the
republic, whereupon he retired from the presidency. In 1856
Baez' supporters managed to recall their leader and make
him president. Baez evened the score with his old ally by

deporting him. But Santana returned in 1857 and ousted Baez, and soon afterward resumed the presidency. In the see-saw politics of these two figures there was little that was edifying. Neither seriously represented any ideal, cause or program. The revenues of the little republic amounted to scarcely a million dollars a year, but they were sufficient to tempt caudillos to seize public office. And opportunities to take land and livestock or to issue paper money were also attractive.

Not until the end of 1860, when the United States began to break up before an impending civil war, was a foreign power willing to assume control of the Dominicans. Spain was the only taker, and her price was high: nothing less than the restoration of the land as an overseas province of the monarchy. By March 1861 Santana was able to announce that Isabel II had consented to reign over the ancient colony established by Isabel the Catholic provided there was unanimous sentiment on the part of the prospective subjects. It was easy enough for Santana to stimulate, or to issue without authorization, requests from various towns inviting the queen to accept them. Spanish troops arrived in April, and Santana was named captain-general. Hopes were high for a moment. In Madrid, Spanish pride was fired by the repentance of a former colony and the possibility of further successes in America. In Santo Domingo, relief from the Haitian menace, orderly government, redemption of paper money, and prosperity were benefits expected of the new relationship.

As it happened, Spain was scarcely able to manage its own affairs effectively or to rule Cuba and the Philippines, much less expand her responsibilities. Only in redeeming paper currency, an accomplishment that pleased the Dominicans who had sponsored the restoration, did the government of Isabel II justify expectations. Though it is true that Haiti was deterred from undertaking outright invasions, the Haitians feared that France might copy Spain, and they incited the Dominicans as much as they dared. Santana and his supporters had anticipated the creation of numerous government positions for their benefit. Instead, Spain dispatched hundreds of peninsulars to take over the province. Commerce improved little, and new capital did not arrive.

Rather, taxes were imposed and business suffered. Further-more, Spanish clergymen were shocked to find how far the Dominicans had lapsed in authorized practices, even to tolerating Protestant missionaries. Severe measures were taken to correct the situation. Spanish soldiers behaved the way occupying troops usually do and created resentment. In less than a year Santana realized that things were going badly and resigned, possibly in the hope of being recalled with enhanced powers. Instead, he was made a marquis and retired. His successor Rivera typified the haughtiness associated in Latin American minds with Spanish colonialism, and he antagonized the Dominicans by seeking to curb gambling and vice. When he tried to institute a system of forced labor for public projects, he created a spirit of revolt.

The War of Restoration, as Dominicans call it, began in 1863 and spread rapidly. Already badly crippled by yellow fever, the Spanish army was unable to strike down the rural bands that multiplied in the mountains. Pedro Santana accepted an appeal to serve the crown in suppressing the rebellion, but he soon felt himself downgraded by Spanish officialdom and protested so passionately that he was on the point of being deported. Before this could take place he died, possibly by suicide. By 1864 the Dominican patriots had organized a government and cleared all but the capital and a few ports of the royalists. In Madrid, where there had always been misgivings about the adventure, the anti-imperialists gained the upper hand. It was obvious that the rebellion would be costly to put down and that Santo Domingo held little promise for Spanish profits in any case. Furthermore, the Civil War in the United States was coming to an end, and Washington had indicated its disapproval of the Dominican affair. In an uncharacteristic display of wisdom, the regime of Isabel II decided to liquidate the enterprise. The last Spanish troops left by July 1865.

Thwarted Revolution in
Puerto Rico   Manuel Maldonado-Denis

Throughout the nineteenth century, liberal Puerto Rican spokesmen chafed at Spanish political restrictions and monopolistic tendencies. Their brief attainment of independence in 1868 and the ideals of the short-lived Republica de Borinquén are examined in this selection. The comparison of the contemporaneous Cuban revolt at Yara with the ill-fated uprising at Lares in Puerto Rico is especially instructive. This selection originally appeared in M. Maldonado-Denis (1972), Puerto Rico: A Socio-historic Interpretation *(trans. E. Vialo), Vintage Books, New York, pp. 39-47. Reprinted with permission of the publisher, Random House, Inc.*

Betances was the chief organizer and the intellectual and tangible inspiration of the Cry of Lares. On July 16, 1867, he circulated in Puerto Rico the following proclamation, which, although signed by "The Revolutionary Committee," seems to be the work of Betances:

Puerto Ricans . . . Your brothers who have left have conspired — and they should conspire — because one day the colonial regime on our island must end; because Puerto Pico must finally be free — like the continent, like Santo Domingo.

They should conspire without any letup, and we with them, because we suffer from lack of action and intervention in public affairs; because, overwhelmed by the weight of taxes which we do not vote for, we see them distributed among a number of inept Spanish employees and the so-called National Treasury, while the natives of the land, more deserving, work only at subordinate or unpaid jobs, and while the island lacks roads, schools, and other means of intellectual and material development.

We ought to conspire, because in exchange for these certain evils
— the insults we suffer daily, the obstacles which everywhere fence us
in, the immorality which slavery sows in its paths — the material order
does not gain and increase in proportion to effort expended, but rather
stagnates or drags along sluggishly. Finally, we should conspire because
there is nothing to hope for from Spain nor from her government. They
cannot give us what they do not have.[1]

Here is a masterful exposition of the complaints against
Spain, joined with a no less vehement justification of the
conspiratorial or revolutionary path. Faced with such a
regime, compromise, accommodation, optimism, and conciliation were not appropriate. On this issue, Betances —
like every other revolutionary — was intransigent. He did
not permit bungling compromises. Like Martí, he considered
that "in her present state and with her current problems,"
Puerto Rico, like Cuba, had reached "the point of understanding again the inadequacy of a conciliatory policy" and
that consequently there existed, as the Apostle (Martí)
expressed it years later in a letter he wrote to Máximo
Gómez, on July 20, 1882, "the necessity of a violent revolution."

In Puerto Rico Betances conspired with several societies
whose abolitionist and emancipative orientation had necessarily to remain secret. The period from the moment of his
exile (July 1867) to the insurrection of Lares (September
1868) was one of intense activity, devoted to collecting
funds, purchasing military stores and weapons, editing
proclamations, etc. Like Martí, Betances did not let up in
his revolutionary activity; like the Apostle, he wanted to
die with his boots on.

The insurrection of Lares was meant to explode on September 29, 1868, the day on which the slaves celebrated their
festival of Saint Michael. The secret societies agreed to work
together to strike the blow at an agreed-upon time. But an
indiscretion caused the plans of the conspirators to be discovered and they were obliged to move up the date of the
insurrection to September 23. The Spanish government went
into action, preventing Betances and his expeditionary force
from getting to Puerto Rico. His ship *El Telégrafo* was
detained at Saint Thomas, and he was personally prevented

from going to San Juan with his liberating army of three thousand men. The unconditionalist chief Pérez Moris also informs us that "one of the reasons why Betances did not come to Mayaguez with men, arms, and munitions at the end of September 1868 was because Báez[2] seized the armaments and prevented the departure of the revolutionaries."[3]

The insurrection was then primarily in the hands of the Venezuelan, Manuel Rojas, and the North American, Matías Brugman. On September 23, 1868, the revolutionaries marched from Rojas' estate in the Pezuela de Lares quarter to the town of Lares and under the motto *Viva Puerto Rico Libre* they declared the Republic of Puerto Rico. The rebels filed by with a flag designed by Mariana Bracetti. They also carried a white flag with the inscription *Muerto o Libertad; Viva Puerto Rico Libre, Año 1868*, and a red flag symbolizing the social nature of the struggle. The revolutionaries took the town hall and forced the parish priest to celebrate a *Te Deum* for the establishment of the republic. Used as a kind of manifesto at this time was a proclamation by Betances entitled "The Ten Commandments of Free Men," in which the immediate abolition of slavery was decreed as well as the end of Spanish despotism in all its forms. In addition, they adopted a "Provisional Constitution of the Puerto Rican Revolution," in which a Revolution Committee of Puerto Rico was constituted as the government of the Puerto Rican revolution. Article 2 of the provisional constitution explicitly stated that "the Committee has as its object the independence of Puerto Rico under a democratic republican form of government."[4] After having duly constituted the government of the Republic of Puerto Rico in Lares, the rebels went toward San Sebastián del Pepino, but there were driven back by Spanish troops. When the Spanish finally succeeded in strangling the insurrection, they immediately instituted harsh retributive measures against the revolutionaries and those suspected of being sympathizers.

The Republic of Puerto Rico, founded that twenty-third of September, 1868, lived only for a short time, but there remains for posterity the example of Borinquén, who had men no longer willing to tolerate the regime of iniquity and exploitation imposed by Spain. A short time later — on

October 10, 1868 — the Cry of Yara burst forth in Cuba, the Greater Antilles thus setting the tone of the West Indian revolutionary movement during the nineteenth century. The fires lit in the rising of Céspedes from his estate in La Demajagua, Cuba, could not be extinguished. The truce imposed in the Peace of Zanjón, ten years later, was a mere interlude in the armed struggle that culminated in the War for Independence in 1895.

Lares and Yara. Aborted revolution and war to the death. Sharp contrasts. Why the difference? Here is a speculation on that matter.

First let us formulate a question. Puerto Rico, no less than Cuba, lived with a situation that carried within it the germ of revolution. The prevailing slave system, the condition of day laborers[5] forced to perform acts of odious servitude to fulfill the demands of the work books[6] (one of the first acts of the rebels was the destruction of these books), the arbitrary increase in taxes which provoked the revolutionary slogan, "Down with taxes" — in short, all the complaints which Betances echoed in his proclamations could have been written by Céspedes, and vice versa. Nevertheless, in Puerto Rico the revolutionary movement did not catch on as it did in Cuba. Why? Putting aside as frivolous the supposed docility of the Puerto Pican as compared to the Cuban, by way of an hypothesis let us take the following factors into consideration.

In the first place, for a simple numerical reason the echo of Céspedes' proclamation abolishing slavery had to be louder in Cuba than that of Betances' in Puerto Rico. When the Ten Years' War began, the population of Cuba was divided in the following way: whites, 797,596; free colored, 238,927; colored slaves, 363,288 (including men and women).[7] In Puerto Rico circa 1863 there were 13,440 slaves, representing a fourth of the free day laborers employed in the countryside. According to Díaz Soler, by 1865 "the class of free workers exceeded the slave class by 56,554 men." And the previously mentioned Committee on Information made the following count (1865): Free population (white), 300,406; free population (colored), 241,037; slave population, 41,738.[8] Even taking into account the difference in number of inhabitants between Cuba and Puerto Rico, the reader can get an idea of the preponderance of blacks in Cuba — especially black slaves. This factor was very important in the whole Cuban revolutionary movement. For despite its decree abolishing slavery, the Puerto Rican revolution did not draw to it the already-freed black masses, as the Cuban revolution would. This was in spite of the fact that there had been brutally repressed slave uprisings during the nineteenth century. Perhaps what was missing was a leader like Maceo or at least a few black rebel generals who — being black — could serve as figures with whom the black population could identify and stand. Very few slaves participated in the Puerto Rican rebellion. Lacking the numerical preponderance of their brothers in Cuba, they did not commit themselves to the liberating step.

In the second place, the revolution of Lares did not sustain itself in the days following the initial uprising, but was snuffed out immediately. Generally the experience of revolution imparts to those in rebellion a clearer, more accentuated revolutionary conscience. That is to say, revolution breaks the vicious circle of oppression, and in the process of seeking their own liberation men discover their own capacity for struggle. Or, in other words, the vicious circle is broken which has determined that there is no revolutionary consciousness because there is no revolution and that there is no revolution because there is no revolutionary consciousness. Unfortunately, the uprising of Lares was aborted at so early a stage in its development that the new consciousness had insufficient time to take root in the masses.

In the third place, there was missing what was so generously present in Cuba: skill in battle. Maceo, Máximo Gómez, and Calixto García were generals in their own right, experienced in the art of war. In Lares the revolt was led by leaders unskilled in miliary matters and was readily crushed by Spanish military power.

Finally, the greater territorial expanse of Cuba made a struggle in the jungle more propitious. This factor should not be underestimated, although one need not thereby be led to accepting a thesis of geographic determinism.

ENDNOTES

1. The proclamation in question is reproduced in Pérez Moris y Cueto's book, *Historia de la insurrección de Lares* (Barcelona, 1872), pp. 282-3.
2. Buenaventura Báez, a Dominican traitor to his own people and a bitter enemy of the Puerto Rican liberation struggle in the nineteenth century. (Author's note to the English edition.)
3. *Ibid.*, p. 52.
4. Lidio Cruz Monclova, *Historia de Puerto Rico* en el Siglo XIX, 3 Vols. (Río Piedras: Editorial Universitaria, 1957-1964), Appendix 9 to Vol. 1, p. 707.
5. *jornaleros* in Spanish. (Author's note to the English edition.)
6. The day laborers' work books (*libretas*) originated with the infamous Police and Good Government Edicts of Governor López Baños (1838) and the Regulation of Pezuela (1849). Cruz Monclova says about these dispositions (*Historia*, Vol. 1, pp. 307, 377: On the Edict of López Baños):

> . . . day laborers were obliged to work personally on repair of the roads in their respective towns, a measure which involved an enormous injustice, for it relieved of responsibility the proprietors, landlords, and merchants, who were precisely those who most benefited from said ways of communication . . . every individual who lacked an income or a profession was declared a vagrant; it [the edict] provided that said individual be condemned to labor on public works if in the period of twenty days he did not provide proof by means of a paper filled out by a proprietor or head of a firm that he had a job; it prohibited all claims to the contrary; and it waived the competency of the high court and other tribunals in cases of vagrancy, which it left to the exclusive control of the municipal administrations.

On the Regulation of Pezuela Cruz Monclova says:

> A day laborer was declared to be a person sixteen years or older who, lacking capital or a business, was engaged in someone else's service — be it in field labor or the mechanical arts, for all or part of the year — working for a salary. The condition of the day laborer was determined by the town judges. Every day laborer was required to enter himself in the registry of the judge in his place of residence; and to provide himself with a work book, renewable each year, which he obtained free from the judge and was replaceable without charge in case of loss. The day laborer was also obliged to carry the work book with him, and if he was caught without it he had to work eight days on any public work, receiving only a half-day's pay. He was likewise required to be constantly employed. When he wasn't, the judge of his town was

to provide work for him on private or public works, in which case he would be paid a full day's pay, according to the custom of the place. Finally, he was required to go live in his respective town before June 11, 1850 (the regulation was dated June 11, 1849), and to build there a shanty or dwelling, except in the case where, before said date, he should present the judge with a paper signed by some estate-owner, farmer or cattleman of the district, declaring that he had contracted to receive the worker on his property as a laborer or subordinate.

Although the work books were abolished by Primo de Rivera in 1874, when the Spanish Republic fell, his successor, General Sanz Posse, reinstituted the custom in his infamous Edict of Vagos (1874).

See Cruz Monclova, *Historia*, Vol. 2, pp. 388-89. Also the essay by Salvador Brau, "Las clases jornaleras en Puerto Rico" (1888), in the book edited by Eugenio Fernández Méndez, *Salvador Brau: Disquisiciones sociológicas* (Río Piedras: Universidad de Puerto Rico, 1956). Consult also the opinion of Baldorioty de Castro on the problem of day laborers in Cruz Monclova, *Baldorioty de Castro* (San Juan: Instituto de Cultura Puertorriqeña, 1966).

7. I take the figures from the "Cuadro sinóptico de los principales censos de la isla de Cuban desde 1768 hasta 1879," as they appear quoted in Melchor Fernández Almagro, *Historia política de la España contemporánea*, 3 vols. 1868-1902 (Madrid: Alianza Editorial, 1968), Vol. 1, p. 453.

8. Luis M. Díaz Soler, *Historia de la esclavitud negra en Puerto Rico* (Río Piedras: Editorial Universitaria, 1965), pp. 137, 141, 259.

Letter to Federico Henríquez y Caravajal, March 1895

José Martí

The poet-patriot José Martí was at his most eloquent when writing about his vision of Cuban independence. In this letter to a compatriot in Santo Domingo, Martí expounds on his identification of the Cuban struggle as a pan-Caribbean campaign, and theorizes, prophetically, that "The Free Antilles will preserve the independence of America . . . and perhaps may hasten and decide the balance of the world." This letter is excerpted from The America of José Martí, *translated from the Spanish by Juan de Onís. Copyright © 1954 by the Noonday Press, Inc. Reprinted with the permission of Farrar, Strauss and Giroux, Inc.*

Friend and Brother:

So great are the responsibilities that devolve upon those men who do not deny their scant powers to the world, and who live to add to the sum of its freedom and decency, that their words are but half-expressed and childlike, nor can a single phrase convey what one would say to a cherished friend with an embrace. This is what happens to me as, standing on the threshold of a great duty, I reply to your generous letter. You did me the greatest good with it, and gave me the one strength great undertakings require, that is to say, the knowledge that a warm-hearted, good man passionately approves them. Rare as mountains are the men who can look down from their heights and feel with the bowels of a nation or of mankind. There is left, after clasping the hand of such a man, that inner cleanliness which should be the reward of winning, in a just cause, the good fight. I deliberately say nothing of the true preoccupation of my spirit, because you have completely divined it; deeply touched, I am writing you from the silence of a home which, perhaps this very day, for the good of my country, is to be left abandoned. The least I can do, in gratitude for this virtue, inasmuch as in this way I do not shirk but come to grips with duty, is to face death, whether it awaits us on land or sea, in the company of one who, as the result of my efforts, and out of respect for his own, and the passion of the common soul of our lands, leaves his loving and happy home to set foot on our enemy-infested country, with a handful of brave men. I was dying of shame — aside from the conviction that my presence in Cuba at this moment is at least as useful as it could be abroad — at the thought that in the face of such a hazardous undertaking I might become convinced that it was my duty to let him go alone, and that a country might allow itself to be served, without scorn and indifference, by one who preached the need of dying without beginning by risking his own life. Wherever my first duty lies, in Cuba or outside Cuba, there I will be. It may be possible or necessary, as seems the case up to this moment, to do both. Perhaps I can contribute to the basic need of giving our reviving war a character that will carry within it the embryo, without superfluous details of those principles indispensable to the good name of the Revolution and the security of the Republic. The difficulty of our wars of independence, and the reason for their slow and imperfect accomplishment, has resided more than in the lack of mutual esteem on the part of their initiators and the rivalry inherent in human nature, in their failure to assume a form that should at once encompass the spirit of redemption and dignity, which, added to the active sum of motives of a less pure nature, launch and maintain the war, and the habits and the human element of the war. The other difficulty which our nations, staid and bookish, have not yet overcome, is that of viable forms of government, after the emancipation, which, without leaving the intellectually superior element of the country discontent, shall take into account — and make possible their natural and growing development — the more numerous and uncultured members of society whom a government imposed upon them, however good and generous, would lead to anarchy or tyranny. I called up the war; my responsibility begins rather than ends with it. For me, country will never be triumph, but agony and duty. Blood is now at the boiling point. Now the sacrifice must be given respect, and a humane and forbearing meaning; the war must be made feasible and invincible. If I am ordered, though my soul dies, to remove myself far from those who die as I would know how to die, I will have the courage for that, too. The person who thinks of himself does not love his country; and the ills of nations reside, however subtly they may at times be disguised, in the barriers or pressures of haste their representatives put in the way of the natural course of events. From me you may expect my complete and unvarying submission. I shall arouse the world. But my one desire would be to stand beside the last tree, the last fighter, and die in silence. For me, my hour has come. But I can still serve this unique heart of our republics. The free Antilles will preserve the independence of our America, and the dubious and tarnished honor of the English America, and perhaps may hasten and decide the balance of the world. You see what we are doing, you with your youthful gray hairs — and I, dragging myself along, my heart broken.

What need is there for me to speak to you of Santo Domingo? In what does it differ from Cuba? You are not a Cuban, and where is there a better Cuban than you? And is not Gomez a Cuban? And I, what am I, and who shall assign me a soil? Was not mine the soul, and the pride which enveloped me and throbbed about me, in your voice that unforgettable and virile night at the *Sociedad de Amigos*? All this is that, and part of that. I obey, and would even say that I accept as a superior privilege, and an American law, the happy need to set out, under the protection of Santo Domingo, for the war of liberation of Cuba. Let us do on the surface of the sea, with blood and love, what the fire of the Andean range does in the depths of the sea.

I tear myself away from you, and leave you a warm embrace, and a prayer that my name, whose only worth is that it is today at the service of my country, will be remembered for whatever justice and charity Cuba may receive.

Whoever loves her, I fervently acclaim as my brother. I have no other brothers than those who love her.

Farewell, and farewell to my noble and indulgent friends. I owe you the pleasure of your loftiness and purity in this harsh and sordid human universe. Raise your voice high: if I fall, it will be for the independence of your country, too.
Your
José Martí

SECTION 6

United States Expansion into the Caribbean: Restructuring the Economy

6.0

Introduction to Section 6

The Spanish–American War not only marked the official entrance of the United States into Caribbean politics, but it similarly signaled a tacit recognition on the part of the British to allow for North American influence to expand hemispherically. The years between 1898 and the formulation of the 'Good Neighbor Policy' in the 1930's, during the presidency of Franklin Delano Roosevelt, witnessed frequent and resented United States invasions and takeovers of Caribbean territory. Although the bitterness caused locally by such actions in Cuba, Puerto Rico, Haiti and the Dominican Republic has been well documented, selection 6.1 views the often-neglected reaction of the United States public to its new-found role in the Caribbean. Freeman Smith's study of Cuba in the early years of American tutelage (selection 6.2) examines the role of the American businessman in that nation's economy. Notwithstanding the 'political independence' guaranteed to Cuba after the signing of the Platt Amendment in 1901, the Cuban economy was clearly dependent on United States sugar quotas and investment capital; where outright invasions failed to establish the desired degree of internal Cuban political compliance, economic sanctions often brought acquiescence.

The United States was not alone, however, in its often self-serving reorganization of Caribbean economies. MacGuire's discussion of the lime industry in the British colony of Dominica (selection 6.3) indicates how poorly planned was the development of interior lands and how sorely neglected were the needs of the local peasantry. The failure of the lime industry in the 1930s, despite the introduction of large-scale capital investment, reveals how dangerous a monocultural economy is and how exposed to the vagaries of climate and

183

market conditions such a crop becomes, even — as in this case — where the traditional sugar production is replaced by the relatively innovative lime industry.

Similarly, Van Soest's contribution on the influence of the petroleum companies in the government and economy of Curaçao (selection 6.4) serves to remind us how impotent Caribbean territories were to counter 'big business'. The compliance of the Netherlands home government with the oil interests, often in direct contrast to the expressed desires of the colony, are indications that the United States was not alone in her manipulative tactics.

Economic conditions worsened in the Caribbean region after the Great Depression registered its effects on metropolitan economies. A series of devastating hurricanes in the 1930s added injury to insult, and against this background of shrinking markets and widespread poverty it is not surprising that powerful strongmen should appear, bringing promises of future prosperity. Both Batista in Cuba and Trujillo in the Domincan Republic represented themselves as 'men of the people', who had first-hand experience with deprivation. Wiarda's assessment of how the 'populist' leader Trujillo sustained himself in power has more to do with strong arm polictics, however, than filling breadbaskets (see selection 6.5).

To understand the initial stages of United States activity in the Caribbean, it is advisable to first study the nineteenth-century power struggle between Great Britain and the emerging North American industrial giant. The nature of this contest is explored in C.J. Barrett, *A New Balance of Power: The 19th Century*. While early reference works on American occupation of Caribbean nations are not lacking, recent monographs tend to be broader in coverage, and, generally, more objective. These include: H. Schmidt, *The U.S. Occupation of Haiti, 1915-1934*; G. Pope Atkins and L.C. Wilson, *The U.S. and the Trujillo Regime*; G.K. Lewis, *The Virgin Islands: A Caribbean Lilliput*. A more emotional account is provided in the eyewitness report of Jesús Galíndez Suarez entitled *The Era of Trujillo: Dominican Dictator*; this frightening portrait of uncontrolled power was published posthumously after the author was murdered, presumably by the dictator's henchmen.

The Press and the Public View
of United States Intervention   John W. Blassingame

An examination of the editorial policies of major North American newspapers at the turn of the century provides important insight into the public mentality behind the expansion of United States' interests in the Caribbean. Blassingame's assessment suggests that 'Manifest Destiny' was interpreted on many different levels within the United States. This selection is taken from J.W. Blassingame (1969), 'The Press and American Intervention in Haiti and the Dominican Republic, 1904-1920', Caribbean Studies, 9, No. 2 (July), pp. 31-34. Copyright © 1969, by The Institute of Caribbean Studies, University of Puerto Rico. Reprinted by permission of The Institute of Caribbean Studies.

Appeals to the Monroe Doctrine rarely represented as much concern for the preservation of Haitian and Dominican independence and democratic government in the Western Hemisphere as it did for the other side of the doctrine: American security. This was the primary reason for American intervention. On April 3, 1905, *The New York Times* reported that most Americans favored a provisional protectorate over the Dominican Republic because "the sending of European warships to collect debts of these republics is distasteful to us. We know that such measures involve consequences that may menace our peace and safety." Likewise, the Chicago *Tribune* on August 2, 1915, called for the United States to "establish an adequate supervision" over Haiti because "from the viewpoint of national security and intelligent self-interest the incurable turbulence of Haiti is our affair . . . Spasmodic

185

and belated police work and a policy of conciliation and drift
gain us neither security nor respect . . ."

Hispaniola's command of important sea lanes and the
threat that European intervention would pose to the
approaches to the Panama canal heightened America's
interests in the island. Many editors feared that European
nations, especially Germany, wanted to establish naval
bases at Haiti's Môle St. Nicholas harbor or the Dominican
Republic's Samana Bay. This would lead to a loss of American hegemony in the Caribbean. Geographical propinquity
placed Haiti and the Dominican Republic within America's
sphere of influence and gave the United States a special
interest in them.[1] The Hartford *Courant* on January 24,
1905, supported intervention because "nature has made the
island on which the so-called Dominican republic festers a
geographical appanage of the United States and probably it is
to become and remain a political appanage." The Chicago
Tribune on July 30, 1915, pointed out that if the United
States did not intervene in Haiti, "the Monroe doctrine and
our hegemony in the Caribbean will be compromised."

A few journalists felt that intervention in the Caribbean
was a sign that America's Manifest Destiny continued un-
abated.[2] The Chicago *Chronicle* declared in 1904 that the
United States "is expanding because it is its nature to do so.
Nothing can and nothing should arrest its progress by leaps
and bounds toward its manifest destiny."[3] In 1915 the
Providence *Journal* praised American progress toward supremacy in "our Mediterranean." The movement toward American control of Cuba, Puerto Rico, the Dominican Republic
and other areas, the *Journal* asserted, had taken "active form
without our seeking . . .. It is now Haiti's turn."[4] The most
influential exponent of Manifest Destiny was the Chicago
Tribune. Reviewing the course of events from 1898 to 1916
in editorials on "American Destiny and Duty," "Force," and
the "American West Indies," the *Tribune* discussed the in-
exorable expansion of the United States in the Caribbean.

Abjuring conquest and annexation but extolling force as
the "germ of life," the *Tribune* was convinced that America
was unconsciously establishing "an unquestioned predominance and an unshakable control" over the West Indies and

spreading freedom from misery, starvation, corruption, disease, and violence in the process. America's imperial destiny, "checked but not evaded," had progressed alike under administrations whose creeds were racist and imperialistic or anti-imperialistic and humanitarian. Without popular discussion or a conscious exertion of will, the United States was forcibly building up an empire in the region flanking the Panama Canal.[5] Americans knew little and cared less about the process of expansion. Nonetheless, "in one fashion or another, by force in one form or another, the United States expands. It pushes its frontiers ahead. Without its people knowing or caring how, it advances . . . The American does not know that we have intervened in Haiti and Santo Domingo; nevertheless, the American destiny goes south, and it is imperial."[6]

Some periodicals went beyond the *Tribune* and fervently endorsed the idea of annexation.[7] In light of the strategic location of Hispaniola, the expense and annoyance of having to keep order on the island to prevent European intervention, and the natives' incapacity for self-government, the New Orleans *Picayune* believed in 1904 that "it probably might save future trouble to annex the island outright and administer its affairs very much as Puerto Rico is governed."[8] The St. Louis *Globe-Democrat* and the Baltimore *American* agreed. The *American* declared: "without further delay we should annex Santo Domingo and set up there a decent and stable government."[9]

The foremost advocate of annexation was *Independent*. Undoubtedly setting a record for editorial consistency, in 1904 and 1914 *Independent* reprinted its 1871 editorials on the desirability of annexing the Dominican Republic. Lamenting the "sad blunder" the Senate had made earlier, the editor of *Independent* urged American to take advantage of every "peaceable opportunity" to acquire territory. The United States had to undertake the onerous task of intervening in the island because it had neglected the opportunity to acquire it earlier. American possession of the Panama Canal made it even more imperative that the United States annex the island in 1914 than in 1870. Since the United States "would like to have possession of all the West Indian islands," and since it was inevitable that they would come under American control, the United States would obviate the necessity of intervention, satisfy its land-hunger, and fulfill its "mission" by annexing the island.[10]

Although Americans would be happy to have tropical fruits in their "natural garden," *Independent* favored annexation because the Haitians and Dominicans needed "energetic Anglo-Saxon influence." It was not enough to expand American power and control under the rubric of "Manifest Destiny." Americans had a higher destiny as philanthropists, Christians and patriots "to extend sound government and stable institutions."[11] On March 3, 1904, *Independent*, summarizing its position, declared that it would like to see the island annexed because

It would plant another star in the blue sky of the flag and plant the flag prophetically in the waters of the Caribbean . . .. If the United States has one 'mission' it is to propagate liberty under the direction of education and morality . . . But it is said that annexation would be the ruin of a negro state. If so, so be it . . .. And if the Negroes or the white men of Santo Domingo, or of the South, under fair laws, cannot swim, they must sink, call it fate or law or what we will. It is best that the best should survive.[12]

Unlike *Independent*, an overwhelming majority of American gazettes favoring intervention rejected annexation. The Hartford *Courant* and the New Orleans *Times-Democrat* were among the most spirited opponents of annexation.[13] While there was some possibility of the United States' acquiring a naval base on Hispaniola, the *Courant* felt that there could be "no thought of annexation." Reprinting Sumner's 1870 tirades against the annexation of the Dominican Republic in 1905, the *Courant* argued that temporary intervention would be less expensive than annexation of the debt-ridden republic. The *Courant* and the *Times-Democrat* were especially suspicious of adding a large Negro or mulatto population to the United States. The *Courant* declared on January 24, 1905: "We are loaded up quite heavily with 'Black Belt' already." Far from wanting to annex Haiti and the Dominican Republic, the United States, according to the *Courant*, "wouldn't open the door if they hammered and begged ever so." *The New York Times* and *Review of Reviews* wanted the two countries placed in a position analogous to that of Cuba because they felt that treaties embodying the equivalent of the Platt amendment would diminish rather than increase the danger of annexation.[14]

ENDNOTES

1. *Review of Reviews*, XLIX (June, 1914), 662; Chicago *Tribune*, Mar. 4, 1904, July 30, Sept. 5 (II, 4), 1915, Dec. 25, 1916; *Harpers Weekly*, XLIX (December 30, 1905) 1924; *Outlook*, CIX (January 27, 1915), 163-65; *Independent*, LXXIX (August 31, 1914), 294; *Review of Reviews*, XXXI (April, 1905), 397-99; *World's Work*, XXXI (April, 1916), 595-96; Hartford *Courant*, Jan. 28, 1905; *Outlook*, LXXIX (February 11, 1905), 366-68; Eugene P. Lyle, "The Control of the Caribbean," *World's Work*, X (September, 1905), 664-69.
2. *Independent*, LXXXIII (February 11, 1915), 311; *Current Opinion*, LIX (October, 1915), 223-25; *Independent*, LVI (February 25, 1904), 454, (March 3, 1904), 507-508; *Literary Digest*, XXIX (September 10, 1904), 310-12; *Independent*, LXXIX (August 31, 1914), 294; Frederic C. Penfield, "Political Phases of Caribbean Dominion," *North American Review*, CLXXVIII (January, 1904), 75-85.
3. Quoted in *Literary Digest*, XXIX (September 10, 1904), 311-12.
4. Quoted in *Current Opinion*, LIX (October, 1915), 225.
5. Chicago *Tribune*, May 5, June 25 (II, 4), July 27, 1916.
6. *Ibid.*, July 27, 1916.
7. *Literary Digest*, XXVIII (March 5, 1904), 319, (January 16, 1904), 69.
8. Quoted in the Hartford *Courant*, Mar. 1, 1904.
9. Quoted in *Literary Digest*, XXVIII (January 16, 1904), 69.
10. *Independent*, LVI (February 25, 1904), 454, (March 3, 1904), 507, LXXXV (March 13, 1916), 368-69.
11. *Ibid.*, LXIX (August 31, 1914), 294.
12. *Ibid.*, LVI (March 3, 1904), 507-508.
13. *Literary Digest*, XXVIII (March 5, 1904), 319.
14. *Review of Reviews*, XXXI (March, 1905), 266-68, (April, 1905), 397-99, *The New York Times*, Sept. 2, 1916.

United States
Businessmen in Cuba
Robert Freeman Smith

Although Cuba was technically an independent nation after the withdrawal of United States occupation forces, the provisions of the Platt Amendment to the Cuban constitution allowed for American intervention in the event of political instability. In this selection Robert Freeman Smith indicates how broadly interpreted those intervention powers were and how the interests of big business were often served simultaneously. This selection originally appeared in R.F. Smith (1960), The United States and Cuba: Business and Diplomacy, 1917-1960, *Bookman Associates, pp. 17-21. Reprinted with kind permission of the Author.*

Between 1898 and 1919 a pattern of Cuban-American relations developed which involved a rather close connection between investments, trade, and Cuban stability. An official of the State Department's Latin American Division — Boaz Long — noted this development in a memorandum to Secretary of State Robert Lansing in February 1918. In a summary statement of the period since 1898, Long enthusiastically reported:

The total trade of Cuba with the United States just prior to the end of the Spanish rule over that island (1897) amounted to about twenty-seven million dollars per annum. During the decade following the termination of our war with Spain the island of Cuba, guided by American influence, increased her trade with us by leaps and bounds and brought it to the startling total in 1917 of something over four hundred and thirty million dollars. This unprecedented development of Cuba may serve as an illustration of what probably would take place in the Central American countries provided this Government extended to them aid of a practical character as it did to Cuba.

190

The "aid" that Long discussed in more detail consisted of the maintenance of stability, investments, loans, and trade.[1]

The protection of investments, the expansion of trade, and the stability of Cuba were mutually dependent parts of the pattern of relationships, and all in turn were linked to the influence of the United States Government. Intervention by various means in the affairs of Cuba, and the reciprocity treaty — which increasingly tied the Cuban sugar economy to the United States — were basic elements in this relationship. The nature of this pattern of Cuban-American relations was clearly illustrated by several events in 1917 and 1918.

Early in 1917 disturbances broke out in Cuba. The United States issued instructions that it would not tolerate armed revolt, and small detachments of marines were repeatedly landed from February to August in response to numerous requests from American business interests.[2] Destruction of property increased during April, however, and by May there was talk of sending a large body of American soldiers. President Mario Menocal disapproved of such a step,[3] but by the latter part of May the State Department had definitely decided to go ahead with this plan and had requested the War Department to begin preparations.[4] In order to salve Cuban feelings, and possibly the feelings of Americans who might disagree with a policy of occupying a friendly country, an artful plan was worked out. It was arranged for President Menocal to "offer" to the United States "sites for training camps . . . if it should be considered desirable to send troops to train in mild winter climate."[5] This would make it possible to "impress eastern Cuba with [the] fact of [the] presence of United States troops" through the guise of "extensive practice marches."[6] The American people were informed that the "friendly offer" had been accepted, and that it was proof of Cuba's desire to assist in the war with Germany.[7] An Associated Press article had hinted at the real reason for intervention and this disturbed the State Department. For, as Minister William Gonzales put it, "such publications . . . are embarrassing to diplomatic work."[8]

Camp sites were rented in Oriente Province,[9] and on August 16, 1917 it was decided to send a regiment of marines

rather than a cavalry regiment.[10] The marines arrived in force
later that month, and the State Department received periodic
"training" reports from the marine commander.[11] Some
historians have contended that this intervention was due to
fear of German attempts to create trouble. There was one
report of possible German activity, but it was received almost
two months after the decision to send troops had been
made.[12] Frank Polk, the acting Secretary of State in July
1917, stated that troops were being sent, "to aid in the
protection of sugar properties and mining properties and in
restoring complete order in the Oriente Province."[13] The
Military Attaché, in a report written in 1921, said that at the
time he was not advised of the reason for intervention but
that it was generally understood that it was to protect American property.[14] In addition the marines acted as strike-
breakers and strike preventers for the Cuba Railroad.[15]

During the summer of 1917 Cuba began negotiations with
the United States for a fifteen million dollar loan. Secretary
of State Robert Lansing informed Secretary of the Treasury
William Gibbs McAdoo that Cuba's application for a loan
offered a good opportunity to bring pressure on that government for a favorable settlement of the claims of the Ports
Company of Cuba and the Cuba Railroad. Lansing noted that
the loan should not be made until these issues were settled.[16]
The Ports Company claim stemmed from the revocation of
the "Dragado Concession" in 1913. The company had obtained a concession to dredge the ports of Cuba in 1911,
and had planned to make over 200 percent profit on the
operation. The Trust Company of Cuba — headed by
Norman H. Davis — was deeply involved with the Ports
Company.[17] The Cuba Railroad claimed that the Cuban
Government owed it $250,000,000 for damages suffered
during the 1917 revolt. The Cuban Government stated that it
was willing to loan money to the company, but that it did
not owe damages.[18]

Pressure was put on the Cuban Government to settle these
claims. In October 1917 the Cuban Congress finally agreed to
settle with the Ports Company, but the railroad claim was
debated until the spring of 1918. The Cuban Government
then agreed to pay the damage claims of the railroad out of

the proceeds of the loan.[19] On April 3, 1918 the Cuban President signed a decree which, in effect, returned to the Ports Company all of its assets while the Cuban Government assumed its debts.[20] The first five million dollar advance to the Cuban Government was approved on March 27, 1918, and the two subsequent advances of like amounts were approved later that year.

During the summer of 1917 the price of Cuban raw sugar on the New York Market increased to 6.75 cents a pound — the highest price since the Civil War.[21] The United States Government then moved to assert control over the sugar market. The Lever Act of August 10, 1917 granted the executive the power to control the marketing and production of foodstuffs, and created the Food Administration. Herbert Hoover was picked to head the administration, and one of his first moves was to organize the machinery to control Cuban sugar marketing.

For all practical purposes Cuban sugar set the price for sugars sold at New York, and any attempt to control raw sugar prices had to eliminate much of Cuba's bargaining power. On August 31, 1917 Herbert Hoover wrote to the British Food Controller and outlined a program to accomplish this purpose. Hoover's plan consisted of several parts: (1) the British were to force the Canadians to withdraw from the Cuban sugar market; (2) the British and American purchasers were to agree to place their purchases with the New York Committee of five men — to be appointed by the United States and Britain; (3) this committee would have the power to set the price for raw sugar purchases and to apportion the Cuban crop among the purchasing nations.[22] Thus, the Cuban producers were to be told that they could sell their crop only to the committee, and for the price set by the committee.

The British agreed to Hoover's plan, and the International Sugar Committee was organized. The British Government appointed two members, and the United States Government appointed three. There was some surprise — and alarm — expressed by Cubans when Hoover picked Earl Babst, the president of the American Sugar Refining Company, to head the committee.

William A. Jamison of the Arbuckle Brothers Refinery and George N. Rolph of the Food Administration were the other two members. American refiners wanted a cheap raw material, and the Cubans believed that the American appointments to the committee were indicative of the influence of the refiner's point of view.[23]

The International Sugar Committee set the price of Cuban sugar at 4.6 cents a pound, plus freight to New York. The producers in Cuba vigorously objected to this price, and on November 20, 1917 the Cuban Minister stated this objection to Secretary Lansing.[24] Four days later Herbert Hoover requested State Department support in forcing the Cubans into line.[25] The American Minister to Cuba informed the department that the price of sugar, as fixed by the committee, would seriously affect the people of Cuba since the price of food — which Cuba imported from the United States — was inflated beyond the purchasing capacity of most Cubans. Minister Gonzales felt that it was only fair to compensate the Cubans with higher sugar prices.[26]

The Cuban producers held out until January 17, 1918, when they finally consented to the price set by the committee. There was some indication that this consent was the result of economic coercion. A report from Cuba in early January 1918, stated that there was no flour in Cuba, and that no bread was available. In addition, the supply of coal was almost exhausted. For some reason the Cubans had been unable to obtain import licenses for wheat and coal from the American Food Administration.[27] As soon as the contract for sugar purchases was approved the Cuban Minister contacted the State Department and urged that imports to Cuba be expedited.[28] The import licenses were soon forthcoming.[29]

During the 1918 sugar shortage hearings, several individuals were quizzed about the tactics used to fix the prices of Cuban sugar. Earl Babst — and others as well — refused to answer the question in public since he said that it would betray the "diplomatic instructions and relationships" of which he was a part. The committee went into executive session to receive the answer, and the veil of secrecy descended.[30]

Thus, the events of 1917-18 illustrate the "practical" aid policy described by Boaz Long. American businessmen helped to interpret this policy, and derived profit from its application. The years 1917-18 represented the zenith in the use of armed force in Cuban-American relations. The pattern of relations, which was so vividly illustrated during this two-year span, had its roots in the Spanish-American War.

ENDNOTES

1. "Memorandum and Arguments Relating to Constructive Steps Which Should be Taken in Central America before the Close of the European War," February 15, 1918, NA 711.13/55. For a similar statement of the relationship of stability, trade, and investments see Chester Lloyd Jones, *Caribbean Interests of the United States* (New York, 1919), 94; Jones's book was written in 1916 and represents the view of a former member of the State Department. NA, here and below, refers to the U.S. National Archives.

2. Lansing to Gonzales, February 18, 1917, NA 837.00/1106a (FR, 1917-1:363). Wilfrid H. Callcott, *The Caribbean Policy of the United States 1890-1920* (Baltimore, 1942), 471-472. A list of the various landings can be found in, U.S., Department of State, *Right to Protect Citizens in Foreign Countries by Landing Forces* (3rd revised ed., with supplemental appendix: Washington, 1934), 101-107. The State Department files contain numerous requests for protection from American business groups, and time after time Gonzales was instructed to "demand" that the Cuban Government protect American properties.

3. Callcott, *Caribbean Policy of the United States*, 471-472.

4. Memorandum: Stabler (Latin American Division) to Secretary of State, June 4, 1917, NA 837.00/1395.

5. Gonzales to Secretary of State, July 14, NA 837.00/1395.

6. *Ibid*.

7. Lansing to American Legation (Habana), August 17, 1917, NA 837.00/1407.

8. Gonzales to Lansing, August 16, 1917, NA 837.00/1407.

9. Gonzales to Lansing, August 14, 1917, NA 837.00/1406.

10. Lansing to American Legation (Habana), August 17, 1917, NA 837.00/1407.

11. Numerous such reports are in the Archives and were read by the author. They reported the areas covered by the patrols and activity encountered.

12. Guantanamo, Cuba to Opnav, Washington, July 17, 1917, NA 837.00/1395.

13. Frank L. Polk to the Secretary of War, July 18, 1917, NA 837.00/1395. Polk to Wilson (President), July 18, 1917, NA 837.00/1395. Polk did not mention that "German threat" to the Secretary of War and told Wilson that "this movement [revolution] may be backed by Germans."

14. Memorandum by General Richards, December 10, 1921; NA 837.00/2183 [?].

15. H.C. Lakin (President of the Cuba Railroad) to Charles Evans Hughes, August 29, 1921, NA 837.00/2155. Marines were camped on the property of the railroad. Lakin, in stating the reason for the intervention in 1917, cited the Bolshevist menace, not the German.

16. Lansing to McAdoo, August 13, 1917, in *Foreign Relations of the United States, 1918* (Washington, 1930), 298.

17. Leland Jenks once described this concession as "the most grandiose attempt at plunder in the history of Cuba." Leland Jenks, *Our Cuban Colony* (New York, 1928), 119. Norman H. Davis was associated with the Morgan Bank and was a leading Democrat. In 1917 he was financial adviser to the Treasury Department in charge of loans to the allies. In this capacity he helped to handle the Cuban loan.

18. Memorandum by John Foster Dulles (Special Counselor, Latin American Division), August 19, 1917, in *Foreign Relations*, 1918, 301.

19. Gonzales to Lansing, July 18, 1918, *ibid.*, 331. The Cuba Railroad ended up getting over three million dollars, and they continued to ask for more.

20. Jenks, *Cuban Colony*, 125-126.

21. *Ibid.*, 197-198.

22. U.S., Department of State, *The World War* (Vol. I), Supplement 2 of *Foreign Relations of the United States, 1917* (Washington, 1932), 655.

23. Gonzales to Lansing, December 16, 1917, in *Foreign Relations, 1918*, 350-353.

24. *Ibid.*, 347.

25. Herbert Hoover to Woodrow Wilson, *Ibid.*, 349.

26. Gonzales to Lansing, December 16, 1917, *Ibid.*, 350-353.

27. U.S., Senate, Subcommittee of the Committee on Manufactures, *Hearings, Shortage of Sugar*, 65th Cong., 2nd Sess., 1918, 1028-1029. (Hereafter cited as *Shortage of Sugar*.)

28. Cespedes to Lansing, January 18, 1918, in *Foreign Relations 1918*, 353-354.

29. Jenks quotes a telegram from Lansing to Gonzales (source given was the newspaper *El Mundo*, January 14, 1918), which, if it is accurate, definitely states that imports into Cuba were stopped in order to convince the Cubans that they should "cooperate" with the United States. Jenks, *Cuban Colony*, 199.

30. Senate, *Shortage of Sugar*, 205. Officials of other refineries testified that the American Sugar Refining Company was favored by the International Committee and profited from the price set for Cuban sugar.

6.3

Dominica's Ill-fated
Lime Industry   Robert E. Maguire

Despite centuries of experience pointing to the inherent
dangers of monoculturally dependent economies, investors
in Dominica, in the early decades of this century, poured
funds into the development of a lime industry. Initially
strong, limes fell victim to the vagaries of the international
market, and, ultimately, provided little real growth for the
Dominican economy. This selection is excerpted from
R.E. Maguire, paper presented at the First Caribbean Studies
Association Workshop Conference, Port-of-Spain, Trinidad,
January, 1977, 'Prelude to a National Park: The Utilization
of Dominica's Interior Lands, 1880–1935'. Printed by kind
permission of the Author.

The enthusiastic support for opening the interior to agricultural settlement cut across the spectrum of those managing
the economic well-being of the island. Any disapproval or
scepticism that did exist over concentrating development
activities on the interior came primarily from resident proprietors with strong vested interests in coastal properties who
were, thus, keenest on seeing development funds invested in
coastal lands. These individuals, however, were seemingly
caught in a dilemma as plans for interior development were
pushed forward by colonial government officials. They
realised that any influx of both development assistance
earmarked for the interior and British settlers with capital
would have indirect positive benefits for them, yet they
saw it unlikely that they would be able to benefit directly in
interior development activities by expanding their holdings

197

inland since local capital was scarce.

Such strong opposition to interior development, however, was not the general rule and, for the most part, was completely ignored by the ultimate decision-makers — colonial officials anxious to transform Dominica into a miniature Ceylon. As interior development activities moved forward, the opposition of local planters was lost in the rush of optimism that seemed eventually to embrace even the sceptics themselves.

After 1900, the growth of the lime industry was spectacular. The planting of lime seedlings procured from the Botanical Station commenced at such a rapid pace that by 1912 Dominica was well established as the largest producer of limes in the world, exporting limes and lime products all over the globe. Hence, a wave of bullish optimism embraced the island. Praise for the interior was common in all that was written about the island, and a host of plans for extending its exploitation came from all corners.

In addition to the extension or introduction of crops, the distinct possibility of cattle raising on 'the extensive Layou Flats, the plains of Castle Bruce, the broad reaches of Grand Savanna, the undulating downs of Lasoye, and the rich district of Grandbay, to say nothing of other localities . . .' was considered.[1] Several proposals to build railroads or aerial ropeways to assist in transporting produce from the interior to the coast were voiced. Suggestions made for meeting increasing labour needs included importing either indentured labourers, prisoners from the Anglo–Boer War, or workers from overcrowded Barbados.

A new element, that of tourism, was also introduced. One writer felt that if the Grand Soufriere Valley were

opened up, and riding paths constructed to it, and suitable accommodation for tourists supplied, it would prove as attractive as the Yellowstone or the Northern Island of New Zealand . . . and make it one of the most frequently visited places by all tourists to the West Indies.[2]

Indicative of general, contemporary attitudes toward agricultural development geared toward plantation export production is the fact that proposals put forth by both decision-makers and those influencing decisions totally ignored possible interior development based on small-scale, peasant exploitation of the land and/or the production of locally needed food crops. The only path toward development was perceived by both colonial officials and local planters and merchants to be large-scale production of tropical export crops. With suggestions pouring in from all sides, the illiterate, powerless peasant, unable to articulate his ideas and desires and lacking spokesmen to champion his cause, remained a silent figure in interior development.

Fear of the dangerous consequences of a dependence on the lime monoculture were generally discarded since it was widely believed that lime production was viable because of the diversity of marketable products it engendered. Indeed, Dominican lime exports went out in the form of concentrated lime juice, raw lime juice, lime juice cordial, green or fresh limes, pickled limes, citrate of limes, essential lime oil, and lime attar. Hence, the extension of lime acreage seemed expedient. By 1918, an estimated 6,000 acres were under lime cultivation.[3] In short, limes were viewed as 'an infant industry with very great possibilities before it'.[4]

From 1916 to 1930, however, a series of disasters that included almost every snare that can trip up a tropical economy destroyed the prosperity fostered by the lime monoculture and had a great negative impact on interior agricultural activity. The much-vaunted diversity within the monoculture, while protecting the industry from a drop in price or demand of any one lime product, was not a safeguard against losses caused by the destruction of the tree itself.

Over four successive six-year periods, starting with 1915 to 1921 and ending with 1934 to 1939, average yearly production of limes fell from 400,000 barrels per year in the first period to 40,000 barrels per year in the last. A number of factors, emanating from both external sources and within the colony, combined to bring about a rapid and almost complete collapse of the lime industry.

The final blow to the lime industry came after 1930 when the United States, to protect its growing citrus industry, placed a tariff against lime juice imports. In addition, the perfection of a cheaper method of extracting citric acid from sugar shortly thereafter practically eliminated the market for concentrated lime juice and lime citrate, two products which had accounted for more than half the value of Dominica's lime exports.[5] The situation facing the lime industry now provoked ominous editorial comment in the *Dominica Tribune*.

What with Plant diseases, falling prices, and the harmful U.S.A. Tarriff, coupled with growing indications that citrate of lime is now being manufactured out of some commodity other than lime juice, the situation of the Lime Industry is indeed desperate.[6]

ENDNOTES

1. F. Sterns-Fadelle, *Dominica: A Fertile Island* (Roseau: Dominican Office) 1902, p. 95. Note that Dominica has only 195,000 acres).
2. Symington Grieve, *Notes (for investors) Upon the Island of Dominica* (London: A. & C. Black), 1906, p. 44
3. Francis Watts, "The Development of Dominica," in *West Indies Bulletin*, 15 (3), 1915, p. 206.
4. *Ibid*.
5. Arlin D. Fentem, *Commercial Geography of Dominica* (Bloomington, Indiana: University of Indiana) 1960, p. 6.
6. *Tribune* Jan. 1, 1929.

6.4

The Pressure of the Oil Industry
on Curaçao's Economy

Jaap Van Soest

That a single industry can often drastically alter the society as well as the economy of a Caribbean nation is dramatically borne out in this discussion of the oil industry in Curaçao. Van Soest traces the introduction of oil refining in the Netherlands Antilles and examines the widespread structural changes which ensued. This selection is excerpted from J. Van Soest (1978), Trustee of the Netherlands Antilles, *Willemstad, Curaçao, pp. 226-230. Reprinted by permission of the Author.*

The economic history of the Netherlands Antilles cannot in general be divided into clearcut episodes, but if one year must go down as a turning point it is 1915. That was the year in which the Royal Dutch/Shell Group decided to extend its activities to Curaçao. It marked the beginning of a new era for the entire Colony, for the whole community, and for all sectors of the economy.

Change did not come about abruptly in 1915. The oil refinery was a small, necessitous industry in the first few years and it was only from 1923 onwards that it began to grow into one of the largest oil-processing industries in the world. A second oil giant followed, and established itself after 1925 on Aruba. In the same way and just as unexpectedly as Curaçao, the previously so tranquil island of Aruba was hauled into the twentieth century. On the other islands of the Netherlands Antilles, by comparison, time seemed to stand still. Here, things became even quieter than they had been before, as many people left to find work on Curaçao

201

and Aruba, whence they kept up relations with those left
behind by means of postal money orders.

Oil brought employment, income, and purchasing power.
Everything connected with oil thrived: trade and the port,
building and the public utilities. But economic activities
which could not cater to the oil industry or its labour force
were doomed to fall into the background: crafts and home-
industry, agriculture and stockbreeding. In addition to the
almost traditional lack of capital and of innovative management, these sectors were now confronted with a dearth of
labour and what was for them an excessively high wage level.

The new prosperity required a complete adaptation of the
infrastructure. Harbours, roads and communications were
improved, education and health care were modernized, the
administrative apparatus was substantially enlarged, and legislation was brought into line with modern requirements. The
ancient desire for financial autonomy was realized, and it
could not be long before the political relationship between
the mother country and its colony was revised accordingly.
Full account was taken of the provenance of the bonanza:
the oil companies were given a vote on the Council of Administration, the Colonial Council, and the Chamber of
Commerce. But Bonaire and the Windward Islands, which the
oil industry had passed by, were rather badly served by the
central governments in Willemstad.

The Royal Dutch Company for the Exploitation of Petroleum Wells in the Netherlands East Indies, formed in 1890,
was engaged in fierce competition with the Standard Oil
Company of New Jersey at the beginning of this century.
The collaboration with Shell Oil, since 1902, and then the
amalgamation in 1907 were directly caused by this competition. Royal Dutch contributed 60% and British Shell 40%
to the new colossus, which soon had a network of companies
under it. The Group did good business but had insufficient
reserves to be able to satisfy demand in the longer term.
Therefore, it began to seek new oilfields around 1910. For
three reasons, these had to be in the middle of the western
hemisphere. Firstly, the existing oil production in Mexico
was threatened by political unrest. Secondly, the fields had

to be not too far from the American market, where the competitive war with Jersey Standard was being waged. And finally, the construction of the Panama Canal foreshadowed more shipping and a higher demand for oil in the region. When Royal Dutch/Shell was approached in 1912 for participation in Venezuelan explorations, it did not hesitate to decide.

In Venezuela, the dictators Castro and Gomez were handing out oil prospecting licences to friends and collaborators. Most of these were speculators, who sold their concessions to foreign companies. One of these companies did not have enough capital to undertake first the exploration and then the exploitation of a large concession it had acquired, and saw a powerful partner in Royal Dutch/Shell. The latter jumped at the opportunity, took the necessary organizational measures, and started prospecting. In April 1914 oil was struck at Mene Grande, near Lake Maracaibo.

Although formally there were three possible locations for a refinery, in fact only two were feasible. Trinidad was dropped because it was too far from the centres of activity, so that the areas around Lake Maracaibo and the Leeward Islands of the Netherlands Antilles remained. Royal Dutch/ Shell first thought of building a refinery in Venezuela and — because Lake Maracaibo was only accessible to smaller vessels — transhipment facilities for refined products on Curaçao. In September 1914 it was decided to build two tanks on Curaçao. It was only on 13 May 1915 that the decision was taken also to locate most of the oil processing facilities themselves on Curaçao. In Venezuela, for the time being, all that was built was a small refinery to satisfy domestic demand.[1]

In 1915 Royal Dutch/Shell had various reasons for locating its refinery on Curaçao. Even before the decision was taken, the local authorities — on the instructions of the Dutch Government — had exempted from import duty all oil and oil products and all materials for the construction and maintenance of plant, offices, housing, recreation facilities, etc.[2] An ideal site with ample room for expansion in all directions lay waiting on the shore of the Schottegat, one of the best natural harbours in the Caribbean. The large number of ships calling at Curaçao formed a potential clientèle for the refinery's principal product, fuel oil. The Venezuelan régime took no action to prevent the choice falling on Curaçao. Dictator Gomez was probably even pleased that for the time being no enclave of industry and prosperity would arise in the State of Zulia, which was far from Caracas and might otherwise grow into a breeding ground for separatist movements or revolutionary actions against his administration.[3] In the Netherlands, on the other hand, the Government did everything to make the choice of Curaçao as attractive as possible. The Government entertained good relations with Shell's top men; the subsidiary of Royal Dutch/Shell which was charged with oil processing had its head office in The Hague; and everyone was well aware that 60% of the Royal Dutch/Shell Group was of Dutch origin. So it was hardly any wonder that Royal Dutch/ Shell took the opportunity of settling on a piece of familiar Dutch territory in extending its activities and spreading its risks through the western hemisphere.

As soon as the decision had been taken, the oil company purchased the Asiento estate and the peninsula which extended from it into the Schottegat.[4] It began by building a few tanks on the peninsula, followed later by the refinery. The extensive lands of the estate were kept in reserve for the time being, and were used only as a water extraction area. Housing for expatriate staff from the Netherlands was built on a small island which was joined to Asiento by a causeway. A few landing stages were built off the coast of the peninsula.

From the opening of the refinery in 1918 until 1922, the Curaçaosche Petroleum Maatschappij (CPM, Shell's subsidiary in Curaçao) was a necessitous enterprise. Shell's main activities in the region were still concentrated in Mexico, the Venezuelan/Curaçao unit being no more than a standby. There was no regular supply of crude oil from Venezuela. Either the wells did not produce enough,[5] or CPM was left in the lurch by the primitive tanker fleet. The marginality of the Curaçao refinery for the Group as a whole is perhaps best illustrated by the composition of the fleet of the Curaçaosche Scheepvaart Maatschappij (CSM, Shell's shipping company in Curaçao) in those early years: simple wooden lighters, in fact no more than big bins which were towed backwards and forwards by tugs between Maracaibo and Willemstad, and later eight converted motor torpedo boats pensioned off after the World War.

There was on Curaçao no working class, in the sense of a group of people accustomed to engage in specific activities of an industrial nature at fixed times. In agriculture, in the port, and everywhere in traditional Curaçao, people worked when there was something to be done — and hence irregularly. In one of his first monthly reports the manager of the oil company complained: "Curaçao labour is very unsatisfactory and unreliable. People come to work when they please and neither good words nor fines can alter them in this respect." It was often the land whose call was heeded: "When a shower of rain has fallen, the blacks run off to their fields for planting."[6] The dubious chance of a maize harvest of one's own was more attractive than the sure wage paid by the oil company.

In addition to its problems with transport and staff, CPM in the first few years experienced teething troubles with the marketing of its products. Owing to a dearth of packing material (the familiar 5-gallon drums), it was at first unable to execute all orders; the poor maritime communications between the islands in the Caribbean were another inhibiting factor. To solve these problems a drum factory was built next to the refinery, and CPM obtained a special steamer for carrying packed products. On the domestic market of Curaçao, Shell immediately had to join battle with Jersey Standard in 1918 — to the advantage of the customer, who benefited from drastic price reductions.

The end of the precarious initial period came in view in 1922. The Royal Dutch/Shell Group began to shift the main theatre of its operations in the hemisphere from Mexico to Venezuela, where new and very large oil reserves were discovered.[7] Other companies also had their eyes on Venezuela at this time, but Shell was well ahead of them. Of all the crude oil extracted in Venezuela before 1920, more than three quarters had been shipped to the Shell refinery on Curaçao, and most of the rest had been processed in the Shell

refinery at San Lorenzo.[8] To exploit its lead, it was important for Shell to market the newly discovered Venezuelan
oil resources as quickly as possible. The installations on
Curaçao were soon operating at full capacity and parts of
them were enlarged. In October 1923, however, it was clear
that Venezuelan oil production was not merely to be increased somewhat but would be of a wholly different order
of magnitude from what it had been before. To match this
development, the construction of a brand-new refinery was
necessary. This was built at Asiento between 1924 and 1926.
But Venezuelan production went on increasing substantially,
and extension of the new refinery could not be avoided.
This third phase was about to be completed when the Great
Depression hit the oil company, in 1930.

The growth of the oil industry which commenced in 1923
appeared for seven years to be unstoppable. The extention of
the existing complex, the building of the new refinery, and the
enlargement of the new plant, succeeded each other almost
without a break. The vigorous expansion affected not only
the refinery itself but also the staff and the complementary
facilities, such as the CSM fleet, the tank farms, water supply,
and housing. It led to a fundamental change in the place of
the industry in Curaçao society. The Curaçao subsidiary of
the oil company also took up a new position within the
Royal Dutch/Shell Group, as witness the transformation of
CPM, which was established in the Netherlands, into the
Curaçao-based Curaçaosche Petroleum Industrie Maatschappij
(CPIM, commonly pronounced 'cépim').[9] The enclosure of
the premises with a high fence further demonstrated that the
pioneering days were gone for good.

Various problems which had dragged on during the initial
phase were now brought to satisfactory solutions. Curaçao
became a showpiece for Royal Dutch/Shell. It no longer
had to make do with patched-up secondhand boats but was
endowed with a fleet of tankers specially built for the Lake
trip. To maintain this fleet, CSM had a floating dock specially
built for it in the Netherlands, a second dock being ordered
later, when the first could no longer keep up with the work-
load.[10] To ensure a regular supply of crude oil for the refining installations, the tank farm was extended, its capacity

in 1930 being twenty times as much as it had been in 1922. Construction of subsidiary facilities further comprised new electricity works, a larger laboratory, an oxygen plant, two ice plants and a new barrel plant.

Large areas of land — all in all some 3000 hectares — were purchased to accommodate the plants, subsidiary installations, and residential quarters, but in particular for the purpose of obtaining well water. When water consumption increased faster than had been anticipated, CPIM began to use distilled seawater in addition to ground water; the first distillation plant was built in 1928. The oil company bought or acquired long leases on so many parcels of land and water in and on the Schottegat that the encirclement of Curaçao's principal port was virtually complete by 1930. In addition, for the shipment of its oil products, CPIM acquired the Caracasbaai and Bullenbaai, on the south coast of the island, where ships of unlimited size could easily moor.[11]

By worldwide custom Shell manned its refinery with expatriate staff, mostly of Dutch origin, resorting to local labour for the lower levels. As more labour was required for new construction and operations than Curaçao itself could supply, the company turned to Aruba and Bonaire, the Windward Islands, and Surinam. When the labour markets of the Dutch colonies began to get tighter and wage levels went up, CPIM began to look further afield in the region. Large numbers of unskilled workers came from Maracaibo and Coro; they lived together on a site near the refinery where no person from Curaçao dared to go — not even the military police — and where the Venezuelan rebel leader Urbina could readily lie low while preparing his successful attack on the garrison (1929). In addition to the Venezuelans, many British West Indians came, from Trinidad and Barbados and especially the Lesser Antilles; they were regarded as very reliable and employed preferentially as watchmen. Only a few dozen workers came to Curaçao from Santo Domingo and from the French and American Caribbean. Finally, in 1929, 50 Portuguese from Madiera landed at Curaçao; they quickly acquired an excellent reputation for their industry, obedience and temperate life style.[12]

ENDNOTES

1. For the first paragraph I have drawn on E. Lieuwen, *Petroleum in Venezuela: A History* (Berkeley, 1954); C. Gerretson, *Geshiedenis der 'Koninklijke'* Vol. 3 (Baarn, 1972); L. Vallenilla, *Auge, declinación y porvenir del petróleo Venezolano* (Caracas, 1973); and J.J. van Soest, *Olie als Water. De Curaçaosche economie in de eerste helft van de twintigste eeuw* (Curaçao, 1976).
2. *Official Gazette* 1914 No. 67 and 1915 No. 46.
3. *Vallenilla* 1973, p. 36.
4. It paid Dfl 40,000 for the estate (130 hectares) and Dfl 50,300 for the peninsula (25 hectares).
5. Figures in *Vallenilla* 1973, p. 70.
6. Curaçaosche Petroleum Maatschappij (CPM) — Monthly Refinery Report, October 1918.
7. F. Haussman, 'Latin American Oil in War and Peace', in *Foreign Affairs*, Vol. 21, no. 2, Jan. 1943, pp. 354-361; *Gerretson* 1973 (Vol. IV).
8. W.G.E. d'Artillac Brill, 'Economische toestand van Venezuela', in *Economische Verslagen von Nederlandsche diplomatieke en consulaire ambtenaren*, vol. 15, no. 17, 1922, pp. 585-619.
9. Deed of 9 March 1925: CPIM became 'Shell Curaçao' in 1959.
10. The Wilhelmina Dock (3000 tonnes, 1927) and the Juliana Dock (4000 tonnes, 1929).
11. Government Orders of 29 June 1925 No. 542, and of 4 July 1928 No. 670.
12. Figures for workers according to year and origin in CPIM's Annual Reports.

Control Through Dictatorship: Trujillo's Dominican Republic — Howard J. Wiarda

In the non-colonial Caribbean, the early years of the century also saw economic reorganization and structural changes, often to the advantage of a single individual or regime. A classic example of this phenomenon is provided by Rafael Trujillo of the Dominican Republic who represented himself to his nation, and especially to labor interests, as a 'populist' leader. Notwithstanding his self-assumed title, Trujillo held control by coercion and managed to use his office to acquire huge assets in the form of personal estates. Wiarda's description of Trujillo's tactics is reproduced from H.J. Wiarda (1968), Dictatorship and Development: The Methods of Control in Trujillo's Dominican Republic, *University Presses of Florida, pp. 174–177. Reprinted by permission of the Publisher.*

The Trujillo regime, 1930-61, was clearly an extremely severe and absolute kind of dictatorship. For thirty-one years Trujillo governed his country in an imperious fashion that has seldom been equaled; only in the last two years of his lengthy rule did the elaborate web of dictatorial controls which he had carefully fashioned and maintained for so long begin to come unraveled. It remains for us in this chapter to summarize the methods and techniques of his control, to recapitulate briefly the theoretical presentation of the introductory chapter and to see where the Trujillo dictatorship might fit within this conceptual framework, and to attempt to arrive at some conclusions as to the implications of the Trujillo regime both for the theory of dictatorship and for the Dominican Republic.

The Dominican Republic, prior to Trujillo's seizure of power, had remained essentially a traditional, semifeudal land. Poverty was widespread and the illiteracy rate was high. The economy was almost exclusively agricultural; the early stages of industrialization had hardly begun. The society was divided into two widely separated classes and consisted of a small group at the top, a large number at the bottom, and only a few in between. Modern kinds of organization such as political parties, a bureaucracy, a professional armed force, and associational interest groups were nonexistent or still in their infancy, and political power was determined most often by competing caudillos, in alliance with rival first family groups, who sought to muster enough force to take office.

Trujillo's own upbringing reflected the society in which he was born. Without much formal education, raised in a poverty-ridden agricultural village, of middle-class parents, Trujillo desired a more important rank both for himself and his nation. Employing his considerable talents as an administrator and organizer, he rose to power through the only channel open to ambitious youths who were outside the dominant elite but who sought to rise in prominence — the military. In 1930 he seized the presidency and during his lengthy tenure exercised dictatorial control over his country.

The primary pillar of Trujillo's control over the Dominican Republic was the armed forces. It was through the Marine-created constabulary that he had risen to prominence, with the backing of the army that he had seized the presidency, and by armed forces might that he remained in power. Under Trujillo the military became a huge, powerful, and well-organized force at the service of the dictatorship. The dictator never allowed the reins of control over the armed forces to slip from his own hands and used this juggernaut not so much for purposes of national defense but to impose a technologically advanced, all-pervasive terror over the domestic population.

The second major pillar of the Trujillo regime was his control over the entire governmental apparatus. With his army's help he gained the presidency and thereafter controlled absolutely the institutional and political machinery of the state. Notwithstanding the façade of constitutionallism and democracy, the constitution, the Congress, the courts, elections, the legal system, local and provincial administration, and the national bureaucracy were manipulated at Trujillo's whim. A single official party functioned as the political arm of the regime fulfilling certain special services for it. The entire system was a constitutional and democratic parody in which, despite appearances, Trujillo alone exercised authority.

The near-monopoly which Trujillo had over the national economy further cemented his hold over the country. The regime not only manipulated the economy for its own enrichment but used its predominance in agriculture, commerce, and industry to destroy or control real or potential opposition. In addition to his conversion of the country into a private fief or corporation, Trujillo kept all socioeconomic groups (the rural peasantry, the rural-urban workers, the middle sectors, and the elite) under his control. No group or association of interests was allowed an independent existence; no organized nucleus could be formed to rival or perhaps compete with the dictator's personal rule.

Trujillo's political philosophy was perhaps not a full-fledged ideology, as is Marxism, for example; and there were only limited efforts on the part of the regime to vigorously indoctrinate the mass of the population in an official set of beliefs. Despite these limitations, Trujillo's ideology did serve some purpose, the importance of which should not be underestimated. The principal ideas — nationalism, the need for peace, order, and stability, the organic state, material progress, corporativism, the deification of the leader and the personification of him as the essence of the nation, "true" freedom and democracy — provided not just a rationale for his own practices but also a set of goals and aspirations which rallied Dominican nationalism and patriotism. Furthermore, his ideology was believed by wide sectors of the population to embody all that was worth knowing, and proved an effective propaganda device for bettering the Trujillo image abroad as well.

The ideology took on added importance when considered in the light of his highly developed system of thought control. Through his monopoly over education, intellectual life, and the communications media, through his extensive use of public relations, particularly concentrated on the United States, and through his mutually supporting arrangement with the Church, Trujillo deprived his people of free choice, forced the cult of the leader to permeate almost all aspects of existence, and maintained nearly absolute control over all aspects of thought. In these respects the Trujillo regime was tending more and more toward modern totalitarianism.

The Trujillo system was, however, eventually overthrown. The string of fallen Latin American strong men tended to make the Dominican dictatorship an anachronism in the late 1950's. The exile organizations increased in strength, and the Galíndez-Murphy affair resulted in a barrage of unfavorable publicity for Trujillo. The sanctions voted by the Organization of American States and the actions eventually taken by the United States further increased the pressure. As the external opposition to Trujillo increased, internal opposition grew as well. Important sectors in the business-professional-landowning elite, middle-sector merchants, elements in the government service, in the Church, and in the armed forces became disenchanted with the regime and began to plot its overthrow. When the external and internal opposition coalesced, the dictator fell; on the night of May 30, 1961, he was brutally assassinated.

The Trujillo regime, as hardly needs re-emphasis, was a very tightly knit dictatorship. The personal power of the dictator was nearly absolute. The elaborate controls which were established over the armed forces, the governmental machinery, the national economy, communications, education, intellectual life, and thought processes, together with the longtime harmonious and beneficial arrangement with the Church, meant that no group, institution, or individual could effectively function independent of Trujillo's controls. The extensiveness of these controls helps explain the longevity of his rule.

Trujillo's total system of control, however was considerably greater than merely the sum of its parts. Trujillo's own considerable talents as a leader and organizer enabled him to weld together the military, political-governmental, economic, communications, educational-intellectual, religious, and ideological aspects of his era into a tightly knit, interlocking pattern which was probably as absolute and as unbreakable as the world had ever seen. Trujillo's dictatorship was, in the words of Robert D. Crassweller, based upon a "honeycomb of power," with all the cells joined together and harmonized and each buttressing the others. The strength and endurance of the various components were as nothing compared with the structure as a whole. The entire system remained under the absolute personal control of Trujillo.

SECTION 7
Caribbean Reactions:
The Awakening of Consciousness and
the Beginning of Nationalism in
the pre-World War II Period

7.0
Introduction to Section 7

One of the most pervasive themes of twentieth-century writing is the desire for self-determination intellectually, politically and economically among colonial peoples. In the Caribbean, such expressions of early nationalism were abundant, although these precocious statements often went unnoticed by the mainstream public. Marcus Garvey, like many early visionaries, was initially vilified for his recognition of the positive contribution of African culture to the shaping of the Caribbean and Afro-American experience. Jamaican-born, Garvey achieved world recognition only after he established himself in the United States and formed the Universal Negro Improvement Association. While critics of the day condemned Garvey for his 'seditious' views, today Garvey is considered one of Jamaica's National Heroes for his positive role in achieving political rights for Afro-Americans hemispherically. Selection 7.1 contains one of Garvey's most famous declarations of his view of future equality.

In Cuba, contemporaneously, Fernando Ortiz was exploring Afro-American themes in his analysis of Cuban culture and economy. His intellectual and literary treatment of such prosaic matters as the sugar and tobacco industries (in selection 7.2) identifies him as an early nationalist writer, more concerned with Cuban than European themes. Many of the writers of this period, such as Luis Palés Matos of Puerto Rico, turned their attention to African culture for inspiration. This writing genre is known broadly as Négritude; the products of such fertile artistic imaginations did much to alert the public to the contribution of the African background in the development of Caribbean culture.

At the same time, nationalistic themes appeared in the rhetoric of formative worker's groups, which eventually emerged as unions demanding political and economic rights. Certainly the syndicalization of labor is not a phenomenon unique to the Caribbean nor is its appearance out of synchronization with the movement globally. However, the emergence of such unions in the British West Indies had several unique elements, not the least of which was the organization of labour, which was more peasant and agriculturally based than industrial. This process, along with the rise of strong labor leaders, is explored in selection 7.3. The student should also bear in mind that in Cuba and the Dominican Republic during this time period, the emergence of populist leaders, with strong labor support, had evolved into full-scale dictatorship.

There are many wonderful works available to read on the awakening of Caribbean consciousness. C. MacKay, *Banana Bottom* is an excellent starting point, as this novel explicitly rejects European themes in favor of local culture. Marcus Garvey's writings and commentaries on his influence have recently been collected and edited by J.H. Clarke, *Marcus Garvey and the Vision of Africa*. The experience of a Caribbean labor leader in the Spanish-speaking islands is the subject of C. Senior, *Santiago Iglesias: Labor Crusader*. Two offerings that explore nationalistic themes and politics in a more recent context are R. Nettleford, *Identity, Race and Protest in Jamaica* and L. Despres, *Cultural Pluralism and Nationalist Politics in British Guiana*.

The Future As I See It — Marcus Garvey

Marcus Garvey's famous vision of the future contains an impassioned plea for economic as well as political independence for black peoples universally. Conscious of the need to release the ties of industrial and commercial bondage, Garvey promoted the establishment of totally black-owned enterprises and pioneered in this goal with the creation of his Black Star Line Steamship Company. This speech is reprinted from M. Garvey (1967), The Philosophy and Opinions of Marcus Garvey *compiled by A.J. Garvey, 2nd edition, Frank Cass and Co Ltd. Reprinted by permission of the Publisher.*

It comes to the individual, the race, the nation, once in a life time to decide upon the course to be pursued as a career. The hour has now struck for the individual Negro as well as the entire race to decide the course that will be pursued in the interests of our own liberty.

We who make up the Universal Negro Improvement Association have decided that we shall go forward, upward and onward toward the great goal of human liberty. We have determined among ourselves that all barriers placed in the way of our progress must be removed, must be cleared away for we desire to see the light of a brighter day.

THE NEGRO IS READY

The Universal Negro Improvement Association for five years has been proclaiming to the world the readiness of the Negro to carve out a pathway for himself in the course of life. Men of other races and nations have become alarmed at this attitude of the Negro in his desire to do things for himself and by himself. This alarm has become so universal that organizations have been brought into being here, there and everywhere for the purpose of deterring and obstructing this forward move of our race. Propaganda has been waged here, there and everywhere for the purpose of misinterpreting the intention of this organization; some have said that this organization seeks to create discord and discontent among the races; some say we are organized for the purpose of hating other people. Every sensible, sane and honest-minded person knows that the Universal Negro Improvement Association has no such intention. We are organized for the absolute purpose of bettering our condition, industrially, commercially, socially, religiously and politically. We are organized not to hate other men, but to lift ourselves, and to demand respect of all humanity. We have a program that we believe to be righteous; we believe it to be just, and we have made up our minds to lay down ourselves on the altar of sacrifice for the realization of this great hope of ours, based upon the foundation of righteousness. We declare to the world that Africa must be free, that the entire Negro race must be emancipated from industrial bondage, peonage and serfdom; we make no compromise, we make no apology in this our declaration. We do not desire to create offense on the part of other races, but we are determined that we shall be heard, that we shall be given the rights to which we are entitled.

THE PROPAGANDA OF OUR ENEMIES

For the purpose of creating doubts about the work of the Universal Negro Improvement Association, many attempts have been made to cast shadow and gloom over our work. They have even written the most uncharitable things about our organization; they have spoken so unkindly of our effort, but what do we care? They spoke unkindly and uncharitably about all the reform movements that have helped in the betterment of humanity. They maligned the great movement of the Christian religion; they maligned the great liberation movements of America, of France, of England, of Russia; can we expect, then, to escape being maligned in this, our desire for the liberation of Africa and the freedom of four hundred million Negroes of the world?

We have unscrupulous men and organizations working in opposition to us. Some trying to capitalize the new spirit that has come to the Negro to make profit out of it to their own selfish benefit; some are trying to set back the Negro from seeing the hope of his own liberty, and thereby poisoning our people's mind against the motives of our organization; but every sensible far-seeing Negro in this enlightened age knows what propaganda means. It is the medium of discrediting that which you are opposed to, so that the propaganda of our enemies will be of little avail as soon as we are rendered able to carry to our peoples scattered throughout the world the true message of our great organization.

"CROCODILES" AS FRIENDS

Men of the Negro race, let me say to you that a greater future is in store for us; we have no cause to lose hope, to become faint-hearted. We must realize that upon ourselves depend our destiny, our future; we must carve out that future, that destiny, and we who make up the Universal Negro Improvement Association have pledged ourselves that nothing in the world shall stand in our way, nothing in the world shall discourage us, but opposition shall make us work harder, shall bring us closer together so that as one man the millions of us will march on toward that goal that we have set for ourselves. The new Negro shall not be deceived. The new Negro refuses to take advice from anyone who has not felt with him, and suffered with him. We have suffered for three hundred years, therefore we feel that the time has come when only those who have suffered with us can interpret our feelings and our spirit. It takes the slave to interpret the feelings of the slave; it takes the unfortunate man to interpret the spirit of his unfortunate brother; and so it takes the suffering Negro to interpret the spirit of his comrade. It is strange that so many people are interested in the Negro now, willing to advise him how to act, and what organizations he should join, yet nobody was interested in the Negro to the extent of not making him a slave for two hundred and fifty years, reducing him to industrial peonage and serfdom after he was freed; it is strange that the same people can be so interested in the Negro now, as to tell him what organization he should follow and what leader he should support.

Whilst we are bordering on a future of brighter things, we are also at our danger period, when we must either accept the right philosophy, or go down by following deceptive propaganda which has hemmed us in for many centuries.

DECEIVING THE PEOPLE

There is many a leader of our race who tells us that everything is well, and that all things will work out themselves and that a better day is coming. Yes, all of us know that a better day is coming; we all know that one day we will go home to Paradise, but whilst we are hoping by our Christian virtues to have an entry into Paradise we also realize that we are living on earth, and that the things that are practised in Paradise are not practised here. You have to treat this world as the world treats you; we are living in a temporal, material age, an age of activity, an age of racial, national selfishness. What else can you expect but to give back to the world what the world gives to you, and we are calling upon the four hundred million Negroes of the world to take a decided stand, a determined stand, that we shall occupy a firm position; that position shall be an emancipated race and a free nation of our own. We are determined that we shall have a free country; we are determined that we shall have a flag; we are determined that we shall have a government second to none in the world.

AN EYE FOR AN EYE

Men may spurn the idea, they may scoff at it; the metropolitan press of this country may deride us; yes, white men may laugh at the idea of Negroes talking about government; but let me tell you there is going to be a government, and let me say to you also that whatsoever you give, in like measure it shall be returned to you. The world is sinful, and therefore man believes in the doctrine of an eye for an eye, a tooth for a tooth. Everybody believes that revenge is God's, but at the same time we are men, and revenge sometimes springs up, even in the most Christian heart.

Why should man write down a history that will react against him? Why should man perpetrate deeds of wickedness upon his brother which will return to him in like measure? Yes, the Germans maltreated the French in the Franco-Prussian war of 1870, but the French got even with the Germans in 1918. It is history, and history will repeat itself. Beat the Negro, brutalize the Negro, kill the Negro, burn the Negro, imprison the Negro, scoff at the Negro, deride the Negro, it may come back to you one of these fine days, because the supreme destiny of man is in the hands of God. God is no respecter of persons, whether that person be white, yellow or black. Today the one race is up, tomorrow it has fallen; today the Negro seems to be the footstool of the other races and nations of the world; tomorrow the Negro may occupy the highest rung of the great human ladder.

But when we come to consider the history of man, was not the Negro a power, was he not great once? Yes, honest students of history can recall the day when Egypt, Ethiopia and Timbuctoo towered in their civilizations, towered above Europe, towered above Asia. When Europe was inhabited by a race of cannibals, a race of savages, naked men, heathens and pagans, Africa was peopled with a race of cultured black men, who were masters in art, science and literature; men who were cultured and refined; men who, it was said, were like the gods. Even the great poets of old sang in beautiful sonnets of the delight it afforded the gods to be in companionship with the Ethiopians. Why, then, should we lose hope? Black men, you were once great; you shall be great again. Lose not courage, lose not faith, go forward. The thing to do is to get organized; keep separated and you will be exploited, you will be robbed, you will be killed. Get organized, and you will compel the world to respect you. If the world fails

to give you consideration, because you are black men, because you are Negroes, four hundred millions of you shall, through organization, shake the pillars of the universe and bring down creation, even as Samson brought down the temple upon his head and upon the heads of the Philistines.

AN INSPIRING VISION

So Negroes, I say, through the Universal Negro Improvement Association, that there is much to live for. I have a vision of the future, and I see before me a picture of a redeemed Africa, with her dotted cities, with her beautiful civilization, with her millions of happy children, going to and fro. Why should I lose hope, why should I give up and take a back place in this age of progress? Remember that you are men, that God created you Lords of this creation. Lift up yourselves, men, take yourselves out of the mire and hitch your hopes to the stars; yes, rise as high as the very stars themselves. Let no man pull you down, let no man destroy your ambition, because man is but your companion, your equal; man is your brother; he is not your lord; he is not your sovereign master.

We of the Universal Negro Improvement Association feel happy; we are cheerful. Let them connive to destroy us; let them organize to destroy us; we shall fight the more. Ask me personally the cause of my success, and I say opposition; oppose me, and I fight the more, and if you want to find out the sterling worth of the Negro, oppose him, and under the leadership of the Universal Negro Improvement Association he shall fight his way to victory, and in the days to come, and I believe not far distant, Africa shall reflect a splendid demonstration of the worth of the Negro, of the determination of the Negro, to set himself free and to establish a government of his own.

Cuban Counterpoint: Tobacco and Sugar

Fernando Ortiz

That the economy exerts a profound influence on the shape of society is apparent in Fernando Ortiz's classic account of Cuba. The differences in the production methods of sugar and tobacco account for the differences in those sectors of the Cuban social structure which dealt with these commodities. The demanding nature of the sugar crop required large amounts of labor and capital and thus, in Cuba, resulted in a reliance on outside funding. For Ortiz, this reliance had clear political implications, and in this selection he argues from a clearly economic nationalist position. From F. Ortiz (1947), Cuban Counterpoint: Tobacco and Sugar *(trans. De Onis), pp. 55-65. Reprinted by permission of the publisher, Alfred A. Knopf. Copyright © 1947.*

The social consequences deriving from tobacco and sugar in Cuba and originating in the different conditions under which the two crops are produced can be easily grasped. The contrast between the *vegas* where tobacco is grown and the sugar plantation, particularly if it is a modern *central*, is striking. Tobacco gave origin to a special type of agricultural life. There is not the great human agglomeration in the tobacco region that is to be found around the sugar plants. This is due to the fact that tobacco requires no machinery; it needs no mills, nor elaborate physical and chemical equipment, nor railway transport systems. The *vega* is a geographical term; the *central* is a term of mechanics.

In the production of tobacco intelligence is the prime factor; we have already observed that tobacco is liberal, not to say revolutionary. In the production of sugar it is a question of power; sugar is conservative, if not reactionary.

I repeat, the production of sugar was always a capitalistic venture because of its great territorial and industrial scope and the size of its long-term investments. Tobacco, child of the savage Indian and the virgin earth, is a free being, bowing its neck to no mechanical yoke, unlike sugar, which is ground to bits by the mill. This has occasioned profound economic and social consequences.

In the first place, tobacco was raised on the land best suited for the purpose, without being bound to a great indispensable industrial plant that was stationary and remained "planted" even after it had impoverished all the land about it. This gave rise to the *central*, which even in olden times was at least a village, and today is a city. The *vega* was never anything but a rural holding, like a garden. The *vega* was small; it was never the site of latifundia, but belonged to small property-owners. The *central* required a plantation; in the *vega* a small farm was enough. The owners of a *central* are known as *hacendados* and live in the city; those of the *vegas* remained *monteros, sitieros,* or *guajiros* and never left their rural homes.

The cultivation of tobacco demands a yearly cycle of steady work by persons who are skilled and specialized in this activity. Tobacco is often smoked to kill time, but in the tobacco industry there is no such thing as "dead time," as is the case with sugar. This, together with the circumstance that the *vega* was a small holding, has developed in the *veguero* a strong attachment to his land, as in the rancher of old, and made it possible for him to carry on his tasks with the help of members of his family. Only when this is not feasible does he hire workers, but in small groups, never in gangs or by the hundred, as happens with sugar cane. The *vega*, I repeat, is merely a topographical denomination; the *colonia* is a term having complex political and social connotations.

For these same reasons, while during slavery Negroes were employed as sugar-plantation hands, the cultivation of the *vegas* was based on free, white labor. Thus tobacco and sugar each have racial connections. Tobacco is an inheritance received from the Indian, which was immediately used and esteemed by the Negro, but cultivated and commercialized by the white man. The Indians at the time of the discovery raised tobacco in their gardens, considering it "a very holy thing," in the words of Oviedo, distinguishing between the mild cultivated variety and the stronger wild species, according to Cobo. The whites were familiar with it, but did not develop a taste for it at once. "It is a thing for savages." The historians of the Indies did not smoke, and some abominated the habit. Benzoni tells that the smell of tobacco was so offensive to him that he would run to get away from it. When Las Casas wrote his *Apologética Historia de las Indias*, in the second quarter of the sixteenth century, he called attention to the unusual fact that he had known "an upright, married Spaniard on this island who was in the habit of using tobacco and the smoke from it, just as the Indians did, and who said that because of the great benefit he derived from it he would not give it up for anything."

It was the Negroes of Hispaniola who quickly came to esteem the qualities of tobacco and not only copied from the Indians the habit of smoking it, but were the first to cultivate it on their owners' plantations. They said it "took away their weariness," to use Oviedo's words. But the Spaniards still looked askance at it. "Negro stuff."

In Cuba the same thing probably happened; tobacco was a thing for "Indians and Negroes," and only later, as it worked its way up from the lower strata of society, did the whites develop a taste for it. But by the middle of the sixteenth century in Havana, where each year the Spanish fleets assembled and set out across the ocean in convoy, tobacco had already become an article of trade, and it was the Negroes who carried on the business. The whites realized that they were missing a good venture, and the authorities issued ordinances forbidding the Negroes to go on selling tobacco to the fleets. The Negro could no longer sell or cultivate tobacco except for his own use; the Negro could not be a merchant. From then on, the cultivation and trade in tobacco was the economic privilege of the white man.

Sugar was mulatto from the start, for the energies of black men and white always went into its production. Even though it was Colombus who brought the first sugar cane into the

Antilles from the Canary Islands, sugar was not a Spanish plant, nor even European. It was native to Asia, and from there it was carried along the Mediterranean by the Arabs and Moors. For the cultivation of the cane and the extraction of its juice the help of stout slaves and serfs was required, and in Portugal, as in Spain and Sicily in Europe, in Mauritania and Egypt in Africa, in Arabia, Mesopotamia, Persia, and India in Asia, these workers were as a rule of Negroid stock, those dark people who from prehistoric times had penetrated into that long strip of supertropical areas and gave them their permanent dark coloring, the same stock that in the Middle Ages invaded it anew with the waves of Moslems, who never felt any hostile racial prejudice toward the Negro. Sugar cane and Negro slaves arrived together in the island of Cuba, and possibly in Hispaniola, from across the sea. And since then Negro labor and sugar cane have been two factors in the same economic binomial of the social equation of our country.

For centuries the workers in the *centrals* were exclusively Negroes; often even the overseers were colored. This was true of the mill workers as well as of the field workers, with the exception of the technicians and the management. It was not until the abolishment of slavery, the influx of Spanish immigrants after the Ten Years' War, and the introduction of the sharecropping system that white farmers were to be found on the Cuban sugar plantations.

The nineteenth century in Cuba was marked by the change in the labor system brought about by the prohibition of the slave trade and, much later, by the abolition of slavery and the substitution for it of hired workers. The abolition was proclaimed by the Cubans fighting a war of secession against the mother country, and later by Spain in 1880-6. The cessation of the slave trade coincided with the introduction of the steam engine, which increased the productive capacity of the mills, and the abolition of slavery (1886) was simultaneous with the use of steel rails and the development of the railroads, which increased the radius of activity of the *centrals*. Cheap labor was an imperative need, so Spain, no longer able to smuggle in slaves or bring in more Chinese coolies or peons from Yucatán, began to export her own white laborers. As a result the proportion of Negroes in the Cuban population began to diminish. In the distribution of colored population in Cuba today the greatest density is to be found in the old sugar-growing sectors, not in the tobacco-raising areas, which were settled in the main by white immigrants from the Canary Islands and peasants of old Cuban stock. Tobacco drew upon the free white population, whereas for sugar cane black slaves were imported. This also explains why there are no invasions of migrant seasonal workers in the tobacco industry, and still less of Haitians and Jamaicans, who were brought in to make the harvesting of cane cheaper.

It must also be set down that the union between sugar and the Negro had nothing to do with the latter's race or pigmentation; it was due solely to the fact that for centuries Negroes were the most numerous, available, and strongest slaves, and cane was cultivated by them throughout America. When there were no Negroes, or even together with them, slaves of other races were to be found on the plantations — Berbers, Moors, mulattoes. The alliance was not between the canefield and the Negro, but between the canefield and the slave. Sugar spelled slavery; tobacco, liberty. And if on the tobacco plantations of Virginia along with the black slaves there were white ones, purchased in England with bales of tobacco, on the sugar plantations of the British West Indies there were also black and white slaves, Irish condemned to slavery by Cromwell, and even Englishmen who had been sold for 1,550 pounds of sugar a head; or, as we would put it today, the price of an Englishman was five sacks of sugar. This did not happen in Cuba. There may have been an occasional white slave there, more probably a white female slave, in the early days of the colony, but not afterwards; and although it is true that there were near-white mulattoes who were still slaves, the whiteness of the skin was always the sign of emancipation in Cuba.

The seasonal nature of the work involved in sugar, in both the fields and the mill, is likewise very characteristic and of great social consequence. The cutting is not continuous, and whereas it used to last almost half a year, it is now almost never longer than a hundred days, and even less since legal restrictions have been placed upon it. All the rest of the year is "dead time." When it is finished, the workers who came to Cuba for the harvest in swallow-like migration leave the country, taking their savings with them, and the native proletariat goes through a long stretch of unemployment and constant insecurity. A large part of the working class of Cuba has to live all year on the wages earned during two or three months, and the whole lower class suffers from this seasonal work system, being reduced to a state of poverty, with an inadequate, vitamin-deficient diet consisting principally of rice, beans, and tubers, which leave it undernourished and the ready prey of hook-worm, tuberculosis, anemia, malaria, and other diseases. This does not occur to the same degree with the tobacco workers, for both the agricultural and the industrial activities require steadier work; but even so, unfortunately for the country, they are also coming to suffer from undernourishment.

The unflagging devotion of the tobacco-grower to his field, his constant concern with weather and climatic conditions, the painstaking manual care the plant requires, have prevented the development of the *vegas* into great plantations, with great capital investments and submission to foreign control. González del Valle writes that "there is not one known case of an American or other foreigner who has grown rich cultivating tobacco in Cuba; as a matter of fact, foreigners who have tried it have lost most if not all of their capital." There are foreign landowners, but they are not the growers, with the exception of a few Spaniards who became quickly naturalized because of their easy adaptability to Cuban ways. Tobacco has always been more Cuban than sugar. It has been pointed out that tobacco is native to the New World, while sugar was brought in from the Old.

Foreign predominance in the sugar industry was always great, and now it is almost exclusive. Tobacco has always been more Cuban because of its origin, its character, and its economy. The reason is obvious. Sugar has always required a large capital investment; today it amounts to a veritable fortune. A century ago a well-balanced *central* could be set up with a hundred thousand pesos; today the industrial plant alone is worth a million. Moreover, ever since the *centrals* were first established in America, all their equipment, with the exception of the land, has had to be brought in from abroad. Machinery, workers, capital, all have to be imported, and this makes necessary an even larger outlay. If the sugar industry was capitalistic in its beginnings, with the improvement in mechanical techniques and the introduction of the steam engine more elaborate mills were required, more canefields, more land, more slaves, greater investments and reserves — in a word, more and more capital. The entire history of sugar in Cuba, from the first day has been the struggle originated by the introduction of foreign capital and its overwhelming influence on the island's economy. And it was not Spanish capital, but foreign: that of the Genoese, the Germans, the Flemings, the English, the Yankees, from the days of the Emperor Charles V and his bankers, the Fuggers, to our own "good-neighbor" days and the Wall Street financiers.

Even in the palmy days of the Cuban landowning aristocracy, which sometimes unexpectedly acquired fabulous fortunes and titles of nobility through their *centrals*, the sugar-planters always suffered a certain amount of foreign overlordship. The sugar they produced was not consumed in our country and had to be shipped raw to foreign markets, where it became the booty of the refiners, without whose intervention it could not enter the world market. The sugar-planter needed the underwriter, and he, in turn, the rich banker. As early as the middle of the sixteenth century the sugar-planters were requesting loans of the brokers of Seville and of the kings, not only to continue with their enterprises, but even to set them up. This was another factor that contributed to sugar's foreignness. Its capitalist character obliged it to seek abroad the creditors and bankers not to be found here or who, when they existed, were merely agents of the brokers of Cádiz or the English refiners, who supplied machinery and financial support but who through their loans at usurious rates could dictate their own terms and prices from London and Liverpool, and later from New York. When María de las Mercedes, the Countess of Merlin, wrote her *Viaje a la Habana*, well along in the nineteenth century, she was amazed at the fact that the rate of interest charged the Cuban planters by foreign loan-brokers was thirty per cent a year, or two and a half per cent a month.

By the end of the Ten Years' War, when through the progress in metallurgical techniques the great mills and the networks of railways were introduced in the *centrals*, the capital required for a venture of this sort was enormous, beyond the possibilities of any one person. This brought about three economic-social developments: the revival of the sharecropping system of cultivation, the anonymous stockholders' corporations, and the direct control of foreign capital over the management and ordering of the *centrals*. And finally, as a result of the financial depression after the first World War, industrial and mercantile capitalism was replaced by the supercapitalism of banks and financial companies, which today constitute the foreign plutocracy that controls the economic life of Cuba. One of the effects of this has been the greater dependence of the tenant farmer, who, according to Maxwell, received his fairest share of returns in Cuba, his gradual disappearance, and, finally, the complete proletarianization of the workers in the *central*, from the fields to the mill, where an executive proconsul holds sway as the representative of a distant and imperial power. The "foreignness" of the sugar industry in Cuba is even greater than that of Puerto Rico, which is actually under the sovereignty of the United States.

The foreign control of the *central* is not only external but internal as well. To use the language in vogue today, it has a vertical structure. There are not merely the decisions of policy taken by the sugar companies in the United States, from that radiating center of moneyed power known as Wall Street, but the legal ownership of the *central* is also foreign. The bank that underwrites the cutting of the cane is foreign, the consumers' market is foreign, the administrative staff set up in Cuba, the machinery that is installed, the capital that is invested, the very land of Cuba held by foreign ownership and enfeoffed to the *central*, all are foreign, as are, logically enough, the profits that flow out of the country to enrich others. The process does not end here; in some of the *supercentrals* even the workers are foreigners, who have been brought into Cuba, under a new form of slavery, from Haiti and Jamaica, or by immigration, from Spanish villages.

This foreignness is further aggravated by absentee landlordism. There were already absentee owners a century ago, who lived at ease in Havana, leaving the mill in the hands of a manager. But since 1882, when a North American, Atkins, bought the Soledad *central*, becoming the first Yankee planter of Cuba, absentee landlordism has been on the increase and has become more permanent, more distant, more foreign, and, in consequence, more deleterious in its social effects on the country.

Before, this absentee landlordism was periodically attenuated by inheritance, through which, upon the death of the planter, this accumulated wealth returned to society through his children and heirs. This is not so any longer, for the planter, if this name can be given to the organization that in the eyes of the law is the owner of the *central*, is born outside the country and dies a foreigner, and even has no heirs if it is a corporation. The great wealth of capital needed for these *supercentrals* could not be raised in Cuba, and the tendency toward productive capitalism could not be held in check from within. And so the sugar industry became increasingly denaturalized and passed into anonymous, corporative, distant, dehumanized, all-powerful hands, with little or no sense of responsibility.

By 1850 the trade of Cuba with the United States was greater than that with the mother country, Spain, and the United States assumed for all time its natural place, given geographical conditions, as the principal consumer of Cuba's production as well as its economic center. In 1851 the Consul General of Cuba in the United States wrote officially that Cuba was an economic colony of the United States, even though politically it was still governed by Spain. From then on sugar for North American consumption was king in Cuba, and its tariffs played a greater part in our political life than all the constitutions, as though the whole country were one huge mill, and Cuba merely the symbolic name of a great *central* controlled by a foreign stockholders' corporation.

Even today the most pressing problem confronting the Cuban Treasury Department is that of being able to collect its revenues by levying them directly against the sources of wealth and their earnings, making no exception of foreign holdings, instead of continuing the indirect taxes that fall so burdensomely upon the Cuban people and fleece it. Cuba will never be really independent until it can free itself from the coils of the serpent of colonial economy that fattens on its soil but strangles its inhabitants and winds itself about the palm tree of our republican coat of arms, converting it into the sign of the Yankee dollar.

The Emergence of Labour Unions in the British West Indies

Zin Henry

The relationship between the unionization process and the development of nationalist politics is examined in this selection. Clearly, the role of union leaders in redrawing social patterns and allegiances in the West Indies is an important theme of the 1930s. The confidence gained during this organizational period is best demonstrated by the call for West Indian federation, raised by regional union leaders meeting in British Guiana in 1938. Reprinted from Z. Henry (1972), Labour Relations and Industrial Conflict in Commonwealth Caribbean Countries, *pp. 37-46. Copyright © 1972 by the Columbus Publishers, Ltd., Trinidad and reproduced by permission of the Publisher and Author.*

The firm roots of trade unionism in British Caribbean territories grew out of the general labour disturbances and riots of the thirties which were alluded to in Chapter 1. While it happened that in general these disturbances originated and expanded spontaneously with neither formal union organization nor leadership behind them, before they ended, potential labour leaders had emerged in the various territories and broad organizational bases had revealed themselves. Emerging from these disturbances also was the leadership pattern which seemed most likely to succeed in cracking the walls of the traditional socio-economic structure. The main qualifications of future and would-be trade union leaders, though unwritten, seemed obvious. They had to be persons with the courage and willingness to denounce and engage in combat with, not excluding physical combat, the propertied ruling class.

In Jamaica, A.C. Bustamante, one of the main agitators during the disturbances in that colony, fitted the specifications perfectly. His dramatic, flamboyant, and charismatic image was custom-built for the vacancy which he automatically filled without application and in temporary absentia; for it was while he was temporarily incarcerated in May 1938 that the dock workers were advised to form themselves into a trade union under the leadership of Bustamante. In Trinidad the messianic T. Uriah ("Buz") Butler, also fitted the specifications admirably but failed to carry through, after the riots, in consolidating workers' agitation into a vibrant trade union movement. Others filled the vacancy instead. About a decade later, "Uncle" Eric Gairy filled similar specifications in Grenada. In some cases middle-class nationalists and professionals tried to fill the vacancies with varying degrees of success.

The riots resulted in, as it were, an overnight mushrooming of trade unions in most of the territories. Even in situations where there was no trade union law giving legitimacy to trade unions, or where the law carried the handicaps of illegal picketing and damages in actions of tort, trade unions were formed. A feeling of power was felt by the masses even if that power was merely imaginary.

It will be recalled that the first phase of rioting began in Trinidad in 1934. In the year of the second phase in Trinidad, that is 1937, most of the unions which were later to become major unions in that country came into existence, despite the fact that the Ordinance of 1932 underwent no change. Among these were The Oilfield Workers' Trade Union, The All Trinidad Sugar Estates and Factories Workers' Trade Union, The Seamen and Waterfront Workers' Trade Union[1] and The Federated Workers' Trade Union. Within a year thereafter, over a dozen trade unions had been registered including, in addition to those mentioned above, the Public Works and Public Service Workers' Union which was second in size only to the O.W.T.U. Of the rest, a Printers' Union, a Transport and General Workers Union, and a Shop Assistant and Clerks Union were the most important ones. In addition, a coordinating Committee known as The Committee for Industrial Organization was formed by the major unions in that same year (1938) which, by mid-1939, evolved into a Trade Union Council comprising some 10 union affiliates and a total membership of over 11,000.[2] It is perhaps of some interest to refer here to a memorandum submitted by the Committee for Industrial Organization to the West India (Moyne) Royal Commission in 1938, because it revealed a nascent trade union movement already seized with a basic philosophy and perspective which augured well for future development. This memorandum emphasized and recommended nationalization of the two main industries of the territory — sugar and oil.

During the war years, that is World War II, most of the major unions in Trinidad and Tobago consolidated themselves into truly workers' organizations with emphasis on economic gains, notwithstanding involvement of some of the leaders in political activities. But perhaps the most striking feature of these formative years, was the number of different unions with which certain top labour leaders were simultaneously associated. For example, A. Cola Rienzi, first President-General of the Oilfields Workers' Trade Union, was at the same time first President-General of the All Trinidad Sugar Estates and Factories Workers' Trade Union. A few Executive members of the Oil union were also Executive members of the Sugar union. John Rojas, President of the Trade Union Council, was at the same time President-General of the Transport and General Workers' Union and Executive Member (later President-General) of the O.W.T.U. Quintin O'Connor, Secretary of the Trade Union Council, was also Secretary of the Shop Assistant and Clerks Union and later President of the Federated Workers' Trade Union; and so on.

As it was in Trinidad, a number of unions emerged in Guyana following immediately upon the riots. Critchlow's British Guiana Labour Union, mainly a union of waterfront workers, was of course already in existence. A sugar workers' union was organized in 1937 by one Ayube Edun. This union, The Manpower Citizens Association, gained recognition in 1939 from the Sugar Producers Association, which was formed in that same year, soon after rioting on sugar estates in Guyana. The formative years of the union were indeed a period of great turbulence and militancy. Within a year after its registration it was engaged in some 37 strikes on one estate only (Leonora Estate) and within the first 5 years of its existence it had passed the 20,000 mark in membership. It was not long in surpassing the British Guiana Labour Union as the leading trade union in Guyana. In 1941 the MPCA acquired a printery and established a newspaper (The Labour Advocate) as its official news organ.[3]

By the end of World War II, however, dissension had set in. An officer had been accused of being an employee of the sugar producers and there was some loss of faith in the Union. In fact, another union, the British Guiana Workers' League, had by then emerged and shared recognition with the MPCA in the sugar industry. Wildcat strikes had become frequent and to the extent that a Joint Estate Council had to be instituted by the Department of Labour in 1945 in order to make possible a dialogue between the sugar producers and workers' representatives.

Certain government employees, mainly railroad and ferry-service workers, were organized into a Transport Workers' Union which, though numerically small, became very strong from the outset. Being an organization of somewhat skilled workers and having been organized on a sound basis, this union flourished and became very effective in representing its members during the formative years. Other government employees were organized into a separate union called The Federation of Government Workers. Then there was the British Guiana Bauxite Mine Workers' Union which was formed in the early forties and which also was built upon a sound organizational base. It however met strong resistance from the Demerara Bauxite Company and did not gain recognition from that Company until 1947. A number of smaller unions also emerged within two to three years after the riots. In fact, when a Trade Union Council was formed in 1941 to work out jurisdictional boundaries among the many overlapping unions, there were some 28 unions which became members of that Council.[4]

In other Caribbean territories, the emergence of trade unions followed a somewhat different pattern from that of Trinidad or Guyana. What evolved in general was a sort of mass movement. In some territories it began nominally as a trade union movement which later created a political entity. In others it began more as a political movement out of which trade unions were later established. The Windward Islands were belated in responding to the riots and, except in the case of St. Vincent where already a Workingmen's Association existed, no labour movement emerged there during the war years. In fact, there were no significant labour disturbances in Grenada, St. Lucia, and Dominica in the thirties.

British Honduras and Antigua both began with trade union organisations. A general Workers' Union was formed in British Honduras in 1938, but its impact was almost negligible until the early 1950s when a political wing — The People's United Party — was established. The Antigua Trades and Labour Union was formed in 1939 with the advice and assistance of Sir Walter Citrine, then Secretary of the British Trades Union Congress and a member of the Moyne Commission; and in spite of the stout opposition it experienced at the outset from a powerful Sugar Planters' Association, which was formed in that same year, it made rapid strides in its early years of existence. Within three months it boasted a membership of almost 3,000 and, by the time it was registered in early 1940, it had recruited over 90 per cent of the sugar workers and had secured wage increases on their behalf. This union experienced a temporary set-back between 1941 and 1943 partly due to its 1941 resolution renouncing the strike weapon for the duration of the war and partly because of the trek of sugar workers to construction work at the U.S. naval base where unionism was made virtually impossible. However, by the end of 1943, there was a resurgence of buoyancy. This was due partly to the union's victory in respect of the payment of a 1943 crop-bonus to sugar workers and partly because of the change of leadership in September 1943 when a more militant group under the Presidency of V.C. Bird, later Chief Minister, took over control.

Organizing efforts thereafter were concentrated upon waterfront workers of whom one Keithly Heath, an employee of the shipping firm of Bennett Bryson, was the undisputed boss. By his influence both with the firm and workers he was able to organize strong resistance to the union and, through patronage to certain workers he succeeded in aborting several strikes planned by the union. This rivalry was however climaxed soon after the end of the war when the union successfully called a strike which lasted for nearly three months and which threatened to develop into a general strike. The issue of rotatory employment over which the strike was called was eventually won by the union and its stocks went up considerably; almost the entire labour force of the island came within the folds of the union soon thereafter.[5]

St. Kitts and Barbados, unlike British Honduras and Antigua, began with political organizations. As it was pointed out earlier, there were quasi-political parties in existence in both places before the late 1930s. In 1939, the St. Kitts Labour League, which by then held elected seats in the Legislature, established a formal trade union known as The St. Kitts-Nevis Trades and Labour Union. It would indeed be misleading to compare the growth of this union in its formative years with that of the A.T.L.U. for it was not truly a new organization which began recruiting around the time of its establishment; it was more or less the same members of the League who comprised the union; the leaders were virtually the same and it was really a case of the political party establishing a formal industrial wing.

The progress of this union in its early years was relatively smooth and it experienced very little harassment from planter-employers, due largely to the fact that during the war years the League had the majority of elected members in that colony's Legislative Assembly. As it was in the case of Antigua, this union resolved to forego use of the strike weapon during the war years. Similarly, a sugar-crop-bonus issue arose in St. Kitts in 1943 where it was agreed to refer the matter to a Board of Inquiry. The Board recommended continuation of payment of the bonus but the sugar planters refused to accept the recommendation and it was only after the St. Kitts-Nevis Trades and Labour Union rescinded its resolution in respect of wartime strikes that the planters capitulated. This was a major victory for the Leeward Islands trade union movement, including Antigua where a similar bonus issue existed, and it put the final touch upon consolidation of the movement.[6]

The Barbados Progressive League in its early post-riot stage was really a three-pronged, all-in-one organization built around a motto of "All for one and one for all". The three identifiable sections were the political, the economic, and the social. Following the riots, major emphasis was placed upon the economic and a major organizational drive, incorporating workers of all categories such as longshoremen, porters, bakers, agricultural labourers, etc., was launched. It was this economic section which was registered in 1941 as the Barbados Workers' Union after Grantley Adams had gained undisputed control of the League. The political wing was later named the Barbados Labour Party and the social wing became the Progressive League Friendly Society.

Francis Mark's account of the first two to three years of the union's history shows a somewhat disappointing start.[7] However, by 1944, following upon a successful strike by the engineering branch, the union began to flourish. In early 1945 membership of its 22 divisions numbered around 5,500. The sugar industry, after an uphill drive, was organized and by the end of 1947 membership exceeded 10,000. With Grantley Adams as President and Hugh Springer as Secretary, the B.W.U. achieved outstanding success during its formative years. Not only did it secure outstanding gains in industrial relations, but also it was able to acquire a property with buildings for union headquarters, a printery, in association with the political wing, for the establishment of a weekly newspaper (*The Beacon*) and to establish a workers' canteen. Between 1944 and 1945 there was some sort of competition experienced by this union from a rival trade union known as the Congress Trade Union. However, the latter's history was shortlived and the B.W.U. was left unchallenged by the end of World War II.

The development of trade unionism in Jamaica during these formative years fell somewhere between developments in Trinidad and Guyana, on the one hand, and the rest on the other hand. Until the 1938 disturbances, the only unions on the scene were the two Longshoremen's Unions, (No. 1 and No. 2) the Jamaica Workers' Trade Union, of which A.G.S. Coombs was President and Bustamante Treasurer, and a couple of other insignificant ones. In June 1938, when there

was a lull in the riots in Jamaica and within a month after his
release from detention, Bustamante announced his plans for
the formation of five unions — one each for maritime
workers, transport workers, factory workers, municipal
workers, and general labourers — with himself as leader of
all. The question of leadership was of course a foregone
conclusion, for while he was in jail, this had been decided.
One author recorded that on May 26, 1938, with Kingston
in chaos and Bustamante in custody, Kenneth Hill recommended to an emergency session of the National Reform
Association of Jamaica that the dock workers should form
a labour union with Bustamante as their leader. This was
enthusiastically assented to; recruitment began and an
operating fund was established to get the union started.[8]

Bustamante however did not follow his announced five-
union plan. He went through a whirlwind campaign of
organization by speeches and strikes and formed the all-
embracing Bustamante Industrial Trade Union in 1938 which
was registered in January 1939. By the time of registration
the union boasted a membership of over 6,500, ranging from
clerks and factory workers to dockworkers and labourers.
So strong and pervasive had the B.I.T.U. become and so
entrenched had been Bustamante's leadership that, in spite of
the leader's internment under emergency (war) regulations
from September 1940 to February 1942, the union neither
flagged nor failed; nor was his leadership threatened or
challenged.[9] In fact, the union's growth during its leader's
forced absence was phenomenal. Membership and assets
more then trebled and the first all-island sugar agreement,
covering some 40,000 workers, was made between the union
and the sugar manufacturers. All this achievement was made
possible however through the intervention of Norman
Manley, barrister-at-law, who became caretaker of the union
during the leader's absence.[10]

At this stage it appeared that Jamaica, like Barbados and
the Leewards, was destined to a 'one-big-union' future. The
Longshoremen's Union had become defunct by then and
the Jamaica Workers' Trade Union had become over-
shadowed by the B.I.T.U. A Trade Union Advisory Council
had been formed with Manley's blessing from as early as

1939 but this was not intended to be a rival union to Bustamante's union. Rather it was formed following a catastrophic strike called by Bustamante and it was for the specific purpose of unifying trade union policy and preventing frivolous strikes or union rivalry. Bustamante himself was named a member of that Council and Manley had already established a political Party, that is, The People's National Party. It appeared then that a giant politico-trade union complex was in the making with Manley as the political and Bustamante as the trade union leader. Bustamante was also a member of the People's National Party.

But this was not to be, as perhaps the name of the union forewarned. The "Chief", as Bustamante was generally described, broke off relationship with Manley and some of the top officers of the union immediately upon his release from internment. In fact, he accused them of malpractices and intentions to sabotage his organization during his forced absence. Shirley, the first Vice President was ousted and an open split between Bustamante and Manley occurred. Shirley took with him a few union dissenters and formed the Jamaica United Workers' Union but by the end of the war this union had passed from the scene.

The separation of Bustamante and his union from Manley and his political party led to the formation of several other unions in 1942. Most important of these were unions of government employees such as railway, public works, and postal workers which were organized by nationalist and politically ambitious middle-class personalities who comprised the hard-core nucleus of Manley's political party. Among them were Ken Hill, Secretary of the Postal and Telegraph Workers Union and President of the Government Auxiliary Workers Union, his brother Frank Hill, President of the Public Works Union, Richard Hart, President of the Railway Employees Union and Arthur Henry, Secretary of the last-named union. Certain events a decade later were to categorize these four as "The 4Hs".

These unions all ran into a temporary setback in 1942 arising out of Governor Richards' application of the Defence (War) Regulations to bar the registration of trade unions comprising government employees in cases where the officers of such unions were not employees of government. In fact, among other nationalists and political agitators associated with the P.N.P., the 4Hs were temporarily detained under the said Regulations. However, the limitation upon registration was revoked within six months and the way was made clear for the unionizing of government employees.

The year 1943 brought glad tidings of constitutional reform for Jamaica. The new constitution introduced a fully elected Lower House based upon universal adult suffrage and general elections were to be held in 1944. This broadening of the franchise stimulated increased trade union organization for trade union membership had become a particularly large electoral base. Both the number of trade unions and trade union membership increased considerably as the figures in Table 1 indicate. With the phenomenal increase in the number of unions, the early trend of 'one big union' was fading fast, though in reality not yet lost because, at the same time, the B.I.T.U. was expanding by leaps and bounds and its membership accounted for well over 80 per cent of the unionised labour force. What seemed totally lost, however, was the hitherto trend of one powerful politico-trade union complex under the political leadership of Manley with Bustamante as the trade union boss; for Bustamante soon announced his intention to form a political party.

The Jamaica Labour Party was launched by Bustamante within a year of the general elections and when the election results were announced on 14 December 1944, he was not only the trade-union boss but also the political chief of Jamaica. Out of 32 electoral seats for the Lower House, Bustamante and his newly formed Jamaica Labour Party won 23, as against four seats won by Manley's People's National Party. By the end of the war it was clear that, if Jamaica was to have a single politico-trade union complex like those of Barbados and the Leewards, it would be a complex under the political and trade union leadership of Bustamante.

Before we leave this formative era, it may be of some interest to note that trade unionism had been so firmly established in the various Caribbean territories, except in the Windward Islands, that at a Conference held in Guyana in 1944 a Caribbean Trade Union Congress was formed. There was, from as early as 1926, an annual Labour Conference held by the British Guiana Labour Union, which delegates from other Caribbean territories attended. But it was of very little significance as a regional trade union organization because trade unions were non-existent in most of the other territories. It was more an annual meeting of political and nationalist movements throughout the Caribbean than it was a trade union conference. The 1944 Regional Congress was different for it was a body to which only registered trade unions were affiliated.

Table 1. Growth of Trade Unions in Jamaica 1937-45*

Year	Estimated Labour Force	No. of Unions	Union Membership	% of Labour Force	B.I.T.U. Membership
1937	261,700	4	1,080	0.4	—
1938	266,300	7	8,500	3	—
1939	270,900	11	12,600	5 (est.)	6,500
1940	275,500	11	10,700	4	10,007
1941	280,100	13	24,000	9	8,133
1942	284,600	16	35,000	12	20,612
1943	289,200	23	46,000	16	28,762
1944	293,800	34	56,400	19	37,112
1945	298,400	27	57,000	19	46,538

*Source: Phelps, *Rise of Labour Movement in Jamaica* (compiled from Tables 2 and 3) pp. 456-7 (see note 8 below).

ENDNOTES

1. A Stevedores Union under the leadership of one Randolph Folkes began in 1934 but faded out soon thereafter. Folkes had spent several years in U.S. where he was an active member of the National Maritime Union.
2. Compiled from records of the Trinidad and Tobago Trades Union Council.
3. Ashton Chase, *A History of Trade Unionism in Guyana: 1900–1961*, Demerara, Guyana: New Guyana Company Ltd., 1964, pp. 85–90.
4. On the question of multiplicity of unions in the formative years, see *Annual Reports of the Department of Labour of Guyana,*

Georgetown: Government of Guyana, 1942-44.

5. For a detailed account of the formative years of the A.T.L.U. see
   Novelle H. Richards, *The Struggle and the Conquest*, St. Johns:
   Workers Voice Printery, 1960.

6. *Ibid.*, 22-23.

7. For a full account of development of the Barbados Workers Union
   see Francis Mark, *The History of the Barbados Workers Union*,
   Bridgetown: Advocate Commercial Printery, undated.

8. O.W. Phelps, "Rise of the Labour Movement in Jamaica", *Social
   and Economic Studies*, University of the West Indies, 1960, Vol.
   9, No. 4, 419-421.

9. Bustamante's detention was not in consequence of any specific
   offence committed by him and he was neither charged nor made to
   face trial. In ordering his arrest the then Governor stated that he
   was detained "with a view to preventing him from acting in a
   manner prejudicial to public safety."

10. Manley, a cousin of Bustamante, had offered his services as a Law-
    yer, without fees, to Bustamante and others who had been arrested
    during the riots.

SECTION 8
New Solutions to Old Problems:
The Caribbean since 1945

8.0

Introduction to Section 8

The problems of economic stagnation, poorly developed infrastructure and lack of fiscal self-confidence did not disappear despite the achievement of political independence by many Caribbean nations. Certainly the years following the end of World War II have seen remarkable changes in the region, but many observers have had good cause to be cynical of the new patterns created.

Perhaps the best known experiment in changing traditional monocultural dependence was the formulation of FOMENTO, known in English as Operation Bootstrap. This development scheme was implemented in Puerto Rico where it stimulated an economic changeover from traditional sugar monoculture (and peasant agriculture) to heavy industrialization. Puerto Rico found itself the producer of integral parts for heavy industry, the products of which would be shipped back to the mainland United States for assembly. When the finished manufactured product was finally available on the island, its price reflected the high cost of overseas shipping involved. Although recent years have seen attempts to change the industrialization pattern to light manufacture, producing fully completed goods for sale inexpensively in local markets, Operation Bootstrap has not lived up to expectations. Gordon Lewis (selection 8.2) indicates what he considers to be the particularly detrimental aspects of the project and why it has aroused so much controversy in Puerto Rico and in the Caribbean generally.

On the other hand, Hugh Thomas (selection 8.3) makes a case for the difficulty inherent in altering the sugar monocultural pattern in post-revolutionary Cuba. Although Castro tried almost immediately to break his nation's dependency on agriculture, the too-rapid move to industrialization almost

249

ground Cuba to a complete halt. The wiser move, in the view of many economists, is to begin the process of diversification by first industrializing sugar itself (which Cuba has now begun to do with modernized shipping facilities and expanded refineries) and then turning earned profits from such expansion into other sectors of the economy.

In many instances, it has been impossible to divorce economic potentialities from political expectations. The fear of a Cuban-style government in the Dominican Republic (after the assassination of Trujillo in 1961) was instrumental in deposing Juan Bosch, a liberal spokesmen for the Democratic Left in Latin America who stood for economic reform. The unseating of Bosch led to the takeover of another political heavy, Joaquín Balaguer, and although the latter was voted out of office in 1978 the Dominican Republic is still recoiling from the effects of the mid-1960s political crisis.

Thus, in today's Caribbean, several economic alternatives have emerged. Rejecting traditional capital-intensive solutions, some nations have opted for economic socialism, but this course has not necessarily been smooth. For Guyana, which underwent transformation into a People's Republic in 1971, the entrance of Great Britain into the European Common Market had a disastrous economic impact. Since the former mother country no longer functions as an assured market for Guyanese agricultural production, this Caribbean nation has been crippled with balance-of-payments problems contributing little to internal harmony. Jamaica (and more recently Grenada) also chose a quasi-socialistic path, recently rejected by the electorate. However, the conclusions reached by former Jamaican Prime Minister Michael Manley (selection 8.1) that the inheritance of the post-World War II period was the backlog of centuries of inequitable economic distribution remains indisputable. The patterns he describes, however, are not unique to Jamaica, nor had they been totally resolved as the 1970s drew to a close.

There is a vast literature on Castro and the style of government he created in Cuba. The new student might do well to consult T. Draper, *Castroism: Theory and Practice.* Two selections on the Dominican Republic highlight the problems unresolved by the 1960s; J. Bosch, *The Unfinished Experiment: Democracy in the Dominican Republic* and H.J. Wiarda, *Dominican Republic: Nation in Transition.* Economic planning for the Netherlands Antilles is explored in the more technical *Government Finance and Planned Development: Fiscal Surveys of Surinam and The Netherlands Antilles* by F.M. Andic and S.M. Andic.

Jamaica's Colonial Legacy   Michael Manley

What is the inheritance of the colonial past? In this selection, former Jamaican Prime Minister Michael Manley comments upon the economic deficits still apparent in the 1940s. The absence of linkages, the lack of control over foreign investment and profit-taking and a 'trader-mentality' evident in the export-import syndrome have all combined to make modernization of Jamaica's economy exceedingly cumbersome. The correlation of economic patterns to socio-cultural developments is also apparent in this analysis. Reproduced from M. Manley (1974), The Politics of Change: A Jamaican Testament, *pp. 78-86. Copyright © 1974 and reprinted by permission of the publisher Andre Deutsch, Ltd.*

To understand many of today's economic dilemmas one must begin with a broad assessment of Jamaica's economic situation as it existed in 1945. After some three hundred years of British rule and more than one hundred years out of slavery, Jamaican society displayed eight basic characteristics. Most of these features are to be found in other post-colonial societies and each represents a challenge to be overcome, or at least mitigated, if a just and efficient society is to be achieved.

EXPORT-IMPORT ORIENTATION

Perhaps the most characteristic of all the common features of colonial economies is the tendency towards export-import orientation. By this we mean that the total of exports and imports occupy a disproportionately large share of the total economy. By comparison, goods and services produced locally for local consumption make up a comparatively small share of the economy. The reasons for this are well understood. Colonial territories were developed to supply raw materials, or, at best, partially processed goods and to act as a market for the sophisticated manufactured exports of the metropolitan powers.

A good example of the extent to which colonial Jamaica was developed in response to its trading patterns with the United Kingdom is to be found in the administrative structure under which the island was governed. The island was divided into fourteen parishes, many of which had a port which existed for the sole purpose of exporting local agricultural products to the United Kingdom and as the point at which British manufactured goods were received. Historians have remarked that the parish capitals which were based on these ports, often had more in common with London than with Kingston, so great was the metropolitan orientation of the economy, the political system and, indeed, the entire society.

Local production for local use was actively discouraged since production of this sort could only take place at the expense of metropolitan exports. In Jamaica's case our exports, even as late as 1945 were exclusively agricultural, consisting of semi-processed sugar, bananas, together with lesser crops such as citrus, coffee, cocoa and pimento. It was a minor but typical irony of our situation that we shipped crude sugar and coffee beans to England where both were processed and re-exported to Jamaica. This pattern had two inevitable consequences. First, it meant that Jamaica like all other post-colonial countries was at the mercy of the adverse movement in the terms of trade between primary producing and manufacturing countries. Historically the prices for primary products such as sugar, bananas and the like tend to be unstable but show no general tendency to rise through time. On the contrary, the prices for manufactured goods tend to be stable within the context of a general upward trend. In consequence, as the generations passed, it took more and more sugar to buy a tractor, a turbine or a motor car. However, the limits imposed by geography on economic acreages that cannot be used to produce sugar, bananas and the like make it impossible to produce more and more sugar. Thus, economies like Jamaica's are trapped in a vicious circle unless they find the means to break out of the pattern which they have inherited.

The second consequence that is inherent in this situation is that of growing unemployment. Granted reasonably full utilization of economic acreages for export agriculture, one can assume at best a constant labour force. It is more likely, however, that there will be a dwindling labour force as producers turn to sophisticated technology in their battle with rising costs and stagnant prices. In this regard the vicious circle can be illustrated with this example. A sugar producer has to import his fertilizers and tractors. As time passes both cost him more. But the country to which he sells the sugar does not pay him more, so he imports a new piece of labour-saving equipment to try to hold the line on costs. This displaces labour. In due course he has to replace the labour-saving machine, but discovers that he cannot finance the purchase out of his depreciation fund, because the price has soared. So he borrows money to purchase not only the replacement but a further piece of labour-saving equipment. This displaces even more labour. And so the disastrous spiral continues. Where the rest of the economy reflects no dynamic growth, unemployment will rise, not only as consequence of population growth, but reflecting absolute displacement of labour, as well.

THE TRADER MENTALITY

The natural concomitant of the export-import orientation pattern is the trader mentality. Custom and habit are polite terms for the unconscious brainwashing of the historical process. For three centuries, the economic horizons of the Jamaican were bounded by the production of basic crops for export, on the one hand, and the importation of the total range of consumer goods, on the other. To this could be added an interest in the professions such as law, medicine and the Civil Service. The peasant farmer struggling to make a living by coaxing marginal hillside land to produce root crops completes the picture.

The trader mentality has had a number of consequences. Partly it is a consequence of colonialism; and partly it has itself contributed to the psychological and economic deformities which are associated with the colonial experience. In fact, when one considers the general effect of colonialism and the specific effect of the trader mentality, one sees an example of a major historical force creating a minor phenomenon which in turn helps to perpetuate the efforts of the major force. It is like a variant of the hen and egg theme.

Of course, the most obvious consequence of the trader mentality is that it limits economic activity to the business of distributing imported goods. This places a severe limit on the capacity of the economy to provide jobs and means, in effect, that we are importing other peoples' productive labour. Also, as is the case with export agriculture, the employment potential in the distribution of imported goods tends to be static since one salesman can take an order for two dozen shirts just as effectively as he can for one dozen. Equally, it may take a very large increase in demand before a merchant needs additional delivery trucks, employing extra drivers and sidemen.

LACK OF CONFIDENCE

Colonialism and the trader mentality have had a number of other, perhaps less obvious, but just as debilitating consequences which we must examine. We have already seen, and indeed much has been written about, the extent to which colonialism undermined the confidence of subject people. This was no less true in the economic field. The trader mentality may have begun as the logical response to a single avenue of opportunity. In the end, however, it became a conditioned reflex. By 1945 it occurred to very few Jamaicans that they were capable of producing for themselves. The entire entrepreneurial class was, with a few notable exceptions, in the grip of a paralysis of attitude. As a group, businessmen lacked the will, the inclination and, I suspect, the confidence to tackle simple productive tasks which would satisfy their own needs and engage our resources. This crisis of confidence went even further. It was reflected in the assumption that we were incapable of working out our own solutions to our problems. As a consequence, we tended to revere the foreign expert, not in any rational recognition of his particular expertise, but rather in the manner of a tribesman expecting the witch doctor to produce a miracle. Bound up with this exaggerated faith in metropolitan performance was an assumption that even if we did produce something locally, it would necessarily be of inferior quality. This latter characteristic persists even to the present where foreign goods represent for consumers a sort of status symbol irrespective of rational comparisons of actual price and quality.

A taste for conspicuous consumption is one of the subtler consequences of colonialism, the trader mentality and the general disconnection from responsibility. It is not easy to analyse the precise roots of the frame of mind which this term seeks to describe. It manifests itself in a tendency to spend without regard to one's capacity to pay; more particularly to buy more rather than less expensive goods with an equal disregard for consequences and, finally, in an almost total disregard of the importance of savings.

This pattern reflects, in the first place, a general state of mind. Self-restraint is learned as much through continuing exposure to responsibility as through experience of the consequences of irresponsibility. If an entire people are disconnected from responsibility, it is unlikely that they will show a marked capacity for self-restraint. To this general psychological background must be added the effect of exposure to the consumer patterns of metropolitan countries with their far more advanced economies and higher standards of living. Part of the indoctrination of colonialism led to the assumption of superior metropolitan values. The consumer patterns of an advanced economy would appear, therefore, to represent a higher order of experience to be emulated at all costs. When one adds the force of supposedly superior example to a general disconnection from the experience of responsibility, it is not too difficult to imagine how the pattern of conspicuous consumption took hold in a country like Jamaica, nor that it should rest upon so fragile an economic base. Obviously, the most disastrous practical consequence of conspicuous consumption is to be found in its effect upon savings. The propensity to save is low, and so the ability to finance our own productive efforts suffers.

THE ABSENCE OF LINKAGES

This brings us to yet another element in the vicious circle. In an export-import oriented economy that is marked by the trader mentality, coupled with a lack of entrepreneurial confidence and a low propensity to save, it is inevitable that our economy should reflect a striking absence of linkages. By linkages I mean industries that exist for the simple reason that another industry exists. For example, the full utilization of by-product possibilities represent linkages. Since Jamaica grows sugar cane we should not only make raw sugar but should also make refined sugar, confectionary, molasses, rum, citric acid, bagasse board and the like. These are all by-products. Equally, industries that exist to provide the means of packaging or transporting a produce represent linkages. Hence, bags for raw sugar, containers for refined sugar, bottles for rum and so on all represent further economic activity that attaches to those products that flow directly from sugar cane itself. In 1945 the Jamaican economy had virtually no linked industries. This was partly because the linked industries were the preserve of the metropolitan power; and partly because in the atmosphere of colonialism it was not easy to come by the will and the resources to tackle these jobs for oneself. Hence, our sugar cane, to take one example, led to almost as many employment opportunities abroad as it created at home.

POVERTY AND VALUE ADDED

It is an economic truism that the further one proceeds along the productive process, the greater is the 'value added' and, hence, the greater the wealth accruing to the supplier of the process. If one traces, for example, the 'value added' at the various stages of the sugar process one finds that it is lowest at the point of reaping the cane and milling to the stage of raw sugar. It is highest at the level of refined sugar, confectionary and the final blending of rum. The same is true as we trace the development of aluminium ingot through its bauxite mining and alumina stages. Obviously then since colonial economies were condemned to the first, or at best the first two stages of production it was inevitable that they were equally condemned to the poorest section of the economic process. When one adds this factor to the factors of export-import orientation and the failure to develop linkages and bear particularly in mind the problems of the terms of trade, one can perceive the basic anatomy of the problem of rich and poor nations. One can also see how important foreign policy is to the economic development of a young nation.

FOREIGN CAPITAL AND FOREIGN TECHNOLOGY

Jamaica is a small island which does not possess great un-explored frontiers in terms of undeveloped land and un-tapped mineral resources. We have copper but not in deposits which are capable of economic exploitation at this moment in the history of copper technology and marketing. The same is true of iron and there is not, as yet, any sign of oil. There-fore Jamaica must assess the claims of political sovereignty and national independence against the background of economic reality. Without these natural physical advantages and with heavy unemployment, Jamaican economic strategy leaves little room for expansive romanticism. For us, survival and progress are matters of margins. We need foreign capital and we need foreign technology. These must be harnessed to our needs with the greatest skill and ingenuity.

Our great problem is to find the proper balance and mix between foreign capital already in Jamaica, the new capital that we need and the institutions of control and systems of ownership which can ensure that economic development is consistent with national objectives.

In the light of the basic economic problems that we have
been discussing, it is hardly surprising that Jamaicans in 1945
should have looked almost exclusively to foreign capital and
technology to supply the answers to poverty and unemployment. With savings and self-confidence both minimal, unemployment rampant and poverty viewed from the perspective of a growing awareness of metropolitan standards of
living, it seemed that something had to be done and quickly.
Foreign capital and the foreign expert loomed as the two
critical elements of a *deus ex machina* that seemed perfectly
suited to the problem. Nor did it seem at the time that there
was any inherent contradiction between the quest for
political independence and the increasing foreign economic
domination that would result from this strategy. Indeed, it
may well be that the excitement of the political quest served
to obscure the inner economic reality. This strategy must,
however, be at least partly judged in context. Already in
1945 much of the Jamaican economy was in foreign ownership with the United Fruit Company of America and Tate
and Lyle of Britain, only two major examples of a substantial
metropolitan economic presence. Two obvious consequences
of this state of affairs were the substantial proportion of
profits that were exported and the number of economic
decisions taken in foreign board rooms which were neither
sensitive to nor particularly concerned with Jamaica's
problems and needs. An increasing dependence on uncontrolled foreign capital, therefore, could only serve to
exacerbate both problems.

IRRELEVANT EDUCATION

An important characteristic which we may mention arises in
the general field of education. The total educational performance was such as to ensure that the population lacked
the basic skills with which to effect the transformation of
the economy. The sons of planters and merchants either idled
through school safe in the knowledge that they would have
the right to do as bad a job as their fathers on the plantation
or in the company's store; or if they were of a more serious

turn of mind, prepared for careers in one of the professions. The rest of the population fell into one of two categories. Either they received education that prepared them for the simple arithmetic that would fit them for a sales counter; or, even worse, emerged from the process barely able to read and write. If we total the skills of an indifferent planter, a lazy merchant, a sales clerk and a semi-literate manual worker, it is unlikely we will find the kind of expertise that can modernize an economy. This explains a paradox of Jamaican history. Great skill in the fields of medicine, the law, politics and even the arts has been demonstrated at the same time as a comparatively weak performance in the area of sophisticated economic growth.

THE GAP BETWEEN RICH AND POOR

The final characteristic which we must note is a consequence of the distribution of wealth. As a consequence of its economic structure and educational system Jamaica con- sisted of three almost self-contained societies in 1945. There were the merchants and planters, the first of which had substantial assets and income and the latter substantial assets and uncertain income. Then there were the profes- sionals who had income but no assets; and finally there were the workers and peasants the first of whom had a little income with no assets and the second, little assets with virtually no income. The gap between the first two groups and the last represented an affront to social conscience.

The period from 1945 to 1972 witnessed the attainment of representative government followed by full internal self- government in 1959 and full independence in 1962. During this period the basic model for economic thinkers and planners was to be found in the Puerto Rican experience. Strenuous efforts, including various kinds of incentives were made to attract foreign capital, both in the areas of import substitution and manufactured exports. Later these inducements were spread to include local capital. The bauxite industry was developed on the basis of total foreign ownership redressed by special taxes and comparatively high wages. Special diplomatic efforts were directed towards price supports for our export crops and various devices were employed to funnel financial support to farmers of various sizes. The institutions of a modern economy such as a central bank, industrial and agricultural development corporations and agricultural marketing corporations and the like were created. However, this remarkable flurry of effort did not substantially affect the main problems of 1945 which were massive unemployment and the serious maldistribution of wealth. In fact, both unemployment and the gap between the rich and poor increased during the period.

The Failings of
Operation Bootstrap   Gordon K. Lewis

Was Operation Bootstrap a success or a failure? In this selection Gordon Lewis provides insights into the original motivation for FOMENTO and comments on whether the decision to diversify monocultural production by switching to industry has been a wise one. The close correlation of the general health of the United States' economy to that of the island has been staggeringly evident in recent years, when recession has produced widespread unemployment in Puerto Rico as well as escalating prices of consumer goods. This excerpt originally appeared in G.K. Lewis (1963), Puerto Rico: Freedom and Power in the Caribbean, pp. 113-116, 118-121, 141-143. Copyright © 1963 by Gordon K. Lewis and reprinted by permission of Monthly Review Press and the Author.

The period after 1945 marks the turning point in the Puerto Rican transformation. The Tugwell governorship had set a pattern for legislative-executive cooperation in common tasks; and the Elective Governor Act of 1947 ended once and for all the distorting influence in local government of the nominated alien executive. The experience in the PRRA and later in the work of wartime organization had helped train a corps of administrative assistants who could become the timber of the Muñoz cabinets. The institutional machinery appropriate to organizing a radically fresh balance between output and people in an underdeveloped economy, to replacing stagnation with growth, had been set up by means of the far-reaching legislative program of 1942. The Social Science Research Center of the University made its own valuable contribution to the general problem — a contribution sometimes too easily forgotten — with the publication of specialist studies in the areas of labor economics, manpower analysis and occupational structure: Dr. Simon Rottenberg's *Labor's Role in Industrialization*, for example, or the study by Ray and Darling on *Manufacturing Occupations in Puerto Rico*. What remained to be done was to direct all of this into the creation of new income-producing processes by means of a planned industrialization program. This, simply put, was the purpose of "Operation Bootstrap," the "battle for production" that gathered its momentum slowly after 1945 and that had entered into a sufficiently rapid rate of growth by the middle 1950's to become the main stimulus in transforming a declining agrarian economy into an expanding industrial structure.

All this was naturally not self-evident at the end of the war in 1945. With a few exceptions due to wartime developments there had been little change in the insular economy, and reports on its sicknesses, like the Bartlett Technical Paper on *A Development Plan for Puerto Rico* of 1944 or even Harvey Perloff's volume of 1949 on *Puerto Rico's Economic Future*, were not much different in their analysis — although startlingly different in their policy recommendations — from earlier reports such as the 1934 *Report of the Porto Rican Policy Commission*. A land-use pattern entering around the sugar monoculture still prevailed, with all of its hazardous consequences — concentration on a lucrative cash crop, the use of the best lands thus for export purposes, the failure to produce subsistence crops for local consumption, the continual extension of cultivation to increasingly marginal soils. The situation had been rendered ever more precarious by the fact that by 1940 the competition of mechanized beet and cane sugar both in the continental states and in the duty-free offshore areas (Hawaii and the Philippine Islands), combined with relatively high production costs as compared say with the Cuban industry, had caused the Puerto Rican industry to come to a relative standstill. It could thus no longer provide a positive stimulus to the other sectors of the economy. The tobacco industry likewise was in a state of decline as a consequence of long-term changes in world smoking habits as the cigar came to yield

in popularity to the cigarette during the 1920's. The traditional high-class Puerto Rican coffee, again, once the delight
of the European gourmet, never recovered from the loss of its
world markets during the First World War, and the loss was
not compensated for by a United States tariff protection
wall (coffee not being an American industry). Nor had any
of this created, in response, an effort to exploit, by the
planned development of a local truck farming industry, the
export possibilities latent in the Puerto Rican fruits such as
avocados, pineapples, papayas, grapefruit (once a flourishing
industry until it was practically destroyed by the competition
of United States domestic producers), guavas and mangoes;
the exaggerated dependency upon the United States export
market had thus created a gross violation of the principle
of regional specialization.

Two additional factors helped to aggravate the situation.
The first was that, apart from the corporate sugar latifundia,
the insular agriculture was characterized by an almost feudal
pattern of technical equipment and skills, since the family-
oriented farm structure inhibited the growth of a rationalistic-
competitive spirit. "Puerto Rican agriculture," The Bartlett
Report observed, "is a picture of extremes. On the one hand
are large sugar corporations employing modern techniques of
scientific management, and on the other is subsistence
farming based on primitive methods. Between these two
extremes there are small-scale commercial agricultural enterprises."[1] The second factor relates to the unbalanced character
of an economy that had very little to show of pure industrial
activity. The cultivation, processing and distribution of
agricultural products remained the chief activity with some
39 percent of the employed population directly engaged in
farming and more than 25 percent of those being employed
in so-called "manufacturing" occupations which dealt in fact
with the processing of agricultural products. Most of the
banking, finance, and large-scale commercial activities were
likewise concerned with the servicing of the agricultural
sector. Nearly half of the labor force, moreover, classified
in the "industrial" sector were overwhelmingly the women
employees of the evil sweatshops of the home needlework
industry financed by absentee mainland capital and managed

by local business entrepreneurs. Nor were the wholesale and retail trades any more genuinely industrial, being in fact little more (as the ubiquitous Puerto Rican highway grocery store showed) than monuments to a high level of disguised unemployment and an extreme inefficiency of distributive arrangements within the island. The hazardous dependency upon agricultural production was graphically illustrated, finally, in the statistics of the insular export trade, with sugar contributing (in 1946) some 48 percent of the total, tobacco some 13 percent, rum just over 7 percent, and needlework products nearly 16 percent.[2] Puerto Rico was clearly in the general category of primary-producing countries exporting for a world market and subject to international price fluctuations and political arrangements beyond their power to influence. Nor was this offset by any sizeable public sector of economic activity more within local control; by 1944 the governmental enterprises of the insular regime accounted for only 1.2 percent of total net income — proving, incidentally, that the characterization by its critics of Puerto Rican economy under the New Deal as one of "state socialism" constituted an extravagant example of poetic license.[3] Furthermore, the society was marked (in 1946) by an income distribution so grossly imbalanced that 11 percent of its families received over 42 percent of its total income while some 2 percent of families commanded 18 percent of the same total.[4] Though not a "sugar island" as perfectly as Barbados or Martinique, Puerto Rico was at the mercy of the same Caribbean sugar industry, and it was just about as true to say of its condition as Márquez Sterling had said earlier of Cuba that "Sugar cane does not make colonies happy, or a people cultured, or republics opulent; and the independence we won in the war against Spain we must consummate in a war against sugar cane, which perpetuated in the golden island, as an inexhaustible tradition, the despotism of the major-domo and the hatred of the slave."[5]   ......

Dr. Teodoro Moscoso has divided the development program into two phases.[6] The first phase, from 1942 to about 1950, was one of government-built and operated plants (cement, glass bottles, shoes, etc.) undertaken primarily as a means of proving to private capital the feasibility of profitable industrial enterprise in the island. Some of the plants — the glass bottle center, for example — were probably conceived erroneously after a false mental image of American capitalism as being an economy of typically huge mass production plants only. In any case, the effort decisively proved the point that if (as in Puerto Rico) the available local capital fights shy of industry and if in turn (as again in Puerto Rico) the government is unprepared to recruit that capital by coercive measures, the sole alternative lies in the invention of measures to persuade the established United States manufacturer to locate in the island. The elaboration of such measures constituted the second and more lasting phase of the program. This has involved the introduction of tax exemption to new industries established in 1947 and after, especially designed in its clauses to benefit the American manufacturer who moves from the continent to the island. It involves also the rental of industrial buildings; the recruitment of specially trained personnel; the negotiation of labor contracts; the maintenance of Commonwealth offices in the leading American cities; the issuance of an imaginative literature on the advantages of setting up shop in the island; and, not the least important, special aid and guidance to the prospective client concerning the general environment of statutory regulation within which he will be obliged to conduct his enterprise. The considerable difficulties of making a real success of all this should not be overlooked. It has meant assiduous planning of a sort even more arduous than that undertaken, say, by Great Britain in 1945; for whereas the British welfare-state planners inherited an already mature capitalism with which to work, the Puerto Rican planners had to start almost from scratch. Established industry is notoriously conservative in the matter of new geographical location; indeed it rarely moves except under the pressure of vast economic dislocation, as in the major industrial societies after 1929. What Dr. Arthur Lewis has said on this score with relation to the British Caribbean applied with equal force for Puerto Rico in the beginning; "They speak frequently," he observed in 1950 of West Indian nationalist politicians, "as if manufacturing in the West Indies offered a large profitable market which greedy foreign capitalists are anxious to rush in and exploit. They discuss industrialization in terms of the close restrictions which they would like to impose upon such capitalists, and they oppose monopoly rights, tax holidays and other incentives which some governments are now considering offering. The facts are exactly opposite to what they suppose. The West Indies does not offer a large market. There are very few manufacturers who wish to go there. Having regard to the highly developed industrial centers which exist in many parts of the world, offering every convenience, and to the many governments which are now trying to attract industry, it would be surprising if any large number of manufacturers were willing to go to the West Indies without being offered substantial concessions."[7]

There is yet another point to be made. Throughout the entire American period of rule, and especially since the New Deal era, the island economy has been to all intents and purposes a subsidy economy. And since the federal contributions have been largely haphazard and ill directed, they have not helped the island toward a genuine planning revolution designed to take care of its long-term economic needs. The benefits accruing from them significantly, have occurred in an almost completely accidental manner, as in the case of the large fiscal returns on the rum tax during the war period and the financing of the vocational training program through the GI Bill of Rights after the war. "The people of Puerto Rico," Professor Perloff has observed, "have become adjusted to an income level deriving in very large part from a flow of funds into the island which is not directly related to the sale of goods through normal channels or returns on investments abroad. This is not a very sturdy foundation, and the reduction of federal emergency outlays in the island can have unfortunate consequences, *unless* the export industries are built up rapidly and the productive plant and equipment is expanded so as to broaden the base of the economy."[8] Those conditions have still not been completely fulfilled, and thus the Fomento planners continue to see migration as a crucial factor in their considerations and clearly anticipate, also, that in the event of any really large-scale desertion of the island by American firms they will be able to fall back upon an extended federal public works program.[9] But both

of these alternatives are peculiarly unsatisfactory. A policy of
dependence on migration is limited on at least three counts:
its continuance is always uncertain, it can generate (as it
already has done) hostile social and political repercussions
in the United States, and it is likely, considering the nature
of the migrants, to affect adversely the productive capacity
of the island. A public works program, likewise, is notoriously deficient anywhere, since it aims at relief (like the old
PRRA before 1940) rather than at removing the causes giving
rise to the need for relief. In spite of these drawbacks, the
Puerto Rican bureaucracy chooses to accept these alternatives. Or perhaps, more accurately, its "choice" springs
inescapably from the single governing fact that whether
with a sugar economy in one generation or an industrializing
one in another the local power has had to fit itself into the
requirements of the American national concern.

In more general terms of course we are witnessing here a
classic example of how the economic laws that govern the
relationships between superordinate and subordinate societies
operate in such a way as to tighten the vise of economic
dependency. There grows up an entrenched institutional
arrangement of commercial and trading connections which
forces the lesser economy into a narrow and one-sided reliance
upon the greater. In the Puerto Rican case not only is the
island frustrated in any efforts to diversify its global trading
relationships, but it is also to this extent made far more
vulnerable to the repercussions of economic recession on the
mainland. The establishment of any firms and technicians
other than American is practically paralyzed by the strict
enforcement of the federal immigration legislation, a fact
recently emphasized by the remarks of the Economic Adviser
to the Italian Embassy in Washington.[10] The relationship
creates an unfavorable balance of trade against the local
economy; and it is not enough to argue here with the Puerto
Rican Planning Board that such an unfavorable balance is not
of necessity an index of economic weakness and to cite as
suporting evidence the case of the United States itself
between 1790 and 1873,[11] for the comparison ignores the
crucial fact that the American economy during that period
possessed massive raw material resources, as yet unexploited,

whereas the contemporary Puerto Rican economy possesses no such reserves of strength. Industrial development, as a consequence of all this, tends (as a Fomento director has confessed) to rely almost exclusively upon imported raw materials, to sell mainly on the continental market, to use local materials rarely, and generally to be integrated into the American industrial structure rather than into the Puerto Rican economy.[12] If to all this there is added the fact that in all of the strategic sections of the economy in its connection with the continental mainland — shipping, air traffic, immigration control, postal communications — the power to make or break rests either with the federal Congress or with one of the federal regulatory commissions, the degree of Puerto Rican subordination to the continental scheme of things becomes translucently clear. The general result is what Gunnar Myrdal, speaking of the problem generally, has termed an "enforced bilateralism," insuring the continuing hold upon the lesser economy even after political liberation from the colonial status has been completed. Despite the very considerable economic advantages that accrue to the dependent country as a result of the connection, at the end of the process it is certain to mean a considerable economic disadvantage, since it tends to worsen that country's terms of trade by artificially restricting the scope of the markets where it buys and sells. The one great asset which final liberation from the economic dependency will mean will be the liberty of the society to regulate its economic life according to the interests of its own people, since it will then be capable of its own intelligent interference with the play of forces in the international economy.[13]

ENDNOTES

1. Frederic P. Bartlett and associates, *A Development Plan for Puerto Rico* (San Juan, Puerto Rico Planning, Urbanizing and Zoning Board, Technical Paper No. 1, January 1944), p. 21.
2. Harvey S. Perloff, *Puerto Rico's Economic Future: A Study in Planned Development* (University of Chicago Press, 1949), p. 137.
3. Daniel Creamer, *The Net Income of the Puerto Rican Economy 1940-1944* (Rio Piedras, University of Puerto Rico, Social Sciences

Research Center, 1947), p. 33.

4. Perloff, *Puerto Rico's Economic Future*, p. 165.

5. Manuel Márquez Sterling, *Las Conferencias de Shoreham: El Cesarismo en Cuba* (Mexico, 1933), p. 26.

6. Teodoro Moscoso, *Logros y Metas de la Industrialización en Puerto Rico* (San Juan, Administración de Fomento Económico, 1955).

7. W. Arthur Lewis, "The Industrialization of the British West Indies," *Caribbean Economic Review* (May, 1950), pp. 37-38.

8. Perloff, *Puerto Rico's Economic Future*, p. 128.

9. Economic Development Administration, Office of Economic Research, *An Appraisal of Fomento Programs* (San Juan, mimeographed, October 24, 1955), pp. 22-23.

10. *El Mundo*, July 16, 1957.

11. Statement of the Planning Board, quoted in *El Mundo*, October 23, 1956.

12. Hugh Barton, *Puerto Rico's Industrial Future* (San Juan, Puerto Rico Economic Association, mimeographed, 1957), p. 1-2.

13. Gunnar Myrdal, *Economic Theory and Underdeveloped Regions* (London, Duckworth, 1957), pp. 58-62. For a discussion of the advantages and disadvantages of "enforced bilateralism" in the special field of balance of payments problems, see James C. Ingram, *Regional Payments Mechanisms: The Case of Puerto Rico* (Chapel Hill, University of North Carolina Press, 1962). The Commonwealth Government, through its Department of Commerce, has recently spearheaded a drive to expand its Caribbean commercial and trading activities. But it remains yet to be seen whether (1) this is anything more than an exercise in Puerto Rican economic imperialism, under the protection of the United States tariff wall and (2) the existing restrictions upon Puerto Rico's freedom of trade will permit Puerto Rican participation in, for example, a Caribbean customs union venture.

8.3

The Harvest of the Ten
Million Tons in Cuba   Hugh Thomas

If heavy industrialization in Puerto Rico has not lived up to growth expectations, the reverse process, that of maximizing monocultural crop production, has also been plagued with problems. In this account of Fidel Castro's attempt to dramatically increase production of Cuba's traditional crop, sugar, Hugh Thomas pinpoints the difficulties of modernizing agricultural sectors; on the other hand, if dependence on sugar has not been broken, in the 1970s significant forward linkages have been created in the expansion of shipping and refining capacities. From H. Thomas (1971), The Cuban Revolution, *Harper and Row, pp. 658-67. Copyright © 1971, 1977 by Hugh Thomas. Reprinted by permission of Harper and Row, Publishers Inc. and Curtis Brown Ltd.*

The political revolution following the capture of power in 1959 was to have been accompanied by, first, an immediate increase in standards of living; second, a rapid industrialization; and third, a switch away from that emphasis on sugar which had played for so long such a large and, as many thought, destructive part in Cuban society. None of these things occurred: Guevara in 1960 spoke of a future in which Cuba would be self-sufficient in steel, while by 1965 industrialization had been indefinitely postponed: in 1960 Castro was explaining how improvements in living standards would come faster than in any other country which had undergone a revolution but two years later the standards of life in the cities had collapsed while at the end of the 1960s most Cubans were living in a very Spartan manner. Finally, while between 1960 and 1962 the role of sugar in the economy was denigrated, sugar has if anything since 1963 played a larger part than before 1959.[1] The 'year of the Decisive Endeavour', 1969-70,[2] was indeed specially geared to the production of ten million tons of sugar, a goal which, because of the innate unwisdom of relying on the production of a large quantity of an already far from scarce commodity, would once have seemed so foolish as to be absurd. In order to expand the capacity of the sugar industry to produce ten million tons of sugar, it was necessary to invest a new $M1,000, a figure which exceeded the total assets of the sugar industry in 1965.[3] With a rigidly controlled economy, however, and the emigration of many technicians, it was obviously easier to concentrate all energies upon this well-tried crop than to launch successfully into other enterprises, at least as a matter of central concentration. In this respect, the Revolution has been fundamentally regressive, and it must have occurred to many Cubans to ask whether it would not have been more beneficial to have achieved a less profound social change if thereby it had been easier to achieve economic diversification.

Despite the special and grand emphasis laid on sugar since 1964, however, harvests have usually been well below the figures achieved in the 1950s and the yield from the cane has also been smaller.[4] These failures are partly attributable to bad weather, but bad management, delay in getting the cane from the field to the mill,[5] neglect of the industry in the early years, sabotage, shortage of machinery, and even shortage of labour have also been responsible. For a variety of reasons, (among them retirement) the professional cane cutters of the 1950s have almost disappeared and voluntary labour, however energetic, has often been less satisfactory. The harvest of 1969 was described by Castro as 'the country's agony,' and totalled 4½ million tons only. But the goal of reaching ten million tons in the harvest of 1970 was proclaimed for such a long time and such stress had been laid on this goal in propaganda ('What are you doing towards the ten million?') that it almost seemed as if the regime would stand or fall by the extent to which this target was fulfilled.

Nevertheless, in the middle of May 1970 Castro bitterly admitted that this target could not after all be achieved and that nine million would be the maximum possible. Even this, however, represents less of a real achievement than it will seem at first sight, since much of the sugar came from cane left over from 1969 or prematurely cut from the harvest of 1971. It is also unfortunately conceivable that the figures were falsified and, providing that Russia assists in the deception (by, for instance, announcing that she has bought from Cuba seven million tons), there is no means of checking the truth of the announcement.[6] Further, even if the ten million tons had been achieved, Cuba would still have been producing less sugar per head of population than she was in 1925, while the long-term costs of this grand Potemkin-type harvest cannot easily be measured.

It was a bizarre undertaking: the news that this harvest of 1970 would begin on 26 July 1969 (with a *zafra chica*) and that Christmas Eve 1969 would be celebrated, because of the activities on the cane fields, in July 1970, are among the most notable surrealistic contributions to Cuban political life. Meantime, a delegation from North Vietnam, not to speak of the Soviet Minister of Defence, Marshal Grechko, and the entire Cuban cabinet have all done their time in the canefields, while government propaganda has spoken of the harvest as if it were a military challenge: 'Every worker should act as he would in the face of an enemy attack, should feel like a soldier in a trench with a rifle in his hand.'[7]

A commercial agreement with Russia signed in January 1964, and the International Sugar Agreement of 1968 (in force for five years from 1 January 1969), assures Cuba of markets in the short term: the Russians agreed to buy an annually increasing amount of Cuban sugar at 6 cents a pound up to 7 million tons by 1970, though in fact Cuba was on a number of occasions unable to meet her part of the bargain.[8] The International Sugar Agreement gave Cuba a quota of 2.15 million tons.[9] But even leaving aside the political consequences of so close a commercial friendship with Russia,[10] the long-term consequences of reliance on sugar in a world able to produce increasing quantities of it are discouraging, particularly when the Cuban sugar industry seems less efficient and competitive than it was even in the 1950s — not to speak of the last century, when it was in the van of technical experiment (Cuba was even overtaken by Brazil as the largest sugar cane producer in 1966).

There is, however, one important recent development: the beginning of mechanization of the sugar harvest. There were admittedly many early difficulties. Thus despite the construction with the help of Czech and Russian technicians, and parts, of 100 cane-cutting and stripping machines from Russia in 1965 and about 5,000 machines for lifting the cane when it is cut, most of the harvest of sugar in 1969-70 was still being both cut and loaded by hand.[11] For the Russian machines, the *Libertadoras*, often broke down, could only work eight hours a day and when there was no dew, and were useless in the rain or on bumpy ground. In 1968, Castro nevertheless explained that mechanization would be complete by 1975, when the Revolution would 'have secured one of its most humane achievements, having changed over for ever from working conditions fit for animals to those which are truly humane' — that is, to complete mechanization.[12] In the following years, several new combine cane harvesters, of Cuban manufacture, for cutting cane, were used, and the harvest of 1969-70 will apparently use over 200 of these *Hendersons* (called after Robert Henderson, its English-American inventor who had been before the Revolution general manager of the United Fruit's Company's mill, *the Preston* — a curious hero for the Revolution but undoubtedly a real one).[13]

Since 1962, the structure of agriculture, industry and labour have all been transformed, so that the still partially bourgeois society which was threatened in the Missile Crisis no longer exists.

In October 1963, a second agrarian reform nationalized all private holdings larger than 167 acres (five *caballería*). Many of these larger proprietors who had been left out of the earlier agrarian reform were said to be leaving their land uncultivated, presumably since they did not see the point of producing anything if they were only able to sell at the low prices offered by the Institute of Agrarian Reform (INRA). But the private sector of agriculture generally had fulfilled its obligations in respect of production more efficiently than had the state farms or co-operatives, so that the second agrarian reform law was a political rather than an economic measure. Many of these private farmers in the middle range were among the opponents of the regime and had taken to the hills, particularly in the Escambray, Matanzas and the north of Las Villas, during mid-1963, in sporadic revolts.[14]

Some 11,000 farms were thereby added to the state domain, which was in consequence responsible for a little over two-thirds of Cuban agriculture.[15] Though the actual acts of state intervention were often carried out callously, there was no widespread fighting, and no deaths seem to have been reported. All expropriated farmers who were not actual opponents of the regime were compensated, at the rate of $15 a month per *caballería* confiscated, up to a total of $250, for a period of ten years. In addition, some private farms remain with up to about 900 acres, mostly estates farmed by a single family.

Even after this reform, however, there remained between 150,000 and 200,000 small farmers in Cuba, or almost 80% of the farmers of the country before the Revolution.[16] These, despite alarms, remained in being at the beginning of the 1970s. About a quarter of these farms, or 40,000, are so small that they produce only for the farm family, with no surplus for sale. These include many of those 35,000 who received title deeds of land shared out under the terms of the unfulfilled first agrarian reform.[17] Some of these farmers remain relatively rich men. But all private farmers are free only up to a certain point. Thus they are members of the state-directed Association of Private Farmers,[18] are allowed to grow certain crops only, and can sell their produce only to the state purchasing agency (ACOPIO). These farmers can also only sell their estates, if they wish to do so, to the state, and the regime apparently thinks that in the long run, all these private estates will by sale come into state hands.[19] Not unnaturally, therefore, there has been considerable anxiety, particularly among those farmers who might seem to come within the next category, 100 to 150 acres.[20]

The small farmers still make a big contribution to the revolution's agricultural programme. They grow most (70%)

of the fruit in Cuba, nearly all the coffee and tobacco (90%), own almost half of the livestock and still grow about 25% of the cane. (Tobacco is grown by about 40,000 private farmers, though the manufacture of cigars and cigarettes is controlled by the government.) It would be a serious mistake if ideological preconceptions were to cause any further state intervention in a department of the economy which, despite many discouragements, is still very productive.

Since 1964 agriculture has been the centre of the regime's attention and has naturally benefited substantially. 25% of the Gross National Product is invested in agriculture.[21] There have been huge imports of tractors from Russia and Czechoslovakia, many irrigation projects, the building of fertilizer plants — one by the English firm of Simon-Carves, costing £M14 near Cienfuegos[22] — several experimental cattle projects (including an Institute of Animal Science[23]) to increase the quality of animals, directed by the English agronomist, Dr Thomas Preston of Aberdeen, greater care of grasses, and much greater use of fungicides and pesticides. Castro's own interests in agriculture have been continuous. The nationalization of most of the cane land, though it has carried with it familiar disadvantages, has at least made possible on a national scale the rational planning of planting and harvesting. The large investment which the Revolution has made in agriculture could certainly assure Cuba of being one of the most modern and prosperous agricultural countries in the world by 1975-80, assuming that wise decisions are made politically. In particular, the future of Cuban rice and of cattle, especially beef cattle, seems promising. Livestock figures are now apparently well over those of 1959, despite the heavy slaughtering which went on during 1959-60.[24] Land under cultivation is said to have increased by 50%.[25] Except for wheat, fats and oils, Cuba could supply all her basic foods, and, in the long run, home-grown cotton and other fibres could presumably supply the domestic clothing industry. But there are dark sides to the situation. Thus, despite efforts to decentralise since 1965, there remains much inefficiency, and the planning powers of JUCEI, the planning boards, and INRA, though much reduced in functions, continue to hamper local managers, even if it is no longer the case, as occurred before 1965, that small items such as nails had to be ordered from Havana. Castro's own obsession with agriculture and his unchallenged position in the country is not an unmixed blessing for agricultural administrators. Thus since 1965 special farms have been assigned to the personal attention of Castro and these have received absolute priority in respect of equipment, often to the cost of other farms. These farms have so multiplied since 1968 that René Dumont, after a prolonged visit in 1969, described the Cuban countryside as 'now divided up in a series of special giant enterprises given over to single crops'.[26] This is a complete reversal of what occurred before 1965, when each People's Farm diversified and grew twenty-five to thirty-five different crops.

There have also been continuous difficulties with the agricultural workers. In 1966 there had to be a nationwide campaign against the withholding by workers on state farms of small plots of land for themselves; 'even the paths between state farms' had been privately sown, state irrigation had been diverted to secret private plots and private cultivation and the keeping of livestock around state workers' houses had begun at an alarming rate. In precisely the same way, the slaves of the past had developed their own *conucos* around their barracoons. It does not seem as if the twentieth-century authoritarian state has in the long run been any more successful than the nineteenth-century private capitalist in preventing agricultural labourers from self-help. How much agricultural time and labour is 'wasted' in this way is impossible to predict.

Finally, agricultural production, particularly if it is intended to be internationally competitive, is increasingly the consequence of a huge combined economic system in which efficiency depends upon industry, science and commerce as much as upon the farmer. Most competitive agricultural countries, such as Denmark or Britain (since 1945), are serviced by a large number of 'para-agricultural workers'.[27] Thus it is not really feasible to concentrate on agricultural development regardless of its implications, and it must be a matter of serious doubt whether Cuba's continued reliance on Russian and East European industry for the tools of her agricultural undertakings promises well, since this industry has in the past been so unsuccessful in serving her own agricultures.

There is also a black market. As early as 1963 the black market was supposed to give food prices at between three and ten times the official figures. For a long time, the regime turned a blind eye to the large number of townspeople who would drive out of the cities at week-ends to buy food direct from peasants and indeed, with the rationing of petrol from the beginning of 1967, and the lack of buying power of all money, along with the virtual disappearance of all goods from the shops, this activity has more or less come to an end. It was replaced by a system of barter, by which hats, for instance, would be exchanged for chickens, or coffee for a barrel of beer, though one instance was reported in 1969 of a pig for a party being bought for $600.

It is fairly clear that agriculture will dominate Cuban life for the foreseeable future, perhaps forever. Castro appears to bank on likely world food shortages to secure for Cuba permanently a market for increased agricultural production.[28] On the other hand, Castro's politics have changed often and other Cuban leaders still seem to expect more traditionally that agriculture in the long run will 'create exports so as to allow us to enter upon industrialization'.[29] In either event, the social consequences are likely to be considerable, since the Cuban regime evidently hopes, at the moment, to reverse the customary drift of labour into the cities characteristic of the rest of the world and preserve, or even expand, the rural population — so attempting to disprove the conventional wisdom that progress and industrialization are synonyms. This romantic plan is not likely to succeed.

ENDNOTES

1. It was on 10 August 1963, before the Institute of Hydraulic Resources, in the Havana Libre Hotel, Havana, that Castro announced 'we are going to develop the cane fields primarily and then the cattle. These are going to be pillars of the economy until 1970.'

2. The years since 1959 have each received a name from the government to suggest the national theme. Thus, 1959 was the year of Liberation, 1960 of Agrarian Reform, 1961 of Education, 1962 of Planning, 1963 of Organization, 1964 of the Economy, 1965 of Agriculture, 1966 of Solidarity with the Underdeveloped World, 1967 of Heroic Vietnam, 1968 of the Heroic Guerilla. As with many things in Cuba, the labelling of years was systematized, not invented, by Castro: thus the year 1953 had been described by Batista as the 'year of the centenary of the Apostle' (that is, of Martí's birth).

3. Michel Gutelman, *L'Agriculture Socialisée à Cuba* (Maspero, Paris 1967, 205).

4. The yield from the cane averaged 10.85% in 1969 in comparison with 12.62% in 1958. In 1969 Castro was speaking of a yield of 12.05% as quite exceptional (interview, 20 December 1969, published *Granma* weekly edition, 28 December 1969).

5. Cane loses sucrose by easily calculated percentages if there is a prolonged delay between canefield and mill. Cane which reaches the mill seven days after being cut has lost 25% of the sugar it would have had if it reached it immediately. In the first part of the harvest, of 1969-70, this seems to have happened quite often.

6. It is true that the faking of statistics is a little more difficult than it might seem, particularly when the separate achievements of the individual mills are all announced and indeed followed by the press during the course of the grinding. But since 1964 Cuba has followed a policy of secrecy about sugar statistics to 'impede . . . enemies of the Revolution'.

7. Castro's speech at the opening of the main stage of the harvest, 27 October 1969 (*Granma* weekly edition, 2 November 1969).

8. Russia agreed to take 2.1 million tons of sugar in 1965, 3 million tons in 1966, 4 million tons in 1967 and 5 million tons in 1968-9. China blamed Russia for forcing Cuba to continue to emphasise sugar in her economy (see *People's Daily*, 22 February 1966).

9. The total sugar available for sale on the 'free market' was conceived as 9.4 million tons, of which 7.7 million were basic exports and 1.65 re-exports from the Communist countries (some Cuban sugar included, doubtless). Other large quotas included Australia, 1.1 million; British West Indies and Guyana, 200,000 and Brazil, 500,000.

10. See H. Thomas, *The Cuban Revolution* (Harper and Row, New York, 1971, 698).

11. See P. Sakun, *URSS*, July 1968, figure for imported cane-cutters. The most frequently used variety of cane, incidentally, remains that used before 1959 — the Javanese POJ 2878, but recently successful experiments have been made with a Barbados variety.

12. Speech, 5 July 1968.

13. The *Hendersons* are cutters assembled (apparently at Santa Clara) on top of bulldozers imported from Russia. They need a cane

collection centre where the leaves of the cane are stripped off before being dispatched to the mill. Some 300 of these were planned for 1971.

14. Carlos Rafael Rodríquez, *La Revolución Cubana y el Periodo de Transición*, Foletto 2, 12.

15. The second agrarian reform expropriated 6,062 farms between 5 and 10 *caballería* (a total of 608,000 hectares), 3,105 between 10 and 20 *caballería* (610,000 hectares), 1,456 between 20 and 30 *caballería* (508,000 hectares) and 592 larger than 30 *caballería* (377,000 hectares).

16. According to the Agricultural Census of 1946 — and there is no later source — farms smaller than 150 acres constituted over 80% of the farms in Cuba.

17. Only 35,000 deeds were distributed under the terms of the regime's promise in 1959 to give 100,000 land titles.

18. *Asociación nacional de agricultores privados.*

19. Castro's speech to the 3rd congress of ANAP, May 1967.

20. René Dumont, *Cuba, Socialisme et Développement* (1964), p. 87.

21. There were 35,000 tractors in 1967 in comparison with 9,200 in 1960 (Castro speech of 2 January 1968).

22. Simon-Carves of Stockport had built chemical or fertilizer plants in other Communist countries before (see Ian Ball, *Daily Telegraph*, 3 February 1967).

23. See the *Informe Anual* of the *Instituto de Ciencia Animal*, 1966.

24. According to one (Cuban) estimate, cattle numbers about 7 million head of cattle, well above the 1959 figure of 5.8 million. The aim is to raise numbers of cattle to 12 million by 1975, permitting an annual slaughter of 4 million and the daily production of 30 million litres of milk (Gutelman, *L'Agriculture socialisée à Cuba*, 79). However, it is fair to doubt whether these targets will be achieved and whether Castro is right in predicting a rice surplus by 1970. Russia, it will be remembered, has not fulfilled a single one of her agricultural plans since 1929.

25. According to Castro, on 2 January 1968, land cultivation in 1958 in Cuba was 2.3 million hectares. In 1967 this had risen by 56% to 3.7 million hectares.

26. René Dumond, Les Cubains trouvent le temps long, *Le Monde*, 9 December 1969.

27. René Dumont and Bernard Rosier, *The Hungry Future*, André Deutsch, London, 1969, 38.

28. Perhaps this at least he has learned from Professor René Dumont, many of whose other suggestions have been unwisely spurned.

29. Dr. Carlos Rafael Rodríguez in an interview to the author in January 1969.

The Lessons of Juan Bosch for the Dominican Republic
José Moreno

Juan Bosch's short-lived government was a clear attempt to break with the caudillo *politics of the Dominican Republic's past. Although at the present there is a democratically elected president in the nation, the issues which Bosch raised, especially effective land reform and greater participation of labor in the country's gross national product, are still to be satisfactorily resolved. Reprinted from J. Moreno (1970),* Barrios in Arms: Revolution in Santo Domingo, *pp. 14-21, University of Pittsburgh Press. Copyright © 1970 by the University of Pittsburgh Press. Reproduced by permission of the University of Pittsburgh Press and the Author.*

After Trujillo's death, his family, particularly his older son Ramfis, kept control of the armed forces and of the country at large. International pressures from President Kennedy and the Organization of American States, and internal opposition organized by the June 14th Movement and the newly founded nonpolitical civilian group Unión Cívica Nacional (UCN) grew steadily. A few months later the Trujillo family emptied the national treasury and went into exile. Joaquín Balaguer, Trujillo's hand-picked president, decided to form the Council of State on January 1, 1962, to rule the nation under this own chairmanship. Six other members, including the two survivors of the group who had killed Trujillo, were selected from the different political groups as members of the council. But two weeks later, the two middle-class organizations, the June 14th Movement and the UCN, brought about the resignation of Balaguer, because of his intimate collaboration with the old dictator. The presidency of the Council of State then was occupied by Rafael F. Bonnelly. Bonnelly had been minister of the interior under Trujillo, and had cooperated with him,[1] but before Trujillo's death he had joined the UCN.

One of the political exiles who returned to Santo Domingo after the death of Trujillo was Juan Bosch, the leader of the Dominican Revolutionary Party (PRD). After twenty-five years in exile in Cuba, Venezuela, and Costa Rica, Juan Bosch had become — with Rómulo Betancourt, Pepe Figueres, and Muñoz Marín — one of the most outspoken leaders of the so-called democratic left in Latin America. While in exile, Bosch and others had organized the PRD, a political organization based on the same ideology as the Cuban Revolutionary Party (Auténtico), the Acción Democrática of Venezuela, and the Popular Party of Puerto Rico. These parties appealed to the large, dispossessed masses with promises of greater participation in the economic and social life of the country, greater freedom from internal dictatorships, and independence for the country as a whole from imperialistic international powers.

When, in October 1961, Bosch arrived from exile in Santo Domingo, both he and his PRD were entirely unknown in the political arena. The UCN and the June 14th Movement had managed to capture the spirit of the forces opposed to the Trujillo family and had forced Balaguer out of power. Actually the UCN had become the party in power after Balaguer was ousted. However, the two parties soon divided. The Unión Cívica became the party of the extreme right, although until 1962 it had harbored some members of the Communist Party. The June 14th Movement became the extreme left, although most of its members were from the upper middle class. Although the political campaigns of the UCN were based on the need to eradicate "Trujilloism" in the country, most of their leaders — as members of the upper or middle class — had been tightly connected with Trujillo and his family. It was a period of bickering and wrangling about which individuals had cooperated most with Trujillo.

The fact was that practically everyone in the country had been linked with the dictator in some way.

Under Bosch, the PRD sought to assert itself by taking an entirely different line. It discussed problems at a national level and debated about the means available to solve them, not about the vices or virtues of individuals. The PRD addressed its appeal to the masses which, Bosch insisted, had never been considered in Dominican politics.[2] His appeal advocated structural reforms in the whole social system.

Free elections in the Dominican Republic were an unprecedented event in the life of most Dominicans. From 1848 to 1962 there had been thirty-two presidential elections, of which only four were free, and of these only two were conducted by direct popular vote. The political atmosphere was charged with great expectations. An electorate of fewer than a million and a quarter people were offered five presidential candidates, and twenty-six political parties. Elections, supervised by the OAS were held on December 20, 1962. From a total of 1,054,944 votes cast, Bosch received 628,044; his opponent from the UCN drew 317,327. The PRD elected 22 senators and 52 deputies: the UCN, 4 senators and 13 deputies. The few remaining senators and deputies were elected from among the other twenty-four parties. Juan Bosch had been freely elected by an overwhelming majority of Dominicans.

The first task before the new government was revision of the constitution. The National Assembly met for four months, and on April 29, sixty days after Bosch had been inaugurated, it proclaimed a new constitution. The Constitution of 1963 was basically similar to many other Latin American constitutions; it especially resembled the Cuban constitution drawn up in 1940 under Batista and under the influence of the Auténtico Party with which Juan Bosch had become familiar while in Cuba.

As the new constitution was implemented, the government became the target of increasing accusations. On May 14, 1963,[3] in a public letter addressed to the president, the leader of the opposition UCN, Dr. Viriato Fiallo, summarized these accusations. Dr. Fiallo suggested that the "committees for the protection of the forest and sugar cane fields" were not necessary since the armed forces could take care of those, and he pointed out that in other countries such committees were known as militias. He criticized the government for supporting an official monopoly of mass media, for awarding jobs only to members of the party in power,[4] and for placing communists in key government positions and letting them use schools and government buildings for their political indoctrination. He concluded his letter by demanding a clear and definite statement on Bosch's position toward the communist ideology.

Still other critics of Bosch were more biased and vitrolic than Dr. Fiallo. Bosch was accused in the press, over radio and television of the following charges.[5]

1. Embezzlement of 70 million dollars in a contract with the Overseas Construction Ltd.
2. Signing secret agreements with the communists, handing the university over to them, and giving them key positions in his administration.
3. Violating the constitution by changing the structure of the cabinet, undermining the autonomy of the university, and interfering with the judiciary.
4. Organizing a coup against his own government to let the communists take over.
5. Creating an armed conflict with Haiti to divert public attention from domestic problems.

By July 1963, the opposition to the government was trying to create the impression of massive reaction of the populace against the policies of the government. Huge rallies of "Christian reaffirmation" were organized all over the country. Truckloads of peasants were brought from the provinces into the capital to show support for action against the communists. (The practice of transporting peasants to the city for demonstrations had been initiated by Trujillo when he had become concerned with national and international public opinion.)

Also in July, the Dominican Congress modified the Law of Public Confiscations, originally passed under the Council of State to expropriate property owned by the Trujillo family and other Trujillistas. The Congress designated itself, and not the judiciary, as the only tribunal for this procedure. When the UCN was in power, the law had been enforced by the Council of State. However with the PRD in power, the UCN was threatened by a somewhat stricter application of the law than before. The law had been praised by the poor city dwellers and by the peasants, but denounced by organizations of industrialists, entrepreneurs, and landowners.[6] It is interesting to note that these organizations denounced the law using an argument that was to be widely applied by all opponents of the government until the downfall of Bosch. They argued that the Dominican Republic could not become a "second Cuba."[7]

The Dominican armed forces, which had been notorious for their cooperation with Trujillo and for their interference in politics since his death, had been surprisingly quiet since the election of Bosch. However, on July 16, Bosch appeared on television to tell the country that the military had put pressure on him.[8] Rumors spread throughout the country. An attempted coup failed, as did a general strike announced by business and shop owners.

Shortly afterward, another general strike was called by the business and shop owners. Scheduled for September 20, 1963, the strike was to protest "international communism and the complacent attitude of the government toward communist groups in the country."[9] Four radio stations were ordered off the air by the government because of their support of the illegal strike and for inciting rebellion. Nor was Bosch successful in handling the left. On the same day that he closed the radio stations, the June 14th Movement published a communiqué blaming the government and the PRD for not taking the steps necessary to curtail the activities of those plotting against the constitution.[10]

Early on the morning of September 25, a coup against Bosch's government was successful. The communiqué announcing the coup was signed by ten generals and fifteen colonels. It blamed the government for not taking a firm stand on the issue of communism,[11] despite the clear warning given to it by the military that the issue of communism had brought the country to the brink of civil war. It indicated that the new government would respect the rights of individuals and associations, especially the right to private property and free enterprise, so that commerce, industry, and banks, free from fears of confiscation, could contribute to the development of the country.[12]

A few days after the coup, Juan Bosch, who had been under arrest, left the country in a navy frigate for the West Indies. From there he went to Puerto Rico where he was to stay for the next two years. The first and only attempt at democracy in the history of the country thus ended after seven months.

ENDNOTES

1. J. Bosch, *Crisis de la Democracia de América en la República Dominicana* (Mexico City, 1964), pp. 71-73. See also Jesús de Galíndez Suárez, *La era de Trujillo* (Buenos Aires, Editorial Marymar, 1962), p. 87.
2. Bosch, *Crisis*, pp. 80-81.
3. CEFA, *Libro blanco de las fuerzas armandas y de la policía nacional de la Republica Dominicana* (Santo Domingo, 1964), pp. 147–53. Bosch explained in his book how the accusations were entirely without foundation and yet they helped to create a false atmosphere that the communists were taking over his government. See *Crisis*, p. 128.
4. Political patronage from those in government is still an endemic practice in most of Latin America.
5. CEFA, *Libro blanco*, pp. 54-64, 286-88.
6. Ibid., pp. 163-65, 266 and 271.
7. The idea of a "second Cuba" is a recurrent theme that was present in the minds of many both in Santo Domingo and in the U.S. from 1963 to 1965, and undoubtedly is still present today. See CEFA, *Libro blanco*, pp. 163-65.
8. *El Caribe*, July 17, 1963.
9. *Prensa Libre*, September 20, 1966, p. 1.
10. CEFA, *Libro blanco*, p. 301.
11. On the issue of being "hard" or "soft" on communism, see Daniel Bell, *The Radical Right* (New York, 1964), pp. 67-68.
12. CEFA, *Libro blanco*, pp. 90-91.

SECTION 9
The Caribbean Future: Hopes and Dour Appraisals

9.0

Introduction to Section 9

Amidst the recognition of commonly shared historical background and future goals, one might expect that the movement toward regional integration would be a natural course of action. Yet the reality is quite the reverse; past attempts at integration have been miserable failures, from the separate paths taken by Cuba and Puerto Rico in the 1890s to the failure of the West Indian Federation in this century. F.A. Barrett (selection 9.1) examines the reasons why political federation materialized in the English-speaking Caribbean, but never operated effectively. Certainly the timing, at the point when many member units were negotiating for their independence, was wrong.

On the more optimistic side, however, recent attempts at economic integration have been partially successful. The existence of the Caribbean Community (which ideally should function as a local equivalent of the Common Market) and NAMUCAR, a Caribbean-Central American shipping line, attest to this fact. Perhaps the Caribbean Development Bank, which operates in the English-speaking Caribbean, has assessed the problem correctly in dividing member nations into LDCs and MDCs (Lesser Developed Countries and More Developed Countries) and awarding grants in accordance with this scale. The fact that many Caribbean nations produce the same materials (sugar and bauxite are good examples) inevitably means that large-scale economic co-operation is far in the future. Still, local-level exchanges (such as the creation of vocational training centres in Jamaica through Cuban funding) are the first steps in this direction.

Seemingly disillusioned with the economic, cultural and political conditions in their countries of birth, many West

Indian intellectuals have forsaken the region for residence abroad in former metropolitan settings. Pockets of Caribbean writers in London, Paris, New York and Toronto are by no means a rarity. Among the better known of these artists is Aimé Césaire, from the French Department of Martinique, who has used West Indian themes to show his preoccupation with finding identity for Third World Peoples. As Gindine comments (selection 9.2) in her analysis of Césaire's *The Tragedy of King Christophe*, the writer has selected this self-styled, and often pathetic, Haitian monarch as a symbol of despair. Césaire, in this work, was apparently much influenced by the African struggles for political independence in the 1960s.

Other Caribbean citizens have left the region for more pressing economic reasons. Louise Bennet's poem *Colonization in Reverse* (selection 9.3) is an ironic look at and insight into the problems of West Indians residing in England. A more sober analysis of the difficulties of migration (legal and otherwise) is provided in González' discussion of Dominicans living in New York. The problems of cultural adjustment, the difficulties of obtaining work and the harrassment from immigration authorities often render past island experiences as utopian visions. Selection 9.4 focusses on the special obstacles faced by rural migrants to an urban locale. In addition, González analyses the valuable role that income earned abroad and sent home can have for Caribbean economies.

The final selection of this anthology contains the Demas address (see Epilogue) with which the volume began. Demas summarizes the basic themes and issues raised in these pages and offers sagacious advice on how a 'new Caribbean' might eventually be forged.

For an overview of the non-Hispanic Caribbean in recent years, the student might consult D. Lowenthal, *West Indian Societies*. A somewhat dated view of regional economic integration is found in A. Segal, *The Politics of Caribbean Economic Integration*; N. Girvan and O. Jefferson (eds.), *Readings in the Political Economy of the Caribbean* offers a more up-to-date approach, but is difficult to obtain out of the region. The question of integration is also discussed in A. Murch, *Black Frenchmen:the Political Integration of the*

French Antilles. The lack of meaningful integration even within national borders is the subject of L. Barrett, *The Rastafarians: Sounds of Cultural Dissonance*; the author is sensitive, however, to the politically important influence that such dissident groups can wield.

9.1

The Rise and Demise of the Federation of the West Indies
F.A. Barrett

From the moment that federation was raised as an issue at the 1938 Trades Union meeting in British Guiana, the idea of pan-regional unity, at least among the Anglophone units of the Antilles, has both fired the Caribbean imagination and caused seemingly endless dissension. In this selection, F.A. Barrett examines the brief history of the Federation and the causes of its failure. In the long run, perhaps the fact that a Federation was actually created among the English-speaking units of the Caribbean is more remarkable than its ultimate demise in 1962. Reprinted from F.A. Barrett (1974), 'The Rise and Demise of the Federation of the West Indies', Canadian Review of Studies in Nationalism, *1, No. 2 (Spring), pp. 248-254, with permission of the Publisher and the Author.*

In 1945, Arthur Creech-Jones, Secretary of State for the Colonies, invited all the official representatives of the British Caribbean colonies to discuss various political options in the region. The Bahamas declined the invitation but all the other colonies — the ten which ultimately formed the West Indies Federation (Jamaica, St. Kitts-Nevis, Antigua, Montserrat, Dominica, St. Lucia, St. Vincent, Grenada, Barbados, Trinidad and Tobago, as well as British Honduras and British Guiana) — were present. After some delay the conference, held in September 1947 in Montego Bay, Jamaica, formed the Standing Closer Association Committee (S.C.A.C.) to investigate the possibility of federation. The conferees recognized that federation was the most secure and "the shortest possible path to political independence and

responsible Dominion status; but political independence
without financial stability was hardly worthwhile and this was
the reason why federation was of supreme importance."[1]

Reflecting upon Franck's levels of federation motivation
presented in the first part of this paper the above rationale
is almost prophetic as to the outcome of the West Indies
Federation. Desires for independence and solvency, while
extremely important in themselves, could not form the basis
for the foundation and maintenance of a federation. The fact
that the Bahamas, located in the northern periphery of the
proposed association were so uninterested that they did not
attend even the preliminary conference, is indicative of one
of the problems confronting the union. Though the United
Kingdom had initiated negotiations immediately after World
War II, desultory talks continued for more than a decade
before the West Indies Federation was constituted in 1958.
This was a long period compared with the speed with which
numerous other nations moved from colonial status to
independence in the 1950s and 1960s. Clearly, the idea of a
federation lacked strong popular support, the result of three
variables. To attain independence by means of a federal
structure was much more complicated than to achieve that
goal as an individual state in which no relinquishing of power
would be necessary. For all their common colonial experiences, many of the partners in this proposed federal marriage
were strange bedfellows. Historically they had been separated,
their communications disrupted, their economic lives at great
variance. As the Barbadian scholar, Hugh Springer, so per-
ceptively noted:

After all, each island was potentially a separate little member of the
British Commonwealth of Nations overwhelmingly, or at least predominantly British in education and culture, more accustomed to
dealing with Britain than with the other islands, not conscious of being
oppressed by any British yoke, but on the contrary dependent for prosperity and indeed survival upon special arrangements with Britain for
marketing of crops too small in quantity, even in the aggregate, to
give much bargaining power in world markets. There was comparatively
little trade between the islands and there had been virtually no communication between Jamaica and the rest until the advent of air travel,
which coincided with World War II. Thus the ties between the islands
themselves were weaker than ties of each with Britain.[2]

Obviously, the British government was not perceived as an enemy. No wonder that the degree of nationalistic sentiment among the colonies varied considerably. Nowhere was it so strongly developed that Britain was seen as a common foe. This very lack of distinctive nationalistic sentiments in some of the territories resulted in a preference for the federalist rather than the sovereign cause. In a sense, the federation came into existence because national awareness was not fully developed among the various Islanders. As we shall see later, however, latent nationalism in some colonies made the ultimate failure of the federation a certainty.

The movement toward federation was painstakingly slow. Even after the Standing Committee's technical papers were digested, it required three more sessions to resolve major issues. It is noteworthy that both British Honduras and British Guiana sent only observers to the second meeting, the London Conference, held in April 1953. The withdrawal of the two largest territorial units in the British West Indies dramatized the lopsided relationship of Jamaica and Trinidad to the other islands. Spatially, the withdrawal of the two mainland units, along with the earlier rejection of the Bahamas for a call to federation, meant that the most northerly, southerly and westerly British Caribbean colonies had opted out of the proposed union. These actions, seen in hindsight, presaged the ultimate failure of the Caribbean federation concept. Clearly the most distant, dispersed, and culturally diverse members of the Caribbean empire had recognized that few ingredients for a successful federation existed. Conversely, the nationalist principle that Springer alludes to in his study, namely, that some day each Island would be a separate member of the British Commonwealth, acted as a positive check against the negative inducement to federate in order to fill a political vacuum. Another consequence of the withdrawal of the Bahamas, British Honduras, and British Guiana was that Jamaica, now the largest and most populous remaining unit, spatially lost its central position and became isolated. As well, the exclusion of British Honduras and British Guiana accentuated existing differences between Trinidad and Jamaica.

One of the prime points in dispute at that Conference revolved around the question of freedom of movement of people and goods between the proposed federated states. While Trinidad was a firm supporter of federation, it was concerned about the smaller Eastern Caribbean members 'exporting' their unemployed to the larger island. Aside from its economic concern, Trinidad's attitude reveals its lack of any national conceptualization on the federal level. A feeling of 'mine' and 'yours' on Trinidad's part was obvious. There was no intimation that a federation 'ours' had as yet developed. So searching was this issue that another conference, held in 1961 was still not able to come to grips with it successfully.

Other problems also continued to plague the conferees. In 1956, the second London Conference was held. This time the main stumbling block was whether the proposed states should form a customs union. Jamaica was very reluctant to surrender its economic power. Her demands for economic autonomy further loosened the proposed federal bond. At this stage Jamaica's distinctive national image was becoming more clearly defined, heralding future problems for the federation.

In January 1957, the Standing Federal Committee issued its report, among other things, on the name of the proposed federation, and on the proposed site of its capital. Unfortunately, the British Colonial Civil Service was over-represented on this commission and offered suggestions that did not appear to be in the interests of the West Indian Federation. They suggested, for example, that the new state be known as the British Caribbean Federation. The delegates rejected this suggestion and chose as their name "The West Indies Federation" instead. As far as the capital was concerned, it had to be close to an already established urban service base; it had to be situated on an island sufficiently large not to lose its identity, and it had to be a centre well suited to inter-island and international transportation and communication routes. These requirements eliminated all of the smaller, less populated islands. In order of preference, the committee suggested:

1. Barbados, the most 'British' of the islands.

2. Jamaica, a poor second choice because the island was too big, but if chosen, the capital would have to be located in the hills, where it would be more congenial to Europeans living in the tropics.

3. Trinidad, which possessed all the requirements but was nonetheless unsuitable because of government corruption and political instability.[3]

Understandably, the delegation from Trinidad was chagringed. Responding to their annoyance, the delegates rejected the Commission's preferential list and chose Trinidad. While it might appear that the anti-colonialist outburst generated by this conference would help to untie the neophyte federation, it did not.

Choosing the site of a federal capital is always a difficult business. All components of a federation quite naturally wish the capital to be located on their own territory, in order to reap the prestige and political advantage associated with the federal capital. It was clear at the outset that Jamaica was the most dubious of all the West Indian states about the new federation. Perhaps if Jamaica had received the capital, the union might have been strengthened sufficiently to alter the outcome of the 1961 referendum. Though only speculation, it is possible that by locating the federal capital far from Jamaica, that island's nationalism was allowed to grow in a climate unwarmed by the enthusiasm bred of proximity to the federal capital. In any case, it is clear that the federal centre was located as far as possible from the weakest link in the federation.

The long preliminary period terminated in January 1958, when Lord Hauley, the Governor-General, arrived in Chaguaramas (Trinidad), the new federal capital. Sir Grantly Adams, a politician from Barbados, became the first federal Prime Minister. The two most formidable political figures in the region, Norman Manley, Prime Minister of Jamaica, and Eric Williams, Prime Minister of Trinidad, both decided to maintain their island positions rather than foray into the uncertain federal area. From the start, their opposing views of the federal function dominated the union. Williams, a strong federalist, believed that local power had to be significantly relinquished for the common federal good, whereas Manley represented the most intense nationalistic viewpoint, and favoured a loosely associated federation. Trinidad's position was that

> . . . since the first objective of the nation must be to build a national economy, the national government must be enabled to do this by being given complete command of all its material and other resources, including its perspective for the future.[4]

Only a powerful and centrally directed economic co-ordination and interdependence can create the true foundations of a nation. Barbados will not unify with British Guyana, or Jamaica with Antigua. They will knit together only through their common allegiance to a Central Government. Anything else will discredit the conception of a Federation and in the end leave the islands more divided than before.[5]

In contrast, the Jamaican position was that

> The power of the Federal Government to intervene in Jamaican affairs should be severely limited. Even the existing constitution . . . gave the Federal Government too large a power to interfere with the industrial development of each unit and with its powers of taxation . . . The constitution should be revised so as to exclude the possibility of federal control, and to leave in the control of each unit the development of industry and the power to levy income tax, excise duties and compensation taxes.[6]

These opposing views typified the classical federal controversy between states rights versus central authority rights. It is little wonder that the federation was doomed to fail.

In January 1960, Manley's thinly veiled separatist designs surfaced once more. While in London, he sounded out the Colonial Secretary about Jamaica's minimal requirements for full dominion status in the Commonwealth. He also took the opportunity to inquire whether Jamaica might hope to achieve this objective on her own hook, not as a member of the West Indies Federation. Colonial Secretary McLeod replied affirmatively. This encouraging response strengthened Jamaica's national image, as well as its bargaining position in the forthcoming discussion with other West Indian governments. Paradoxically, Jamaica's internal political configuration at the time temporarily played into Manley's hands.

The opposition to Manley's People's National Party, the Jamaican Labour Party, was led by the experienced Sir Alexander Bustamante. Sir Alexander's party decided to oppose federation. As a result, Jamaica's official party, which favoured a loose federal association, had as its official opposition in the legislature an outright opponent to federal union. National independence was, therefore, becoming an increasingly popular alternative for Jamaica. Capitalizing on this grass roots sentiment in Jamaica Manley went to the Intergovernment Conference in May 1961 held in Port-of-Spain, and succeeded in significantly altering the nature of the federation. The only two points that remained were federal control over the development of industry and over taxes on incomes and profits. Both of these points were strongly opposed in Jamaica.

These contentious issues had surfaced somewhat earlier. On his first official visit to Jamaica in December 1958, Sir Grantly Adams, the Federal Prime Minister, had chided Jamaicans and threatened to introduce retroactive federal taxation. The reaction to the statement was reflected in a letter to Kingston's largest newspaper the *Gleaner*:

I am shocked that now Jamaicans can be dictated to by 'small islanders' even under the guise of creating a large nation.[7]

By 'small islanders' the writer meant that Adams hailed from Barbados. Both sentiments were typical reflecting the antipathy that existed between the various islands. They typified the growing nationalism most clearly developed in Jamaica but becoming increasingly evident among other island members of the federation.

Under the pressures of growing regional nationalisms the federation began to crumble. Upon his return from the Intergovernment Conference, Manley decided to place the question of Jamaica's continued participation in the West Indies Federation to a popular referendum. On 19 September 1961, 54% of those who voted cast a negative ballot. Manley accepted the mandate and proceeded to initiate independence negotiations with the Colonial Secretary. Four months later, the government of Trinidad, fresh from an electoral victory, passed a resolution not to participate in a Federation of the Eastern Caribbean. In Williams' arithmetic book ten minus one equalled zero! On 31 May 1962, after only four years, the federal parliament of the Federation of the West Indies ended its legal existence.

ENDNOTES

1. Lloyd Braithwaite, "Progress Toward Federation, 1938-1956," *Social and Economic Studies*, (June 1957), p. 147.
2. Hugh W. Springer, *Reflections on the Failure of the First West Indian Federation*. Occasional papers in International Affairs, No. 4, (Cambridge, Mass., 1962), p. 42.
3. Braithwaite, *ibid*.
4. Springer, *ibid*., p. 15.
5. *Ibid*., p. 16.
6. *Ibid*., p. 17.
7. *Ibid*., p. 20; citing letter of 5 December 1958.

Aimé Césaire's La Tragédie du Roi Christophe

Yvette Gindine

Disenchanted Caribbean intellectuals run the gamut from Naipaul to Fanon. One outstanding literary figure in this category is Aimé Césaire, whose Tragédie, *based on the life of Haitian monarch Christophe, is examined in this selection. Yvette Gindine finds that the despair expressed in this work extends beyond the Antillean setting; Césaire obviously saw analogies between Caribbean history and the political processes evident in Africa of the 1960's. Reprinted from Y. Gindine (1974), 'The Magic of Black History: Images of Haiti',* Caribbean Review, *VI, No. 4, pp. 28-29. Published at Florida International University. Copyright © 1974* Caribbean Review *with permission of the Publisher and the Author.*

As dramatized by the Martiniquais Aimé Césaire, *La Tragédie du Roi Christophe* (Paris: Editions de Présence Africaine, 1970. Translations mine) and by extension the tragedy of Haiti — must be recognized as analogous to the African upheavals of the 60's, even though it anticipated by a century and a half the disasters now befalling many of the new-born Third World states. Césaire boldly interprets Christophe as a paradigm of the Third World leader, trying to defend his young country against the general hostility of the former masters, imposing on his people a ferocious discipline meant to insure the collective survival. Yet the Black leader is inexorably rejected and ultimately destroyed by those he wanted to protect.

From the very start Césaire imposes a reading of past Haitian developments in terms of the present through the systematic use of anachronism and a deliberate simplification of the political context. Without forcing Christophe into an allegory of the sacrificed leader, Césaire retains enough concrete references so that the two sets of coordinates — Haitian and African — are simultaneously accepted and a constant comparison established between the two. Thus Christophe's political Westernization appears as an early instance of the mimetic syndrome described by current analysts: in the absence of specific solutions geared to the particular problems of the emerging nation, there seems to be an unavoidable return to the conventional system inherited from the colonial power. When Christophe decides to institute a Sovereign Empire and to crown himself King Henry the First, he borrows from the enemy the sole conceivable model of political structure, the only respectable formula of Government. Conversely the search for personal identity — Négritude or Antillanité — a key preoccupation of the newly emancipated peoples, finds a counterpart in Christophe's fabrication of an instant nobility: by creating hereditary titles, he grants an exalted selfhood to men who had been robbed of their very names during the Middle Passage. And on the top of a mountain, the Citadel stands as symbol in stone of Black challenge, restoring pride among the people — "for these men kept on their knees, a monument which makes them stand up!"

In this continuous mirroring of past and present, lyrical and somber passages alternate with comic and ironical moments. Thus appears in a lighter vein the plight of the leader having to forge posthaste a national cultural consciousness: to encourage and accelerate the production of Native Poetry. Henry the First must endure the dreary declamations of his National Bard, the historical Chanlatte, whose patriotic zeal is couched in the then-prevailing 18th century neoclassical style, brilliantly parodied by Césaire. With the same touch of self-mockery addressed to mandatory chauvinisms, Christophe commands that Champagne be replaced at official banquets by the local rhum Barbancourt. However the tone becomes more sardonic when the King receives from "Tesco", in the guise of Technical Assistance, an expert in Etiquette who directs the rehearsals of the Coronation ceremony and imposes complicated ballet steps onto the reluctant dignitaries. Not only is the desultory help of Inter-nation organisations generally ridiculed but the French exportation of cultural values finds itself specially singled out with the delirious invocation to Form intoned by the same Protocol Officer in a language suffused with Valéry and Malraux overtones.

Still, for the new leaders, then as now, Time is pressing and Christophe cannot wait, in spite of Wilberforce's prudent advice about nations being the slow fruition of slow ripening. Seized with a racking sense of urgency, conscious of the enor-mous handicap imposed by slavery, the leader wants to skip whole stages of history even though he is at times aware of the futility of such a design and sees himself as a teacher threatening with a stick a whole nation of dunces. Voluntary, democratic participation is out of the question: at the cost of his popularity he will "ask from the Blacks more than from others because . . . they have more duties than others." Hence the authoritarian methods of the despot escalate; orders, repression and terror threaten miserable and baffled peasants for whom the mystique of work means only a return to slavery. Meanwhile, undeterred, Christophe is determined "to teach a lesson to those Blacks who believe that the Revolution is winning when they take the place of the Whites." But his vision of an economically self-reliant, strong nation is accompanied in practice by a dictatorial scheme resented by the rich as well as the poor. According to the cynical bourgeois commentators, Christophe thrives in serving freedom by the means of slavery. And when the land-less peasants agitate for the breaking up of large estates, the king refuses adamantly to change his agrarian policy: "Who will buy? If it is the big shots, I pity the poor people. And if it is the peasants, I pity the poor country. I can already imagine the anarchy of millet and sweet potato crowding each other out in tiny lots."

Like the Rebel, sacrificial hero of Césaire's first play and his brother in defeat, Christophe will be the victim of his own people, and his enterprise destroyed from within by what he calls "the sad army of termites." Forced to admit that he cannot raise a united front against external dangers, he becomes now the bitter spokesman for Césaire or even Fanon — two lucid and powerless observers of African conflicts — mourning the shattered hope of Pan-Africanism and Haiti's future blighted by internecine wars. "Poor Africa, I mean to say poor Haiti! It's the same thing anyway. Over there the tribes, the languages, the rivers, the castes, the forest, village against village, hamlet against hamlet. Here blacks, mulattoes, griffes, marabouts, what else, clan, caste, color, suspicion and competition, rooster fighting rooster, dogs fighting for a bone, battles of fleas!"

The ultimate catastrophe does not proceed from the physical paralysis of the King or even his stoical suicide, but from the unrelieved awareness of total failure which makes him conclude with despair: "The very fabric of man is to be remade. How? I do not know." Seen in a literary perspective, this doomed leader recalls the 19th century tradition of heroes entrusted with a mission, Extraordinary Envoys, solitary and sacrificed prophets destined to be martyrs of the cause they serve. As embodying Césaire's 20th century view of history, he suggests a profound pessimism which the gloating, hypocritical lament of the "Tesco" dancing expert underlines in the most deliberate gallows humour: "One can't really do anything with the Blacks!" In spite of its ultimate sustained threnody to the dead King whose ashes are translated to the sacred burial ground of Ifé, this play, written after the murder of Lumumba, reveals Césaire's depths of disillusionment and makes no allowance for the future, except in the bleakest terms.

Colonization in Reverse   Louise Bennet

Dialect writing is never more effective than in the poetry of Jamaican author Louise Bennet. In this poem she takes a jaunty yet perceptive look at the social and economic problems of Jamaicans resident in Great Britain, subtly suggesting that there is irony in the resettling of colonial peoples in the mother country. Reprinted from L. Bennet (1966), Jamaican Labrish, *Sangster's Book Stores Ltd. Reprinted with permission of the Publisher.*

Wat a joyful news, Miss Mattie,
I feel like my heart gwine burs'
Jamaica people colonizin
Englan in reverse.

By de hundred, by de t'ousan
From country and from town,
By de ship-load, by de plane-load
Jamaica is Englan boun.

Dem a-pour out o' Jamaica,
Everybody future plan
Is fe get a big-time job
An settle in de mother lan.

What a islan! What a people!
Man an woman, old an young
Jusa pack dem bag an baggage
An tun history upside dung!

Some people don't like travel,
But fe show dem loyalty
Dem all a-open up cheap-fare-
To-Englan agency.

An week by week dem shippin off
Dem countryman like fire,
Fe immigrate an populate
De seat o' de Empire.

Oonoo see how life is funny,
Oonoo see de tunabout,
Jamaica live fe box bread
Outa English people mout'.

For wen dem catch a Englan,
An start play dem different role,
Some will settle down to work
An some will settle fe de dole.

Jane say de dole is not too bad
Because dey payin' she
Two pounds a week fe seek a job
Dat suit her dignity.

Me say Jane will never find work
At the rate how she dah-look,
For all day she stay pon Aunt Fan couch
An read love-story book.

Wat a devilment a Englan!
Dem face war an brave de worse,
But I'm wonderin' how dem gwine stan'
Colonizin' in reverse.

Peasants' Progress: Dominicans in New York   Nancie L. González

The life of a Caribbean migrant is seldom without difficult and often costly adjustments, whether the land of relocation is Canada, France, the United States or Great Britain. Some Caribbean nationals arrive seeking political asylum; others, as in the case of Dominicans residing in New York, are more aptly described as economic refugees. The departure of thousands of citizens can have significant consequences for the home nations, as González points out, as well as for the country of destination. From N.L. González, 'Peasants' Progress: Dominicans in New York', Caribbean Studies, 10, No. 3 (October), 166–70. Copyright © 1970 by the Institute of Caribbean Studies, University of Puerto Rico. Reprinted by permission of the Institute of Caribbean Studies and the Author.

The average *campesino* or lower-class urbanite sees New York as the promised land. Many migrants go to New York with the idea of making a sum of money which they can then invest in the Dominican Republic to better their future there. Some case histories show persons who have saved what seem at first to be fantastic sums — from $15,000 to $20,000 or more. Such persons have returned to their country to build large modern houses complete with all sorts of electrical appliances, expensive furniture, elaborate plumbing fixtures, etc. Often they will start a store, or buy a truck and set up a hauling business. In other cases they buy land and either rent it out on "shares" or farm it themselves using hired employees. Some have bought cattle and others have invested in urban real estate, the rental of which may provide a very good income. Such persons usually retain their immigrant visas, making return visits as needed to augment their capital by working for a few months, to bring in expensive items either for their own use or for resale at tremendous profits, and to keep their visas in good standing.

Actual figures on the amounts saved in the United States seem impossible to verify, partly because of a reluctance on the part of the individual to discuss this delicate subject. Local gossip seems always to exaggerate the figures, but observations of the kinds of investments made by returned migrants indicate that amounts ranging from $5,000 to $25,000 over a period of fifteen to twenty years are possible. Since these migrants earn in the range of $60 to $90 per week, with some managerial positions paying up to $125 per week, it may be difficult for the average middle-class American to understand how such savings are possible. Investigation in the Dominican Republic indicates that many Dominicans in New York actually live in a far different fashion from native Americans or acculturated Dominicans. Informants say that husbands and wives may leave their small children to be raised by grandparents while they themselves go to New York and share an apartment with a similar couple — often kinsmen. The two families may pay $100 per month rent. They eat inexpensive foods. Those who work in the restaurant trade usually eat on the job and also manage to bring home leftover food for others. They learn from their friends and relatives in the garment industry how they may buy goods and ready-made clothing rejected as "seconds" from the factories. Some who work in the sorting process see to it that the "seconds" they take home are actually first-class products. These are used to clothe themselves, and to make a profit on the side by selling to others. Sometimes an individual will bring a suitcase full of such clothing or goods to the Dominican Republic. Unless he gets caught in customs, this can more than pay for the trip itself.

Ambitious Dominicans in this class do not become involved in buying simply to keep up with their neighbors. Sometimes they invest in property in the United States which they then rent to others while they themselves live in

less expensive quarters, thus realizing another profit. They do
not buy insurance, since they are surrounded by numerous
kinfolk who will take care of them in case of emergency or
death. They do not buy cars but depend upon buses and sub-
ways. Often they hold two jobs, or work overtime for as long
as twelve or fifteen hours per day. Money saved is invested or
placed in savings accounts where it draws interest. In these
and other ways, the Dominican who wants to save money
manages to do so. Although he will never achieve middle-class
status within the United States society in this fashion, this
goal does not motivate him. He is far more concerned with
his status in the Dominican Republic, both at the moment
and in the future. He has already gained some respect at
home by simply having secured the visa and made the trip. If
he can return with a large sum of money and invest it wisely,
he will have established himself and secured his future.

Not all Dominicans adhere to the above pattern. In fact,
informants say that quite often the young person who goes
to New York never returns to his homeland except to pay
visits. Some get so involved in the American way of life that
they spend their money as fast as they make it. Such individuals may return to the Dominican Republic for vacations.
They bring presents for relatives, and sometimes leave their
children with the latter until they are ready for school, but
ultimately they return to the source of their income New
York. These persons are frequently instrumental in supporting
those left behind. It is rare to find families without some
members living in the United States. There are whole villages
for which remittances from the United States are one of the
primary sources of income. Not only do they send money for
be used for living expenses by their relatives, but they also
help support community projects such as churches, schools,
etc. At the time this was written, the Dominican colony in
New York was helping to raise money for a large dam and
hydroelectric plant considered by many to be the only salva-
tion for agriculture in the northwestern part of the Cibao.

Remittances from absent relatives may continue even after
the emigrant's death, as in the case of survivor's benefits from
the social security system. The United States Consulate in
Santiago handles approximately 75 checks a month for

Dominicans from the Cibao alone who have either worked in the United States, served in the U.S. Army, or who have deceased relatives in these categories. The total amount of these checks for one month was $4,747.90 in a count made by this writer in February, 1968. The range for social security checks was from $35.00 to $129.50, which indicates something of the time spent and salaries earned by Dominicans in New York. The checks for veteran's benefits ranged from $19.60 to $167.00.

Some Dominicans are required by U.S. law to pick up their checks in U.S. territory, which means trips to Puerto Rico on a fairly regular basis. Other informants say that they retain their U.S. address long after they have left the country just so their checks will continue to be mailed there. Relatives then forward the checks directly to the Dominican Republic. There is no way of determining the magnitude of these latter sources of funds, but it seems reasonable to think that they form an important source of dollar income for the peasants and for the country as a whole. Actually, few of the dollars which enter in this way ever go through the central Dominican bank to increase the dollar reserve. Most are sold on the black market for an extra 5 to 15%, thus further increasing the income of the recipients.

In terms of the movement of the *campesinos* themselves, the effects of the migration to New York seem to be several. First, let us consider the individual *campesino*. Migration gives him a new field for employment by means of which he can support himself and those he leaves behind. If he stays in the States for any length of time, he can eventually bring his children and provide them with a better and less expensive education than they could obtain at home. The migration itself, and the money earned, which he may use both for consumer's goods and investments, will increase his social standing — he will be known as a clever person, and possibly also as hardworking and thrifty. He will also be able to improve his level of living considerably, whether he stays in the U.S. or returns with his savings and accumulated goods. Finally, the very possibility of migration provides a dream, a hope, and a form of relaxation for the less privileged peasant or slum dweller.

From the point of view of the Dominican nation, the migration serves some rather important functions. First of all, it provides an outlet for excess population. Although only a trickle at present, the migration will probably increase in spite of attempts by the United States to curb the flow. As in the case of Puerto Rico, the fact that a high percentage of the migrants are young adults would soon be reflected by a lowered birthrate in the Dominican Republic as these young couples have their babies in the States rather than at home.

Given the custom by which all children inherit equally, landholdings become increasingly fractionated in each generation to the benefit of no one. Migration serves to drain off some of the population in the countryside, thus reducing population pressure. At the same time the increased income received through remittances allows those left behind to improve their condition. Savings may be used upon return to increase the size of small holdings, providing a more secure economic base for agricultural endeavour.

A third advantage to the country is that a whole generation of Dominicans is being educated in the basic skills which will be useful to the country in its later development. At the present time there are few skilled workers, but even fewer jobs for them to fill. If industrial development proceeds, more persons familiar with machine operation and factory work can be absorbed by the economy. Similarly, service personnel and maintenance workers will be needed, as well as a larger number of white-collar workers. Many of these will probably be recruited from the returned migrants or the children of migrants, if the Puerto Rico situation is comparable, as I think it probably is.[1]

Finally, the migration itself provides employment opportunities for Dominicans at home. Getting a visa and arranging for trips to the United States, translating documents, facilitating business and legal matters for those who migrate — all of these require paper work, know-how, legwork, and time. Many people prefer to pay someone else to take care of these things for them, and therefore the profession of agent or broker arises. In one sense it could be said that this type of employment results from inefficiencies in the system. But at the same time it must be recognized that in a highly populated, underdeveloped country where lack of employment is a crucial matter, this type of system helps distribute the income among a larger number of people than would otherwise be the case. I am here referring both to the undercover agent who works illegally or semilegally, and to the individual working in plain sight and within the law, either on his own or for the government. The operations of these agents or brokers also helps to relieve the anxieties of a person unfamiliar with any of these processes (the *campesino*, the very young, the foreigner, as well as the illiterate), and enables him to take part in a system which he might otherwise misunderstand, fear, and avoid.

This leads us to a consideration of the term "peasant" (or "campesino") and its meaning in the world today. Peasant society, as described by Redfield,[2] Kroeber,[3] Foster,[4] and others, seems to be breaking down in the Dominican Republic. The small, isolated, rural communities of primary agricultural producers, working without the aid of fuel-driven machinery, but dependent upon a local market for the interchange of agricultural and manufactured products, will probably be pushed out gradually by the larger, medium-sized farmer who aims at efficient and mechanized production for a national or international market. If we consider some of the characteristics usually assigned to the peasant as a person, certain differences from the modern farmer are obvious. The farmer is neither unsophisticated in the ways of the outside world, primarily dependent upon personal relationships, nor more influenced by the sacred as opposed to the secular; nor is he dependent upon knowledge transmitted through oral traditions.

In fact, the migrants to New York — even those who remain there for many years — are often closer to the classic description of "peasant" than is the modern farmer in the underdeveloped country today. Upper-class Dominicans recognize this when they speak of *campesinos*. Although the word *means* countryman, it is used to refer to the uneducated, unsophisticated, usually poor, individual of the lower classes. Even though there are actually many *campesinos* who have migrated to Dominican cities, many upper-class citizens overestimate their number, assuming that they can always tell a *campesino* by his clothing, by the way he speaks, by his "simple" airs. García's study, for example, showed that many people in a *barrio* thought to be made up of migrants had actually been born in the city.[5]

An analysis of social structure is different from a consideration of how people adapt themselves to changes in that structure. Some social scientists have emphasized the differences between rural and urban living patterns, and others have dwelled upon the migrants themselves. It is clear that some individuals, under some circumstances, suffer trauma and anomie when faced with the urban scene,[6] while others adapt with little or no difficulty.[7] Obviously, not all cultures, cities, or individuals are alike, but it is the task of social science to explain variations in behavior in terms of something more basic than idiosyncrasy (whether in reference to the character of people or cities).

It may be that the structure of the very large metropolis permits (though does not necessarily determine) a kind of protective pluralism which the smaller city cannot. Individuals, depending upon their previous life circumstances, may then fit into one of several kinds of urban living patterns. Thus, the peasant in cities like New York *may* survive very well using the social techniques and social structures with which he grew up back in the rural Dominican Republic. He is still dependent upon primary ties, especially those of kinship ties, his knowledge of the world beyond that seen during his own daily activities is limited, he is largely dependent upon oral tradition — even to the extent of learning how to get a visa to go to the United States. When and if he returns to his home country, he fits right in again with the patterns he left behind. Even though change is going on all around him, he has changed only his relative position within the framework already familiar to him, which is still basically a non-industrial, or traditional one. If he has gone into business, it will probably be in small-time commercial activities, not industry. If he has bought up larger amounts of land, he will probably still cultivate it on the old-time basis of sharecropping, rather than with modern techniques, or he may utilize it as pasture for cattle purchased with his capital, but will not go into modern dairying. In short, he remains a peasant operating under a peasant system which is fast disappearing. His children, however, because of their different experiences and broader education begun earlier, may very well move out of that world to become successful farmers, businessmen or even industrialists, in what for their fathers, in spite of having lived in a city most of their lives, is still a foreign environment. On the other hand, for some, it may take more than one generation for the change to occur. Probably we can expect the peasant system to persist side by side with the more modern so long as it is at least partially supported by wage labor, whether at home or abroad.

ENDNOTES

1. José Hernández Álvarez (1967) *Return Migration to Puerto Rico*. Population Monograph Series, No. 1, University of California, Berkeley.
2. Robert Redfield (1941) *The Folk Culture of Yucatan*. University of Chicago Press, Chicago.
3. A.L. Kroeber (1948) *Anthropology*: Harcourt, Brace & Co., New York, p. 284.
4. George Foster (1953) "What is Folk Culture?" *American Anthropologist* 55: 159-173.
5. César Garcia (1967) "Como se vive en un barrio de Santiago." Colección "Estudios." Universidad Católica Madre y Maestra, Santiago, República Dominicana.
6. Jacob Fried (1959) "Acculturation and Mental Health Among Migrants in Peru." In *Culture and Mental Health*, Marvin Opler, ed., New York, Macmillan; Lewis Wirth (1938) "Urbanism as a Way of Life." *American Journal of Sociology* 44: 1-24.
7. D.S. Butterworth (1962) "A Study of the Urbanization Process Among Mixtec Migrants from Tilan-Tongo in Mexico City." *America Indigena*, 22: 257-274; Oscar Lewis (1952) "Urbanization Without Breakdown: a Case Study." *Scientific Monthly* 75: 31-41; William Mangin (1960) "Mental Health and Migration to Cities: a Peruvian Case." *Annals of the American Academy of Political and Social Sciences* 84: 911-917.

SECTION 10
Epilogue

The New Caribbean Man William G. Demas

The counsel offered by William G. Demas in his address to the 1970 graduation exercises at the University of Guyana summarizes the issues and themes considered in this anthology. The 'New Caribbean Man', in his view, is necessarily a young person who must come to grips with his history, the place of technology in his nation and its relationship with the former mother country, as well as the role of his country and the region in the international context. Demas posed a formidable challenge for the 1970s, one which has not yet been overcome; perhaps the 1980s will be better able to meet it head-on. The address appeared in W.G. Demas (1971), 'The New Caribbean Man,' Caribbean Quarterly, 7, Nos 3 and 4, and is reprinted with kind permission of Caribbean Quarterly and the Author.

The theme of my address to you this afternoon is "The New Caribbean Man." I have chosen this theme for two reasons. The first reason is the concern of many Caribbean figures to define and create a New Man. The two most prominent Caribbean names associated with this endeavour are, of course, Frantz Fanon and Che Guevara. Fanon came from Martinique while Guevara, although born in Argentina, closely identified himself with Cuba. It is also not too fanciful to suggest that in the late nineteenth century Jose Martí "the Apostle of Cuban Independence" when he asserted the moral equality between Black and White Cubans, was implicitly concerned with the creation of a New Cuban Man.

My second reason for choosing this theme is the present preoccupation in the Caribbean with the creation of a New

Society in the Caribbean. This contrasts with previous efforts by Caribbean intellectuals and activists to create a New Society in countries outside the Caribbean.

In the 1920's Marcus Garvey of Jamaica sought to create a new society for the Black American in Africa. In the 1930's and 1940's C.L.R. James and George Padmore, both of Trinidad and Tobago, sought to create new societies for the Africans in Africa through liberation from British imperialism. In our own time Stokeley Carmichael, also of Trinidad and Tobago, has sought to achieve the redemption of the Black American on American soil while Frantz Fanon sought to create a consciousness and a frame of reference for all the peoples of the Third World.

But today we must be concerned with the creation of the New Society here in the Caribbean. And, since this must be created by men, it is pertinent to ask what sort of person, what sort of New Man will build the New Society here in the Caribbean.

YOUTH

The most outstanding fact is that the New Caribbean Man is and must be a young person. This is so partly because of coincidence and partly because of inevitability. Coincidence makes it so because in the entire demographic history of the Caribbean the percentage of young people in the total population has never been so high. In many of the countries of the Region about 60% of the total population is less than 25 years of age.

It is inevitable that the New Caribbean Man will be a young person because Youth is or ought to be the vanguard of change in all societies. Caribbean Youth of today have clearly thrown off many of the psychological shackles and complexes that so distorted the personality of the older folk in the Region. Caribbean Youth have shown a readiness to reject many of the irrelevant values, preconceptions and attitudes of the metropolitan countries and are now actively seeking new values to replace the old. Further, Caribbean Youth in terms of sensibility and the common quest for a new ideological framework have achieved de facto unity, in spite of the dividing factors of sea and political boundaries in the Region. They have achieved integration ahead of our statesmen, businessmen, trade unionists and economists. They are truly a vanguard. They have the advantage of being better educated and more prosperous materially than their parents and grandparents. They are certainly more stimulated by events outside of the Region than previous generations, for in this technological age, as has been aptly said, the electronic mass media have reduced the world to a "global village".

FOUR TASKS

What then are the tasks before the new young Caribbean Man in creating the New Caribbean Society? They are many and formidable. Although all are inter-related, four can, I think, be identified.

First, the New Caribbean Man must know, understand and come to terms with his history. He must be intensely pre-occupied with the History of the Caribbean. We often hear the Philistines in our midst urging us to turn away from the contemplation of our past experiences. This view is so extremely superficial that it does not even deserve the effort of refutation. I shall therefore limit myself to two observations. In the first place, we cannot create a New Society unless we know who we are and we cannot know who we are unless we know where we have come from. In the second place, to be acquainted with our history and to know that we have survived the moral and psychological travail of slavery and indentureship, Crown Colony Government and cultural deprivation and have retained our vitality, our elan and our creativity (although here and there, especially among the older folk, some psychological sears are still left) ought to give us a tremendous amount of self-confidence. We ought to feel elated rather than depressed by knowing that we have the greatest gift a group of human beings can have — moral and psychological resilience.

The second great task facing the New Caribbean Man is the creation of a distinctive Caribbean Society. The fundamental point to be grasped here is that Caribbean political independence can be justified only if this independence is used to create something new — a better society with an identity of its own. If we do not use our independence to do this, then we will simply have changed our status as outposts of the British Political Empire to outposts of the North American Economic Empire.

THE TECHNOLOGICAL TRAP

In assessing our potentials and capabilities for creating a new and better society in the Caribbean, we should not suffer from any undue inferiority complex because of our shortage of resources, both physical and human, and our inadequate mastery of modern technology. For Europe and America have recently made the startling discovery that Technology is the God that failed. The most advanced Western societies find that human action and human creativity in shaping their social, political, economic and even physical environment nearer to the heart's desire is frustrated by the apparently autonomous power of Technology. Western Man now seems to be engaged in a losing battle with a highly deterministic social process. Instead of Man freely making his own choices and shaping his own society, human action is the dependent and man-made Technology the independent, variable in the process of social change.

More generally, we can say that in many ways the advanced Western countries have not been remarkably successful in ordering their societies, not so much through lack of will as through the devil's compact which they made in the nineteenth century with the fiend of Technology. They have now discovered in the second half of the twentieth century that Technology is not neutral in terms of human values, as they once believed, but that Technology can actually triumph over human values. This disenchantment with technology, organization and bureaucracy lies at the heart of the revolt of the youth of Western Europe and North America and is perhaps the most important factor in the emergence of the New Left.

It is one of the great tasks of the New Caribbean Man to

escape this trap. From the very beginning the New Caribbean Man must see and put Technology in its true place as a servant of human values. To say this is not to adopt a romantic attitude or to reject the desirability of material progress. The New Caribbean Society will fail to develop its technological skills at its own peril. The first priority of the New Caribbean Society must be to meet the basic needs of all the people in the society for work, food, shelter, clothing, education and recreation, and to ensure that these goods and services are equitably distributed. Even to achieve this modest goal would demand considerable application of Technology, and a very large number of both high and middle-level technologists drawn from among the New Caribbean Men. Rather, what I am suggesting is that we so construct our economic, political and social institutions that our New Society is susceptible of control by our own human will and conscious activity rather than by the blind force of Technology.

All of this means that the New Caribbean Society must rest on an indigenous and not an imported ideological basis. If we are to create a distinctive society in the Caribbean, we must formulate the intellectual and moral bases of this society in the light of our own situation, our own history, our own possibilities and our own aspirations. The New Caribbean Man must look inwards for ideological inspiration.

METROPOLITAN RELATIONS

This brings me to the third great task confronting the New Caribbean Man. He must devise ways and means of reducing the negative aspects of the metropolitan impact on the New Caribbean Society and of turning to his own advantage the opportunities presented by contact with the metropolitan countries. In other words, the New Society must be selective in its contacts with the metropolis — no less in economics, than in ideology, culture and values.

I shall not say much on this occasion about the economic aspects. Suffice it to say that, while the Caribbean clearly needs to have extensive economic intercourse with metropolitan countries, it has to guard against the danger of economic absorption into the powerful economies of these countries. But two aspects of contact with the metropolis other than the economic, need to be singled out here. The first is the cultural penetration through the electronic mass media and the second is the drain of our trained manpower out of our countries.

Properly conceived, the role of the electronic mass media in Third World countries ought to be the preservation and strengthening of the national cultural identity and the promotion among the people of attitudes conducive to racial cohesion and national development. Instead we find that in many Third World countries, particularly in the Caribbean and Latin America, the electronic mass media, especially television, play a role which is destructive of national cultural identity and of autonomous and independent economic and social development. This role arises not only from the advertising of imported goods but also from the actual content of the programmes which brainwash the population into accepting and wanting the way of life of the affluent societies. The New Caribbean Man will have to change the role of the electronic mass media if he is to build the New Society. This is not really difficult.

Much more elusive of easy solution is the problem of "the brain drain". I obviously on this occasion cannot go into the intricacies of this problem. Suffice it to say that unless the New Caribbean Man can devise measures to retain the highly trained and the highly skilled for work in the Caribbean, then the New Society will never be created. We shall remain outposts of economic empire — forever dependent on the metropolitan countries.

EXTRA-CARIBBEAN ROLE

The final task among those which I have identified facing the New Caribbean Man is to convert the Caribbean from being the Third World's Third World (to use Vidya Naipaul's witty but uncharitable phrase) into being a self-respecting and respected society, exercising a certain moral influence over the Third World generally and Afro-America in particular.

Let me elaborate this point. As I pointed out earlier, many distinguished sons of the Caribbean have played an extremely important part at both the intellectual and activist levels in creating the Third World and in developing self-awareness among Black Americans. In the future the Caribbean will have a somewhat different role to play.

First, since the Caribbean is the only part of the Hemisphere where Black people (originating from both India and Africa) control the State, what the Caribbean does by way of creating a new and better society cannot fail to be an inspiration to all the other Black peoples of Afro-America in their travail. The New Society in the Caribbean can instill among the dispossessed coloured peoples of the Western Hemisphere a sense of pride in the moral achievements of the New Caribbean Societies controlled and run by children of Africa and Asia. We should not forget that the creation of the State of Israel and its successes have done more than anything else to give the Jews in the Diaspora a sense of pride in themselves. In this profound moral sense, then, the New Caribbean Man stands at the vanguard of the Afro-American struggle for dignity.

Second, by founding the New Caribbean Society on the basis of solidarity between African and Indian, the New Caribbean Man can help directly but no less powerfully — through the force of moral example — to contribute to the solidarity between Asians and Africans in the wider Third World.

I have great hopes that the New Caribbean Man will be equal to these formidable tasks. I am convinced that Caribbean Youth hold out brilliant promise for the future of the Caribbean. But there are certain danger signs on the horizon. Most of us will agree that one of the saddest spectacles to contemplate is that of an individual who never fulfilled the promise of his early brilliance. If the Caribbean Youth of the 1970's do not fulfil the promise of their early brilliance, it will mean that we in the Region will have to wait yet another generation or possibly more for the creation of the New Society and for the emergence of the New Caribbean Man.

POSSIBLE OBSTACLES

Is it possible to identify the factors which may stand in the way of Caribbean Youth fulfilling its present high promise? I shall attempt to identify a few of them, but I do so with the greatest diffidence since in the 1970's it is almost heretical even to appear to be slightly critical of youth not only in the Caribbean but in the world as a whole. In attempting to point out some of the pitfalls into which Youth may fall, one runs the risk of being deemed a reactionary, or a counter-revolutionary. One runs the risk of appearing insensitive to the aspirations and thoughts of the new generation. My diffidence is however qualified by the fact that I have a foot in each camp — somewhere between youth and maturity. (Perhaps many of you will not agree with me, since it sometimes appears in the Caribbean today that anyone more than twenty-five years of age is beyond redemption!)

First, the New Caribbean Man must set about the task of building the New Society rationally. Here again I am not trying to inject a dose of conservatism into the ardent and impatient blood of Youth. Both the revolutionary and the conservative can be rational. Rationality falls into the category of means and not ends. If we reject rational means — and what is rational depends always on the specific situation and the specific time — then we shall compromise the achievement of our ends. Rationality must always guide and discipline emotion. For to be rational is to be human.

In the second place, the Youth of the Caribbean is doing neither itself nor the society any good by rejecting the older people. To seek to excommunicate everyone over forty and in some cases even thirty is not only wrong but silly. Discrimination by age is no more justifiable than discrimination by race or by sex. Moreover, while it may be true that many of the older people have not achieved the degree of psychological liberation in many ways in which the majority of the younger people have, the older folk, although limited by metropolitan values, have proved themselves and have in their own way shown themselves of great moral and social worth. Some of you are not so young as to have forgotten the old type of West Indian headmaster who is now rapidly disappearing from the scene. How many examples are there today among the younger people of this kind of integrity, commitment and dedication? Persons such as these may have been building badly designed structures; but they built well. Today many young people are rejecting what now appears to them to be ill-designed structures but they have not designed a new structure even in outline nor do some of them seem interested in building anything.

The third factor I would like to identify as a possible pitfall for youth is lack of discipline. And by discipline I mean not only old fashioned discipline — which is indeed important — but also moral and intellectual discipline. I see certain signs of self-indulgence developing among the young people of the region; and here I am referring not to the indulgence of the sensual appetite but to an absence of intellectual toughness and of moral integrity and authenticity. How far are some of the rebellious postures of Caribbean Youth authentically and genuinely felt and reasoned through? To what extent are attitudes of dissatisfaction being stimulated? To what extent do they derive from the knowledge that youth is angry and dissatisfied in other parts of the world?

VIOLENCE

Let me end by turning to the fourth possible pitfall — the misunderstanding about violence. The spread of the cult of violence as a means of resolving social and political problems in the late 60's and 70's throughout the whole world will certainly be noted by future historians when they come to write about our times.

Let us being by noting that violence is and has been a means of effecting political and social change. No intellectually honest person can escape this conclusion when he reviews the several cases where violence has brought about social and political change — in Europe, in America and in Third World Countries. Violence (or the desire on the part of those who hold power to avert violence) let us admit at certain specific times and in certain given circumstances, is probably the only means of achieving change. I say "probably" because, history being an irreversible process, we can never be sure that non-violent means may not have succeeded in achieving the same objective.

Where one has to take issue with many of the young exponents of the cult of violence all over the world is with respect to the glorification of violence as an end in itself. This particular line of thought can, of course, often be traced back to the writings of Frantz Fanon. Fanon's greatness as a political theorist and as one of the forgers of the conscience of the Third World is indisputable. His writings display a rare blend of vision, insight and commitment. But to my mind his work is deeply flawed by his strange attitude towards violence. It is the irony to crown all ironies that Fanon, who called on the peoples of the Third World to make a total break with Europe, should in glorifying violence be merely reflecting a certain strand of contemporary European thought. This strand of thought derives largely from French Existentialism which boldly proclaims and insists on the autonomy and freedom of choice of the individual. No one can quarrel with this, but certain Existentialists have elevated individual self-expression to the point where the violent killing of another human being is claimed to exalt or purify the individual killer who is held to assert his manhood by exercising his free choice.

Merely to state this doctrine is to show how absurd it is and how much it derives from certain decadent aspects of European Existentialism. It is more than time that some commonsense were introduced into the discussion. Among human beings violence can only be a means towards certain ends, never an end in itself. An African guerilla who kills a Portuguese soldier in Mozambique does so not in order to purify himself but in order to liberate Mozambique. If he were purifying himself, he would probably stop fighting after killing two or three soldiers. Fortunately, the African guerilla has more commonsense than an Existentialist philosopher. If we count the number of times in modern history when the oppressed have killed the oppressors, then we should by now have a highly purified and exalted human race.

Having thus expelled this alien body of the Existentialist-derived cult of violence for its own sake from Fanon's thought, we in the Caribbean can take up the noble invocation at the end of his great work.

For Europe, for ourselves and for humanity, comrades, we must start afresh, develop a new way of thinking and bring into being a new man.

A Guide to Selected Literature

F.M. Andic and S.M. Andic (1968), *Government, Finance and Planned Development: Fiscal Surveys of Surinam and the Netherlands Antilles*, Institute of Caribbean Studies, University of Puerto Rico, Río Piedras.

L. Barrett (1977), *The Rastafarians: Sounds of Cultural Dissonance*, Beacon Press, Boston.

C.J. Barrett (1970), *A New Balance of Power: The 19th Century*, Caribbean University Press, Barbados.

J. Bosch (1965), *The Unfinished Experiment: Democracy in the Dominican Republic*, Praeger, New York.

S. Brau (1967), *La Colonización de Puerto Rico: desde el descubrimiento de la Isla hasta la reversión a la corona española de los privilegios de Colón*, Instituto de Cultura Puertorriqueña, San Juan, Puerto Rico, 4th edition.

J.H. Clarke (ed.) (1974), *Marcus Garvey and the Vision of Africa*, Vintage Books, New York.

H. Cole (1967), *Christophe, King of Haiti*, Viking Compass, New York.

S.F. Cook and W. Borah (1971), *Essays in Population History Vol. I: Mexico and the Caribbean*, University of California Press, Berkeley.

N.M. Crouse (1943), *The French Struggle for the West Indies, 1665-1713*, New York.

P. Curtin (1955), *Two Jamaicas: The Role of Ideas in a Tropical Colony*, Harvard University Press, Cambridge, Mass.

P. Curtin (1969), *The Atlantic Slave Tade: A Census*, University of Wisconsin Press, Madison.

L. Despres (1967), *Cultural Pluralism and Nationalist Politics in British Guiana*, Rand McNally, Chicago.

L. Díaz Soler (1965), *La Historia de la Esclavitud Negra en*

Puerto Rico, Editorial Universitaria, Río Piedras, Puerto Rico.

T. Draper (1965), *Castroism: Theory and Practice*, Praeger, New York.

R. Dunn (1972), *Sugar and Slaves: The Rise of the Planter Class in the English West Indies, 1624–1713*, University of North Carolina, Chapel Hill, N.C.

C. Gibson (1966), *Spain in America*, Harper and Row, New York.

N. Girvan and O. Jefferson (eds.) (1971), *Readings in the Political Economy of the Caribbean*, New World Group, Kingston, Jamaica.

C.C. Goslinga (1971), *The Dutch in the Caribbean and on the Wild Coast, 1580–1680*, University of Florida Press, Gainesville.

W.A. Green (1976), *British Slave Emancipation: The Sugar Colonies and the Great Experiment 1830–1865*, Oxford University Press, London.

D. Hall (1971), *Five of the Leewards, 1834–1870*, Caribbean Universities Press, Barbados.

G.M. Hall (1971), *Social Control in Slave Plantation Societies: A Comparison of St Domingue and Cuba*, Johns Hopkins University Press, Baltimore.

C.H. Haring (1952), *The Spanish Empire in America*, Harcourt, Brace and World, New York.

B.W. Higman (1976), *Slave Society and Economy in Jamaica, 1807–1833*, Cambridge University Press, Cambridge.

C.L.R. James (1963), *The Black Jacobins: Toussant L'Ouverture and the San Domingo Revolution*, Vintage, New York.

F.A. Kirkpatrick (1946), *The Spanish Conquistadores*, Meridian Books, Cleveland.

F.W. Knight (1970), *Slave Society in Cuba During the 19th Century*, University of Wisconsin Press, Madison.

G. Lamming (1971), *Water with Berries*, Longman Caribbean, Trinidad.

K.O. Laurence (1971), *Immigration in the West Indies in the 19th Century*, Caribbean Universities Press, Barbados.

G.K. Lewis (1972), *The Virgin Islands: A Caribbean Lilliput*, Northwestern University Press, Evanson, Illinois.

Lowenthal, D. (1972), *West Indian Societies*, Oxford University Press, Oxford.

C. MacKay (1933), *Banana Bottom*, Harper and Row, New York.

M. Maldonado-Denis (1972), *Puerto Rico: A Socio-historic Interpretation* (trans. E. Vialo), Vintage Books, New York.

V. Martinez-Alier (1974), *Marriage, Class and Colour in 19th Century Cuba: A Study of Racial Attitudes and Sexual Values in a Slave Society*, Cambridge University Press, Cambridge.

E. Montejo (1968), in M. Barnet (ed.) *Diary of a Runaway Slave*, Pantheon, New York.

M. Moreno Fraginals (1976), *The Sugar Mill: The Socioeconomic Complex of Sugar in Cuba 1760–1860* (trans. C. Belfrage), Monthly Review Press, New York.

A. Murch (1971), *Black Frenchmen: The Political Integration of the French Antilles*, Schenkman Publishing, Inc. Cambridge, Mass.

R. Nettleford (1972), *Identity, Race and Protest in Jamaica*, William Morrow, New York.

R. Pares (1936), *War and Trade in the West Indies, 1739–1763*, Clarendon Press, Oxford.

O. Patterson (1967), *The Sociology of Slavery: An Analysis of the Origins, Development and Structure of Negro Slave Society in Jamaica*, MacGibbon and Kee, London.

G. Pope Atkins and L.C. Wilson (1972), *The U.S. and the Trujillo Regime*, Rutgers University Press, New Brunswick.

R. Price (ed.) (1973), *Maroon Societies: Rebel Slave Communities in the Americas*, Anchor/Doubleday, Garden City, New York.

L.J. Ragatz (1928), *The Fall of the Planter Class in the British Caribbean, 1763–1833, A Study in Social and Economic History*, The Century Co., New York.

J.A. Saco (1932), *Historia de la esclavitud de los indios en el nuevo mundo, seguida de las historias de los repartimientos y encomiendas*, Colección de Libros Cubanos, Havana.

H. Schmidt (1971), *The U.S. Occupation of Haiti, 1915–1934*, Rutgers University Press, New Brunswick.

A. Segal (1968), *The Politics of Caribbean Economic Integration*, Institute of Caribbean Studies, Río Piedras, Puerto Rico.

C. Senior (1972), *Santiago Iglesias: Labor Crusader*, Inter-American University, Hato Rey, Puerto Rico.

R.B. Sheridan (1974), *Sugar and Slavery: An Economic History of the British West Indies, 1623-1775*, Caribbean University Press, Barbados.

J.G. Suarez (1973), *The Era of Trujillo: Dominican Dictator*, University of Arizona Press, Tucson.

H.J. Wiarda (1969), *Dominican Republic: Nation in Transition*, Praeger, New York.

Further bibliographic references may be found in:

S.A. Bayitch (1967), *Latin America and the Caribbean: A Bibliographical Guide to Works in English*, University of Miami Press, Coral Gables.

L. Comitas (1977), *The Complete Caribbeana, 1900-1975: A Bibliographic Guide to the Scholarly Literature* (4 vols.), Kraus-Thomson, Millwood, N.Y.

General bibliographies:

E. Huiwitz (1975), *Caribbean Studies*: Part I, *Choice* (June 1975), 487-502; Part II, *Choice* (July/August 1975) 639-647; Part III, *Choice* (December 1975) 1271-1276.

Index